# COUGHING
## THE DISTANCE
CYCLING FROM PARIS TO ISTANBUL WITH CYSTIC FIBROSIS

www.coughingthedistance.com

Published and printed by: CreateSpace
Second Edition
ISBN 978-0980-592-016

Layout and cover design: Megan Rozynski - www.seventyfivedesign.com.au
Editing Support: Kathryn Whitfield and Dace Shugg
Cover photograph: Walter J.J. van Praag
Other photos: Heather Lea, Cindy Brazendale and Walter van Praag
Blog entries: Heather Lea

A Centre of the Universe Production
2 Rose Court, Devonport,
Tasmania 7310, Australia
www.cotu.biz
info@cotu.biz

Also available:
Coughing the Distance documentary on DVD, produced by Lucas Li and the children's edition called Walter and the Mucous Monsters by Katherine Hitch and Pip Valentine. More Information on www.coughingthedistance.com or search on www.createspace.com

In 2009 Walter was surprised with a medal of the Order of Australia for service to community health through raising the awareness of Cystic Fibrosis.

# Prologue

The idea behind this book is to encourage people with CF to not give up. It is very common for a young person with CF to grow up as a 'sickly child' and as a result go through periods of depression. I have been there and found myself asking what was the point in studying hard or carrying on, and instead just concentrated on living it up and partying – not a good idea when your health is at stake and you are particularly susceptible to serious lung infections.

This book would never have been possible if not for the many people who insisted I should record the whole experience. Hans and Marjan from Rotterdam, for instance, told me right from the start that this book needed to be written! I have always wanted to write books, and here was my chance. It is my first book, and it is written from the heart. During the ride, I was too busy enjoying myself to take down notes and my memory was aided greatly by team member Heather Lea's fantastic blog entries, many of which I have included in the telling of our story. Without my best mate and our navigator David Barz this book would have been seriously lacking detail as his GPS's record of our ride proved to be a most valuable aid to my memory! Google and Wikipedia have also aided my research greatly by shedding light on locations that we bumped into along the way. When you ride 4395 kilometres along a route where people speak dozens of different languages it is also impossible to research all the interesting locations along the way and accordingly we often found it next to impossible to find out what we were seeing en- route! This made the ride particularly exciting as we never knew exactly what was around the next corner.

I thank my parents for bringing me up the way they did: not treating me as a sick child; letting me have my way and allowing me to go and have my adventures. I am sure my father would have been very proud – he always loved it when I travelled and saw things that he had only read about. I am also grateful for the help received from my brother, Frank, and mother, Connie, as well as the entire family in Holland, especially my uncle Bernard and his Rotary Club of IJmond were invaluable.

Thanks also to the Hitch clan in the USA and my friend Brent Reynolds President of the Mad Bomber company for sponsoring me, Martin Quelle for providing the support vehicle and helping finance film equipment and for coming along with the team for weeks of cycling; Batavus the Dutch bicycle manufacturer for providing our bikes and Cor Mellisant Fietswereld for outfitting them; Patagonia for dressing us; All the people from Tasmania who helped raise funding for the airfares for the support team; Troy Baggett and the Deck Café staff and their suppliers for their huge contributions; Tiina, Kim and Alix for 'allowing' their partners to ride with me; CF Tasmania for their support and the Adult CF team of the Hobart

Hospital for their energy and for treating, teaching and supporting me; Jenny Busch, their team's coordinator, for actually making it to Paris to see us off with a team of Australian fans all wearing homemade COFE T-shirts; Cath Levett of The Observer newspaper for making me a logo – onya Cath! And all the dozens of special people who helped us along the way.

A very special thanks to Dace Shugg from Hobart for the hundreds of hours she spent helping me – from fund raising to editing drafts of this book. She is a whirlwind of energy despite claiming to be of retirement age. Kathryn Whitfield for patiently helping me style the final format of this book to make it much more acceptable and easier to read!

I am very grateful to everyone for all their support, without which I could not have coughed the distance.

Katherine my wife is the one who not only supported me through all these times, allowing me to be absent for months and months, but also sacrificed pretty much all of her ambulance-officer income on the trip and helping finance the documentary and the books that followed. She stands by me through thick and thin and I love her very much. She is the bestest wife!

# Sponsors

Thank you for the generous donations and support of the following companies and organisations: Mad Bomber Company, Batavus, Patagonia, Fietswereld, The Deck Café, Freney First Aid, The City of Devonport Lions Club, the Southern Cross Club in Canberra, Tasmanian Forestry, Cradle Coast Tours, Rio Tinto Mining, Coles Devonport, East Devonport Fruit Market, Annette Tyson Arts and Crafts, Dunelm Wines WA, Harvey Norman Devonport, the Ball and Chain Grill, the Cascade and Boags Breweries, Banjos Bakeries from Devonport and Salamanca, Tony Muir Massages, Suzie Smith, Coles, Eastern Shore Hobart, Crown Jewels Hobart, Sharon Radcliff Jewellery, Alan Tyson Sing-along, Liga Veska Art, The Beachfront Hideaway Cairns, Phoenix Accounting, Canoe 'n' Surf, Paul Pritchard Books, Ian Wallace Photography, Leah Orr Books, Alice Hansen Books, Simon Martin Whips & Leather craft, Hawley's Gingerbread House Wines, Joyce Simmons from the Sarrit Centre in Nairobi (Kenya), Lindisfarne Hotel bottle shop, Devonport Pizza Hut, Bakers Dozen, Tiger Ranch Wines, the Burnie HHH, House of Anvers, The Australian Institute of Sport shop, Dace's army of sandwich makers and many many more businesses and individuals who have supported me in raising funds for The Great COFE for CF.

I hereby also apologise if some people feel I used the wrong name for their ethnic group, especially the Gypsies who might like to be referred to as Roma people. They may have been unfairly stereotyped in this book. Although we found all Gypsies that we met friendly we were warned about 'the Gypsies in Romania' in several countries by people who have probably never even been to Romania. Nonetheless this fear was put into our minds! It also did not help that my dearly departed grandmother often blamed (unfairly or not) crime on a Gypsy camp near where she lived during my informative years (1970s).

And finally, the comments and opinions expressed in this book are my own personal opinions and do not necessarily represent those of the entire team. Events depicted in this book are as accurate as I can remember, but it is always possible events are out of chronological order or sometimes even in the wrong location. Some names had to be made up for readability or to protect the innocent! This is not a guidebook and people intending to ride from Paris to Istanbul should not take this book as an accurate guide. And also, this is not a beer and schnitzel guide to Eastern Europe, despite the regular occurrence of schnitzels and beer.

This edition is brought out after the special early edition of the book which was printed in time for the ANZ CF Nurses Conference (2008) held in Hobart Tasmania in August 2008. Many typos were removed after feedback and my brother Frank's efforts! I am not a perfectionist, so I appreciate all the help I can get.

# ABOUT THE BOY

If only someone had licked me when I was born, it may have saved me a lot of trouble. Though I seemed a healthy baby, the first born and born just shy of nine months after my parents' marriage. We lived in Leidschendam, a suburban area near The Hague in Holland. Just over two years later my little brother, Frank, was born, but it wasn't until he was out of nappies that I started to develop a bit of a cough and a regular fever.

My condition quickly deteriorated and I became a sickly child with a permanent cough and diarrhoea. I was not growing as fast as perhaps I should have been – and my farts were already noticeably smellier than anyone else in the family! Doctors often prescribed me antibiotics and anti-diarrhoea medication. My tonsils were removed but I still got lots of infections. A polyp was removed from my nose, but doctors did not realise what was really wrong with me. I grew to 25 kilograms in my first eight years and stayed there for almost three years.

My parents moved to Noordwijk, a Dutch seaside town, thinking that the fresh salty air would be good for my lungs. They were very concerned and went from doctor to doctor, not believing that I was just a sickly child – they wanted concrete answers. Surgeons offered to open me up and look inside me, they wanted to take liver and lumbar punctures to see what was going on but my parents would not have me subjected to these painful tests unless they thought there was a good reason to do them.

By the time I was 10, Hugo Heymans, a doctor friend of the family, happened to be studying paediatric gastroenterology. He offered to carry out a detailed non-invasive process of elimination to find out what was wrong with me at the Amsterdam Academic Hospital, warning that it might take up to two months. Three weeks later he returned with a diagnosis: Cystic Fibrosis (CF). My parents were sat down and told about CF. The news was not good: I was not likely to live out my teens; I could not eat fats, not even chocolates; and my cough would worsen over the next few years, eventually killing me!

Cystic Fibrosis, or CF, is a recessive hereditary disease that affects the lungs, sweat glands and the digestive system. It is the most common genetic disease among people with European ancestry and if both parents carry the faulty gene, a newborn has a 1 in 4 chance of having CF. Symptoms usually develop during early childhood. The lungs and pancreas of people with CF produce abnormally thick mucus which can result in pneumonia and permanent lung damage. People with CF usually die from lung or heart complications. With improved medical care people with CF now commonly survive past their teenage years, but develop other complications such as diabetes and osteoporosis.

At the time, in the early seventies, my parents kept a brave face, and the nurses were very nice. I was told they had discovered what was wrong with me, and we should all be happy. I jumped with joy, running through the children's ward until I fell over – so hard, they thought my shoulder was broken! It took a few weeks to feel better again. Before I was discharged many young trainee doctors had filed past to look at my finger clubbing, my distended belly, my barrel chest, my thin arms and legs – all classic symptoms of CF, none of which had been recognised by my previous doctors. It was important that the new trainee doctors would not miss these obvious symptoms in future. Above all, my skin tasted salty – this only happens with CF. In England, an old midwives' saying had it that if a baby tasted salty he was doomed.

I was immediately put on a mountain of vitamins and minerals, especially fat soluble ones. I had to take granules of enzymes, counting out 25 of them for each meal. And, as I was not digesting fats, all my meals became low fat: no more butter, no more cheese. Aided by the treatment my digestion improved, my cough got better and my weight increased and best of all, I started growing again.

Three years later, our family moved to Australia, to Canberra – a city without heavy industry. The air there is clean and dry, the climate is great, and my father was convinced I'd do well there. I was called 'Dutchy' at school and, despite being of slight built I was occasionally picked on by bullies and got into fights. I never bruised easily, so when the teachers pulled me and my foe apart I would appear to be the 'winner'. I got a reputation as being a tenacious skinny guy not to mess with. I felt far from tough; I had coughing fits after anything exciting – including fights – and any physical activity.

I did not like Physical Education much in school, so my parents got an Irish Setter dog to encourage me to go running. And run I did – every morning with Mindy the dog. I joined little athletics and even did a milk-delivery run. I also rode my bicycle a lot. I started on a super-strong steel three-speed bike which I had brought from Holland, but I smashed it into a car one day and I had to buy a regular 10-speed. At age 16, I rode around Tasmania protesting in the Ride for Wilderness against the proposed Gordon-Below-Franklin dam. I hardly knew what was going on, but loved the excitement. When mountain bikes were invented I immediately saved up for one. I rode my bike daily. I ran in the odd marathon, and did a lot of bushwalking and hiking with the Canberra Family Bushwalkers. I was very fit. My parents had not forgotten the dire prediction that I would not outlive my teens, but kept their fingers crossed as I seemed to be doing well.

By this time, the official CF diet had changed from low-fat to high-fat. The reason being that as people with CF did not digest fat, they were missing out on its benefits. So bring on the fat and take plenty of pancreatic enzymes to help digest it! Antibiotics and other treatments were getting very good too, and the life expectancy for people with the disease had increased to their twenties. I tried to ignore Cystic Fibrosis. I refused to go to CF clinics and to hospital. If I got an infection, I would take antibiotics and go out for a walk or run as soon as I could. This turned out to be a life-saving choice as it was later discovered that the antibiotic-resistant bugs that grew in CF lungs were very communicable between patients. The most common place to get these bacteria was at the clinics where patients mixed socially. Now hospitals are very careful to keep CF patients separate and to ensure equipment, furniture and fixtures are sterilised thoroughly. CF kids' camps are no longer held.

The life expectancy of CF patients has been increasing over the past 40 years. When I was diagnosed in 1975 at age 10, I was not expected to live past my teens yet I know of at least two people with CF in Tasmania who are older than me; the past president of the Cystic Fibrosis Association of Tasmania is one. He is in his fifth decade and doesn't look his age. Then there is a fellow Hash House Harrier from Hobart who steadily out-runs me with his own lungs! Statistics show that children with CF who were born in the 1990s now have a 50 per cent chance of living more than 35 years and studies show that the life expectancy of children born today with CF will exceed 40 years. Life expectancy of individuals with adequate pancreatic function can now be expected to live more than 50 years.

I don't like the term 'sufferer'. People with CF do not suffer: we live with CF. It is not all rosy, but it is not suffering. We get sick sometimes but most of the time we can manage our condition. We don't suffer: we cough! After 42 years of coughing I am pretty comfortable with it. It's not pleasant, though, and neither is having to take medication and spend time nebulising –the process of making medicine into a breathable mist so that I can inhale it into my lungs. Unfortunately some of us do suffer, and some of us do die. This is perhaps inevitable and maybe there is a 'luck of the draw' factor. There are numerous CF genetic mutations, some worse than others. Some people with CF also suffer from other ailments which make life more complicated. My CF mutation is classified as W128X/? and I have no idea what exactly that means!

Of the many medicines I have to take, the worst for me are the antibiotics, which medical opinion says I should always take. Pancreatic enzymes are, I believe, bits of dried pig's pancreas – they may not be kosher, but I have no real problem taking them. Side effects of the pancreatic enzymes are sneezing and glassy (sparkling) eyes, which I read in the MIMS (the Australian bible of medicine) after 15 years of sneezing! The asthma drug, Ventolin, which I put in my nebuliser, is, I think, pretty harmless, although I only take the light version of it as the regular doses make my heart beat out of my chest. The saline and the Seretide (a long-acting bronchodilator), the Pulmozyme, the vitamins... I can handle them. For some reason I am scared of antibiotic resistance and prefer not to take them. This is perhaps irrational because would I prefer permanent lung damage instead? It is a tough question for me, but a no-brainer for the medicos who tell me the antibiotics that work well for me are 'candies' compared to the heavy artillery they have in the wings for when these stop working for me.

# THE BUG BITES

By the time I began university in 1986 at age 18, I had taken the need to keeping moving to the next step and was a constant traveller – addicted to the adrenalin! It took 10 years to complete my degrees – BA in Philosophy and BSc in Mathematics – at the Australian National University in Canberra as I was away so much travelling. Even before I started university, I took a year off. I bought a one-way ticket to Europe and started with an eight-week Top Deck Tour through Scandinavia and Eastern Europe before backpacking on my own till the money ran out. As a Dutch national, I was still able to work in Holland and I earned enough money there to catch a train (the Trans Siberian) to China. I then worked in Hong Kong to save up for the final leg back to Canberra.

I wrote up my numerous travel tales as 'Adrenalin Trips' in Woroni, the university (ANU) newspaper, covering my adventures of climbing into a Greek jail, getting busted in Russia, driving to the North Pole for Christmas, stock broking in Hong Kong, visiting refugee camps in disputed border areas between Thailand and the former Burma, working in a kibbutz and getting in trouble with Egyptian authorities. Once I even ended up in hospital in Siberia with a lung infection. Many readers thought the stories were fiction.

Years later, the editor of Woroni asked me if it was true that I had CF. I could not believe that this man whom I had known for so long did not know. He thought I was taking illegal drugs when he saw me popping pills and must have thought I had smoked a lot of bongs to make me cough so much. When he found out I had CF he said: 'Ah, which explains why you live every day as if it is your last and take the risks that you do!' It had never occurred to me before that maybe, subconsciously, there was an element of truth in his words.

I finally graduated from university just as the world recession hit Australia. With my health issues I could never work for long periods. I had to concentrate on running, cycling and going to the gym. I did a lot of temporary work in the public service and ran my own business. The first business I set up was an after-hours delivery service (Moonlight Express) and the second one was a computer consultancy. I had also worked as senior technician in a computer shop in Canberra. Eventually, I was given the opportunity to work for a friend in Papua New Guinea as a Branch Manager for his new IT Company, and ended up staying in PNG for three years. I then went to work for another friend in the USA. Working for friends is ideal as they understand my situations and give me a very flexible work schedule, often allowing me to work from home as well. Other employees within their organisations could not always immediately see what was going on, except that I was the boss's mate and was given preferential treatment. I always looked a picture of health, though with a cough and lots of pills. I had to stay fit in order for my lungs to survive – great motivation to get out of the house and do some exercise. People with CF often look the same as other people their age, if only people could look behind the scenes.

In America, I met and married my princess bride, Katherine. An outdoorsy type, a functional chic: no make-up or fancy dresses for her. She was an accomplished mountain climber and a volunteer medic in the USA. She is a 'doer'. She prefers a tent to any hotel. On the night we met, we drank a few pints of Guinness before she drove me home in her pick-up truck – a whole 200m from the pub. She had impressed me with the car as well as with the Guinness. I joined the Volunteer Fire and Rescue Service of Middleburg so I could come with her when she got called out of bed in the middle of the night. We married shortly after the 9/11 catastrophe and moved to Australia. Eventually we ended up living in Devonport, a small port city in north-west Tasmania, where Katherine joined the Ambulance Service and I potter around making myself useful by volunteering in the community. I have taught a little at the local Adult Education facility, and regularly help friends and colleagues with their IT needs. My biggest job is to survive: to go out and kayak, walk, run, cycle and stay fit. In Tasmania this can be done all year round in clean fresh air.

# THE DAY IT ALL BEGAN

One day in early 2005, Katherine and I picked up a fancy brochure about an Orient Express cycling holiday from our local bike shop. The trip seemed awesome – though, by no means, cheap. Not that we were tempted to do a structured tour, but the brochure mentioned a Danube Cycle Trail, the longest bike route in the world. We thought it would be a great ride to do. Katherine is also a keen cyclist and commutes to work on her bike. We have cycled a great part of the rugged 500km Tasmanian Trail together and even rode around Holland for part of our honeymoon.

We figured we would need a couple of months for the Paris to Istanbul ride – too much time for Katherine to take off work. So we invited my mate David Barz in Canberra to take part – riding with me from Paris to Budapest in Hungary, where Katherine would join us for the final leg to Istanbul in Turkey. David was the only person I knew who could possibly want to take on such adventure. We have known each other for many years, since university in Canberra. After that David worked as an Ambulance Officer and his late shifts meant that we could often go out during the day to do sport. He eventually qualified as a paramedic and moved to tropical Queensland where he first worked as a helicopter paramedic, before accepting a senior position on Thursday Island in the Torres Strait. He came back to Canberra looking to change careers and started afresh in the police force, where he is now a highly trained officer. David, who is 42-years old, has to stay extremely fit for his work so this ride was right up his alley. David agreed immediately and our preliminary preparations began.

A few months later, during my regular check-up at the Adult Cystic Fibrosis Clinic in Hobart, I mentioned to my doctor, Dr David Reid that I was planning the epic bike ride across Europe. His reply changed everything for me: 'You'll need to do that for CF awareness!' Next thing I was dreaming up ideas for the project, thinking about possible team members, strategies, sponsors, plans of attack, dates and destinations. We had started something big. Worst of all Dr. Reid does not exactly remember what transpired during that conversation and certainly did not think I would actually attempt, or for that matter complete, the proposed ride.

First things first. A name. What shall we call it? As we would be following the Paris to Istanbul route traditionally travelled by the Orient Express train, I coined the term COFE for CF. COFE stood for a jumbled Cystic Fibrosis Orient Express. And COFE sounded like COUGH, which is something I would do plenty of on the ride.

I devised the route in a matter of hours with the help of Google Earth and the Michelin website. My journalist friend, Kathy Whitfield, who is based in London, told me that CF was a hot topic in Britain at the time as the then Chancellor, Gordon Brown, had a baby son born with CF. She suggested that if I were to leave from London, she would have a better chance of getting me press contacts and possible sponsorships. It was a tempting offer, but increasing the distance and making the name obsolete (London to Istanbul is not the Orient Express route) was too much of a bridge to cross.

Her colleague, Cath Levett, a graphic designer at The Observer newspaper, created the Great COFE for CF logo. It has the Rose for CF (Cystic Fibrosis sometimes called sixty-five Roses) and a bicycle wheel. Kathy also promised to come to see me at some point along our journey.

Being an IT-minded person, I knew we would need a website. No worries! But the trick was to direct people to the site. Pledgepage.org to the rescue. This website hosts anybody's cause and, as a long established website, is instantly findable by search engines. So with half-decent html skills, I whipped up my project pages, using the Pledgepage template, with a link to more information on my own existing websites.

I received a beautiful necklace in the mail from Joyce Simmons in Kenya who had read my Pledgepage website. The necklaces, made by 'ill women trying to make a living for their families', are normally sold to raise money for these women. Joyce suggested I auction the necklace to raise some funds for my trip. I posted it on eBay as a fundraising item and put the jewellery shop that won the bid in touch with Joyce, so hopefully they have sold more of their wares. I was receiving emails

and letters from people from all over the world to wish me well. Donations were received via my PayPal account. Friends and family proved to be very generous. I soon passed the A$1,000 mark, but I had a long way to go – I estimated the trip would cost about $50,000. It seemed appropriate to seek sponsors for The Great COFE for CF and to raise money for CF research – I even devised a complicated plan to ensure that the monies raised in different countries would be distributed to those countries' own CF Research projects. My background in mathematics made it look simple to me, but I think it was too convoluted for people to really understand. Besides, in order to distribute money fairly among research projects, perhaps I needed some money first! Was I counting the chickens before they were hatched?

We prepared dozens of sponsor packs, wrote letters, sent emails and made calls. Most letters went unanswered, some came back with apologetic replies. Some companies offered me 10-20 per cent discount on their services. Kind gestures, but where would the money come from? And extra cool, all the way from San Francisco, USA, I received an anonymous Great Smile card from http://www.helpothers.org complete with a contribution of US$10. Whoever you are, it was a wonderful letter to get in my mailbox.

# DUTCH COURAGE

I visited Holland on the way back from a holiday to see Katherine's family in the United States in August 2006. I wanted to look for maps of the proposed route and get contacts for the big ride. Once in Holland I borrowed and rented bicycles and visited relatives and friends with my mother – who caught trains! I spoke at my uncle's Rotary Club of IJmond, I visited Hugo Heymans, the doctor who first diagnosed me with CF, I trawled bicycle travel shops and map shops and visited motor associations. I also caught up with my old mate Martin Quelle, a Dutchman who – among other adventures – had travelled with me on the Trans Siberian Railway. He had recently sold out of his business interests and planned to visit me in Tasmania soon. The last 20 years of hard business life had worn him out and he needed some fun. My specialty!

Once back in Australia, training started in earnest. I had to be road fit if I was going to survive the 4,000km ride, so I entered the Tullah Challenge, an annual multi-sport contest on the remote west coast of Tasmania in the hills surrounding the small town of Tullah. The previous year I had competed in the challenge as part of 'Team of Mass Destruction' – the other two members being Paul Pritchard, a well known climber who now also lives with a disability, and Greg Schwartz, a doctor from Hobart. The team name was a reference to our state of health, but in the published results it was misprinted as the 'Team of Mass Seduction'. That time I just did the cycling leg, this time I did all three legs myself: cycling 30km, kayaking 5km and running 7.5km. Although I was close to last in most events, it was loads of fun and hard work. Needless to say I coughed the whole way!

I also enlisted the help of Hans Krellmann a keen road cyclist, who became my coach – although he never really knew he was my coach! We went out on rides once or twice a week, ranging from 20-50km at around 15-20km per hour. I still did my regular kayaking, walks, hikes and breathing exercises morning and night. David, my mate from Canberra, had given me a heart-rate monitor and it made me train a little harder as it beeps when you exercise too slow. I was getting fitter and fitter. The doctor has switched me to new drugs and I felt like a million dollars.

# THE TEAM

Most importantly, the team was also starting to take shape. I managed to convince Heather Lea, a 32-year-old Canadian writer, climber, skier and rafting river guide (and basically all-round athlete) to join the team to chronicle our adventures. Heather had met my wife, Katherine, on a climbing expedition to Bolivia in 1998. I got to know Heather on a camping trip to New Zealand two years ago. David was able to take long service leave from the police force to sign up for the entire trip, so he was to become the team medic. I still needed a support vehicle driver... and a support vehicle – how was I going to raise that kind of money?

Another thing that bothered me was that I was not able to get official 'non-profit' status from the government. That meant donations were not tax deductible. Ways around this were too difficult so I opted to just go ahead without the government's blessing. I started getting a little desperate about the whole situation. Time was ticking away and I had nowhere near enough funds or support to make this trip a success.

The new year, 2007, arrived and with it a boatload of guests arrived: first my brother Frank and family, then Stevie a friend from Canberra, Katherine's parents and her uncle came and then Martin from Holland. Good thing I am a househusband –it was a full time job looking after our guests. Fortunately I love showing people around and it is great to keep me fit and moving. I took Martin and Stevie for a hike, and then dragged Martin up to Queensland, north-eastern Australia, to go on a sailing trip with David. We spent two weeks on the boat sailing the Muddy Strait next to Fraser Island and had a good bonding time. During one of our alcoholic evenings, Martin offered his new car as a support vehicle for our Great COFE for CF and said he would join us for a few days or perhaps even a few weeks cycling along.

By now it was almost April, and I was due to start the ride in July. It was all really going to happen: I was well equipped; a vehicle had been promised to me; I had a new mobile phone to replace my rubbish pre-paid one. Things were looking up!

# MAKING NEWS

The publicity machine was starting to kick into gear. I was making the odd newspaper item, the odd mention in a newsletter and even a radio interview here or there. People started getting more interested in our adventure.

The public relations branch of the Royal Hobart Hospital put out a press release on my behalf. I had to go to Hobart for the occasion and cycle up Mount Nelson to meet the press pack there. It was an exciting prospect, my first real press conference. On the three-hour drive to Hobart, my mind was racing as I tried to remember all the important points that I wanted to get across to the media. I have never done well in test situations, and my mind was going into 'test mode'! At the base of the mountain, I met up with Dace Shugg, who is the honorary assistant editor of the Cystic Fibrosis Worldwide Newsletter, and her husband Charlie, who were keen to see me off to a good start. I first met Dace when she contacted me to write an article in the CF newsletter about my upcoming bicycle adventure. She has inspired and helped me tremendously. I popped in to visit her whenever I was in Hobart to discuss each step of the project – and was subjected to culinary delights from her garden and kitchen. Of course, I brought some selected home brews to share with her husband and fellow beer-brewer, Charlie.

I left from the bottom of Mount Nelson in my lowest gear. Half way up the hill the first TV crews came to meet me. I was coughing and spitting and fighting for my breath. I had to stop to get my breath back before they could speak to me and ride alongside of me. I never had this much attention in my life. On top of the hill the CF crew from the hospital were there to welcome me with more press. After the press left, we all went to the Mount Nelson pub for a debrief, but unfortunately none of us had brought wallets up the mountain, and we scraped loose change together from our pockets. That was my first lesson in organisation for the ride. I made it on TV and in a couple of papers. The Royal Hobart Hospital newsletter, InFocus, also published a good story on The Great COFE. Good thing Katherine and I had whipped up a T-shirt with home-made iron-on logos. Just before we left for Europe, David organised to get some cycle gear professionally printed with our logos. It was not cheap, but it made us look like a real team and we were to be easily recognisable.

I still needed a major sponsor though, so I decided to make one more mega-attempt, emailing a hundred or more people regarding sponsorships and sending off letters to 50 bike-makers around the world – many of whom specialised in alternative designs. I explained that the trip would be a perfect way to get publicity for their designs. We were not carrying heavy gear and we were only planning to cycle a conservative distance of about 80-100km on the average day. I said I would love to ride something different and – apart from a unicycle – would have no problem riding anything with pedals!

With sponsorship proving elusive, I had to accept that the idea of fund raising for CF research was a bit of a dud. This was going to be an awareness exercise. We thought it would be great to at least take camcorders with us and film the trip so we could make a small documentary out of it to show children with CF that they can still do fun and exciting and challenging things!

Coughing the Distance was decided as the documentary title. I borrowed money to buy two hi-tech pocket-sized camcorders and a bike-helmet camera for us to film the trip and received an 'Idiot's Guide to Filming' in the mail from Vanessa, a good actor friend who works at the ABC. I also borrowed books from the library about filming and got in touch with Tony Lomas, a professional filmmaker from Heartland Media in Hobart, for advice. An expert at Devonport's Southern Cross TV told me they would be able to handle the high definition footage on our return to make it into a one-hour documentary for broadcast, something they do professionally –it could easily cost about $30,000 to produce it commercially. It even turned out there were grants available for such endeavours, but unfortunately time was running out now and we were not able to apply. Through team member Heather, we found a documentary-maker who agreed to help us do the filming and I enthusiastically booked his flights from Canada. Unfortunately he broke his hand and had some other obligations that became more important so he had to cancel in the end. But nothing was going to dampen our spirits.

I had recruited 30-year-old Troy Phillips, a good mate from Devonport and also our local mechanic. Troy said he'd love to drive the support car for us. I did remind him it would be a bit of a job and less of a holiday – he would be in the car scouting out places to stay and helping us with breakdowns, while we rode the bikes. I said we'd do our best to let him ride occasionally. I knew Troy would be great to have on the team: he is easy to get along with, has good people skills, is an accomplished mechanic and has a lot of other talents. He is also an active volunteer with the local state emergency service and generally a very fit young man. It took Troy all of about three seconds to decide to come along. He was so quick in deciding that I asked him again a couple of times over the next few weeks to make sure he really meant it. Troy doesn't get holiday-pay where he works so he sold his motorbike and caravan to fund the trip – that's when I knew he was really serious! But in the end, his employer, Wiggies Radiators and Welding, gave him a decent sized cheque to help fund his ride

All of the team said they would help pay their own way. Still I promised them that I would do my best to at least pay their airfares if we had enough donations. I also started to realise that the trip was going to cost a lot more than we had calculated.

# GET ON YER BIKE

Suddenly, our luck changed. One of the emails I had sent out landed in the inbox of an organisation called The Association of the European Two-Wheeler Parts and Accessories Industry who lined me up with Batavus, the quintessential Dutch bike brand. If only you could see their range of traditional Dutch bikes! Makes me drool! This company is the bike innovator of the world and they had tentatively agreed to supply us with five AM-400 mountain bikes. As you can imagine we were ecstatic to be supported by Batavus and could hardly wait to putting the bikes to the test. Having a bicycle manufacturer on board was a sign, a good omen, an indication that other sponsors might follow, we were getting this show on the road! The bikes we had been planning on bringing were all reasonably old and cheap. My own bike was more than six-years old and the other team members either had no bike or were planning to dust off some old bike from their shed. So Batavus's sponsorship was a real godsend. We were starting to look professional now, and the team could feel that the ride was going to be something big.

Meanwhile my friend Martin in Holland was arranging the art work to cover the support vehicle – his own personal car – in our signs and logos and I was quick to tell him to add Batavus to the list. He had also offered to pay for the artwork himself. Martin even volunteered to collect the bikes from Batavus for us. The Batavus factory is about a four-hour drive from his house – a day's trip. When Martin also pointed out that we would need to prepare the bikes for the ride – put lights on, bells, mirrors, trip computers etc – he offered us the use of his workshop, but in the end took the bikes to his favourite bike shop, Fietswereld (Dutch for

Bike-World), to get the work done. The shop not only did a fantastic job and fitted special touring tires, but they also contacted Batavus who subsequently paid the bill for all the accessories! We were super-impressed. It was like a dream!

David had arranged for the bike jerseys and vests to be printed so we really were going to look like a team. In fact he was getting excited now too and even managed to get two custom-made first-aid kits donated from Freney First Aid. One kit was for us to take and the other was for our fund-raising efforts. It was great to have an Australian company sponsoring us and we were very grateful for their generous contribution.

More good news. We signed up a spare support driver, Cindy Brazendale, from Turner's Beach in north-west Tasmania, for the hardest part of our trip. Forty-eight-year-old Cindy, a hairdresser by trade, was a fellow Hash House Harrier from the Devonport Hash group. The Hash House Harriers are an international running phenomena – people meet once a week for a social run and have a few drinks afterwards. We jokingly refer to the Hash House Harriers as Drinkers with a Running Problem. She was going to meet us in Vienna in August and help us through to Istanbul in October. It also meant we had an extra hand filming for the documentary.

Next, great news: a Canadian van Praag family connection put me in touch with a kind Patagonia executive who offered to equip the team. We were told we could choose our clothing from their range. This was like Christmas! Patagonia is so good and fashionable that we sometimes refer to it as Pata-Gucci! We got a huge parcel in the mail with enough gear for all of us. We were going to be warm, dry and cosy.

# SHOW ME THE MONEY

'To ensure a nutritious diet and an occasional soft mattress for the team', The Mad Bomber Company (that makes cold weather hats), based in Virginia in the United States, pledged US$7000 to our fund. The offer was even more remarkable when you consider that his company had just recovered from a fire in its warehouse. Brent Reynolds, the Mad Bomber himself, wrote to say he was proud to be associated with a 'Mad Dutchman riding a push-bike through Europe for Cystic Fibrosis Awareness'. If the money were not enough, he also sent a few Mad Bomber hats for a planned fund-raising auction. I first ran into Brent while travelling with my Dutch friend Martin. The three of us wound up taking the Trans Siberian Express together in 1985. We stayed in touch over the years and I ended up working for Brent as his IT and Communications Manager for Mad Bomber for three years.

Every day parcels kept coming through my door: from small battery-operated hard drives and extra memory cards to tripods and filters for the video cameras which I had purchased from my local Harvey Norman department store.

Pharmaceutical company Roche offered me $1,000 to finance a portable nebuliser and a portable fridge to store my Pulmozyme, an expensive but also extremely important medicine for people with CF. The drug, which is manufactured by Roche, is inhaled for 10-minutes every night – vaporised in a specialised nebuliser. As taking a fridge to Europe was out of the question, Roche agreed that I could buy two nebulisers instead as long as they both ended up with the Tasmanian CF community. I gave one to the Adult CF Unit in Hobart and took the other one with me on the trip, donating it afterwards to the CF Association of Tasmania.

Our fund-raising efforts were also in full swing. The Adult CF clinic in Hobart suggested I have a few movie nights. Rowan Bridley, a CF specialist nurse at the clinic, had been involved with one before and offered to make inquiries for me in Hobart. I made an appointment with the sole cinema in Devonport and the manager there advised me to book a premiere showing. With Shrek the Third on offer, to me the choice was easy. I made some posters and had them emailed, printed, and distributed around town.

Dace Shugg, Rowan and the Adult CF crew, meanwhile, were sorting out the movie night at a Hobart cinema. It was hard work keeping track of ticket sales and I had to organise door prizes and nibbles for the events. The Hobart film team was extremely successful in securing a huge amount of food and drink, some excellent prizes, including a trip for a family by police car to the wharf followed by a cruise on the police vessel and back home in a police car.

Not expecting much, I was delighted to start receiving offers of door prizes: petrol vouchers, family passes from Forestry Tasmania to visit their fabulous wilderness tourist attractions –Dismal Swamp and the Tahune canopy airwalk. Local shops came to the party with great prizes, we had a beautiful painting donated by Dace's sister Liga Veska and a life-sized blow up Shrek from Coles in Hobart.

Tasmania author Alice Hansen gave us signed copies of her children's book, A Devilish Tale which is aimed at raising awareness about and funds to help eradicate Tasmanian Devil Facial Tumour Disease, which is threatening to wipe out our island's famous small black mammals. Alice also wrote an article on The Great COFE for CF for Bicycling Australia magazine.

Another author, Leah Orr from the USA, donated six signed copies of Kyle's First Crush – the first ever Cystic Fibrosis children's book. All the profits of this book go to a Cystic Fibrosis Foundation. I passed a few copies to the CF unit in Hobart where they were very much appreciated and will be read by many affected parents and children with CF. The staff at the local Harvey Norman store's staff were as enthusiastic as I was about my ride. They not only helped me with photocopying and printing for the movie fundraiser, donating auction items for the dinner, but they had also negotiated with their suppliers to get me a good price on the two Panasonic high definition camcorders.

The Hobart fundraising movie was a great success, bringing in A$2,300 due to a full theatre, thanks mostly to Rowan, Dace and Jenny from the Hobart Adult CF Unit. In the audience were the renowned Tasmanian landscape photographer Ian Wallace and prizewinning author and rock climber, Paul Pritchard. Both Paul and Ian had provided me with signed copies of their own books and encouraged me to write a book about my trip.

The Devonport Shrek movie premiere was also an awesome event. Thanks to the great effort people put into ticket sales we managed to get 150 odd people to come and this resulted in almost $1,800 profit. Plenty of beer was supplied by Tasmanian brewers Cascade and Boags, groceries were sponsored by Woolworths, some food donated by Pizza Hut, Banjos and Bakers Dozen, a dozen bottles of fine Tasmanian wine were donated by Tiger Ranch Wines. Door prizes from Coles and Forestry Tasmania, chocolates from House of Anvers, sweatbands from Canoe 'n Surf, petrol vouchers from Rio Tinto. Cheese was supplied by the Burnie Hash House Harriers.

The movies were preceded by a small speech that I had prepared about my big plan. It was a real thrill to address an audience of hundreds of people who had come for me! The best part was handing out the fantastic door prizes. My prize, though, was raising CF awareness. Everybody knew that we were raising money for a team to travel to Europe for a 42-year-old with Cystic Fibrosis to ride 4,000km. Our message was getting out!

And the press showed their face too. I even got into the RACT (Royal Automobile Club of Tasmania) magazine for June 2007 and in the Sunday Examiner newspaper. We seemed to be gaining momentum.

# I'M WITH THE BAND

On Sunday, 8 July, I turned 42 and celebrated with the final fundraiser for the ride – and a $7,000 boost to our kitty. This final event was an amazing dinner auction night at the Deck Cafe in Devonport, which – at no cost to us – was arranged for me, and their suppliers provided everything necessary for a three-course meal with matching wines free of charge. The restaurant, our favourite in town, holds a fundraiser every year and this year, the owner, Troy Baggett, offered to do it for us. When he told me that even his staff were volunteering their services for the night, I tripped over my jaw, that is how low it dropped!

With the help of friends at the Tasmanian Ambulance Service, we secured 17-year-old singer-songwriter Ben Curtis to play at the event – Ben's father is one of the paramedics that Katherine, my wife, works with. Ben's biggest solo hit was Just Breathe, a pure coincidence! I liked his music so much that I asked if we could use his music – an eclectic style of indie infused with pop – for our documentary.

Just Breathe will end up as the title track for the Coughing the Distance documentary. Who knows, he might even write another song called Coughing the Distance.

A few weeks after the event Ben and I appeared on an ABC drive-time radio show together to chat about the ride, and rumour that he was providing a soundtrack for a film!

Around this time I also came to know Brian Summerfield, who had ridden 25,000km around Australia, raising funds in every town he came to for the children of Tibet. Brian turned out to be a very interesting man. We met up on a few times and he gave me some valuable tips on travelling by bicycle, such as having a good mirror and tyres – he told me that a couple from Germany who he had met on his travels had not had a flat tire for thousands of kilometres because they had particularly good tires.

Brian couldn't make it to our Shrek fundraiser because he was busy – he had a private audience with the Dalai Lama (!) in Melbourne. But he was an obvious choice for guest speaker at the Deck Café dinner and his fascinating tales of his journey were truly inspiring.

Geoff Phillips, manager of the local Hooker Real Estate franchise, was our ace auctioneer on the night and did an incredibly good job at teasing the crowds. He interpreted anything that members of the public did (or did not do) as a bid. If he looked at someone and they sat still that was a sign for him, if they specifically nodded no that was a sign for him too. Of course he did not sell items to non-serious bidders, but he sure got the crowd to pay attention and join in. He sold everything on the list including a lot of personal tax-return vouchers from Phoenix Accounting, accommodation vouchers, petrol vouchers, massages, food hampers and paintings.

With nothing left to sell, he was handed a restaurant plate signed by a celebrity that only minutes previously had been hanging on the wall of the restaurant, and which was quickly put under the hammer. The night was great fun and a huge success. Our kitty had now increased to about A$15,000 and I was able to buy some airfares for our team members.

# GUYS LIKE US

Meanwhile, on the other side of the world, another 42-year-old Dutchman with Cystic Fibrosis was planning an amazing challenge. Marc Bastiaensen was about to embark on a 2,200km walk across Europe, carrying his backpack all the way from his hometown of Nispen, a small village in the south of Holland, to Rome in an effort to raise €100,000 for Cystic Fibrosis Worldwide and to aid in setting up CF clinics in India, where the mean age of people with CF is only 12. He estimated that his walk would take four months. Although our planned routes cross each other in

Germany, sadly he would arrive there about two weeks before I would and neither of us could change our plans. But it made me realise that there were more people with Cystic Fibrosis going on extreme adventures.

On the internet I found several healthy people doing serious feats for Cystic Fibrosis. Take Noel Webb for instance, he was going to paddle 4,000 km in a kayak, clockwise around the UK. Not to mention all the other people on trips to raise money and raise awareness for other great causes. No wonder that many of the large companies I approached for sponsorship were not able to respond to my letters and emails. I was not the only one.

# CONNECTIONS COUNT

As I have often found, one thing generally will lead to another, and this was the case when my search for a camcorder led me to a cameraman. I had been having a hard time trying to find a third camcorder that could be used in conjunction with a video head-cam that I had ordered from the US. After ordering several models from local shops that turned out to be incompatible, scouring the internet and calling about 50 other shops around Australia without luck, a salesman from Ted's Camera Store, Michael Deeble, who had taken an interest in our mission, found a camcorder that would do the trick. As we chatted, I mentioned that our Canadian filmmaker had cancelled and Michael thought he might just happen to know a possible replacement.

Next thing I knew, I had a call from 22-year-old Lucas Li, from Canberra. He had completed a degree at Australian National University a few years earlier and now specialised in Production Management. He told me he was a competent cinematographer and editor – apparent in his entry in the Getup.org.au film competition: Oz in 30 Seconds – he was very keen on the project, he could ride a bike and he really wanted to come. In fact he was so keen, that within a few days he had found an investor to help to pay his airfare. So we had a new team member on board. Qantas was very prompt, efficient and friendly in cancelling the flights for our Canadian filmmaker and booking Lucas on the same flights to Europe as us.

With Lucas, the team was complete and we were getting ready to go. They were an interesting and diverse group. I knew them all – except for Lucas – but none of the others had really met each other before. And they were about to spent 72 days together.

# WHAT HAVE I DONE!

I can hardly breathe without coughing. I am miserable and just want to cry. There's barely a week to go before I set off on the bicycle ride of a lifetime, almost two years in the planning, and I have been struck down with a lung infection.

I am supposed to leave for Europe for an incredible 4,000km bicycle ride from Paris to Istanbul. A whole team of friends are ready to cycle with me, plane tickets have been bought, sponsors have provided equipment, the community has helped with funding – and I am sick with a terrible fever that bathes me in sweat each night. I have pneumonia and am too sick to fly. I have to face facts: I have Cystic Fibrosis. What have I done!

I am Walter van Praag, diagnosed at 10, now aged 42. Even with the best of care, people with Cystic Fibrosis have an average life expectancy of only 35 and, without a daily barrage of antibiotics and medicine, most would not live past their teens. I now only have 50 per cent lung capacity, yet this infection is the only thing stopping me from setting out with my team of friends on my planned 72-day bike ride that will take us across 11 European countries.

I still have a gazillion things to do before we leave – if we leave. But I am sleeping with towels to soak up my feverish night sweats now and I am worried. I grab straight for the one-week's reserve of antibiotics I always have at home for such emergencies and make a doctor's appointment at the East Devonport Medical Centre to get a new prescription for more antibiotics. The doctor asks me to go past the nearby North West Regional Hospital in Latrobe to get a chest x-ray to bring with me.

I am terrified of hospitals – with so many sick people about they pose the greatest risk of getting dangerous bacteria into my lungs. I sneak into the hospital through the back entrance and straight into Radiography to avoid the sick waiting rooms, but they insist that one of their emergency doctors sees me before I go. With my x-ray in my hands I am told to take a seat in the casualty waiting room.

It's been 20 minutes already and I am starting to get freaked. The waiting room is a bacteria breeding ground. What am I waiting for? What are they going to say? Take antibiotics, probably – but I am already taking them. Or are they going to order more tests? The hospital is so tiny it can't carry out all the tests they would need to.

This is not the first time I have been sick and this is not the first time I have had these symptoms – I've had Cystic Fibrosis for over 40 years now – but it still feels terrible. Everything is just building up. We have so much falling into place: the weather is great for cycling, the sun is shining upon us. But now I am getting sick – the timing is terrible. I am sitting at the hospital with tears welling in my eyes. The staff are trying hard to keep me here, promising the emergency doctor will see me soon. But it's now been an hour and I just can't handle it any longer so I run out the door.

Typically, with bouts of infection like this, people with CF get hospitalised for intensive IV antibiotic treatment, physiotherapy and other treatments. I spent a week in 2001 undergoing 'maintenance' – a course of large doses of antibiotics and physiotherapy to clean the lungs of excessive infection, which most people with CF need at least twice a year. I had been diagnosed with a Pseudomonas aeruginosa lung infection. It was awful, just lying around for a week. One afternoon I 'escaped' to try to go for a jog around the hospital, but my muscles and lungs had lost so much condition from lying around that I had trouble even walking. When I left the hospital after that week I came out with great lung function, but four weeks on I came down with a huge infection again.

The truth is that I had also been under a lot of stress at the time – my father had passed away and it had been very difficult for me to give the eulogy at his cremation. And the respite centre where my father had spent the last night of his life was not the best place for someone with CF to be as many of the bacteria that cause pneumonia in patients with severely compromised immune systems – such as in end-stage cancer – can infect us PWCF (People With CF) as well.

As my coughing becomes worse this time too, I know that my poor health now is probably due to a culmination of all the stress, pressures, excitements and disappointments of the past three months. When I go to see my regular doctor, Dr Afrujul Alam, of the East Devonport Medical Centre, a few days later, he checks out the x-rays and confirms what I already know: I have a serious lung infection. He prescribes me more antibiotics. I have not tested positive for the Pseudomonas aeruginosa bacteria lately, which is a blessing. You rarely get rid of that bacteria, and it most likely still lurks inside my lungs somewhere (indeed that is what was troubling me as it turned out, well after I returned home).

Slowly, a little at a time, I can feel the infection clearing. As the combination of antibiotics that I was given start to work, I get back out running, riding and walking. A journalist interviewing me a few days ago asked me what my next adventure after the ride would be, and then, at the height of my infection, it seemed to me that it would probably be a lung transplant. The paper immediately quoted me as saying my ride was the last big adventure for these lungs! I hope not.

My lung function had come down to 38 per cent of that expected for my age/height – some people would need oxygen with that much impairment. Lung damage is pretty much irreversible, but after the antibiotics, lots of exercise and an asthma spray called Seretide, I have just tested as having just over 50 per cent lung function again. Numbers and facts in medical science are hard to explain sometimes. How can my lung function fluctuate so much if lung damage is irreversible? Doctors explain these things, I am not a doctor!

The Great COFE for CF is back on, and while I am elated, I am also terrified of what will happen while I am away. While I know I can't live in a bubble, the fear of getting a nasty infection is always there. At home, I am even in danger from the bacteria that live in compost bins and grow in sour milk. What can I expect in Europe? Will I get infected with something really bad? And, if that happens, will I get over it again or will it kill me?

The day before leaving a fellow member of the City of Devonport Lions club comes to my door presenting me with a $500 donation towards the ride and 10 Lions Flags of the Devonport Club to swap with Lions Clubs along the way. Having the flags is a great introduction to any Lions Club as the traditional flag exchange is seen as a token of friendship and camaraderie which emphasises the Lions Club's International nature. Each club always proudly displays their collection of flags at each meeting. Receiving the 10 flags was pretty much a ticket to valuable support on foreign soils; it is going to be a great asset for the ride.

# BLESSINGS...

I am standing in Devonport's tiny airport with a Saint Christopher talisman, the patron-saint of travellers, and a scarf blessed by a Tibetan monk. The gifts, from my neighbour and mate Brian, are talismans for our long journey ahead. There are a few tears and a few beers as Troy, the mechanic, and I say goodbye to our families and friends.

At last we are truly on our way. We watch from the plane window as the tiny airport becomes smaller and smaller, and all the while we know we are heading for something big. We can feel it in our bones.

David Barz, the team medic, has flown down from the Australian capital, Canberra, and is waiting for us when we touch down at Melbourne airport. David had been on board since the start of the project. After many years of hard work in the police force, David was ready for an adventure in Europe – not that his job was not exciting, this ride would probably be a welcome break from the excessive exercise he gets with his work chasing criminals

I even manage to find Lucas Li, the cameraman, at the airport without even knowing what he looks like! Lucas is a cool dude of Thai appearance with long hair and is already clearly in travel mode. I have a good feeling about him immediately. Lucas, the last addition to the team, was very excited to be asked along – even at such short notice – and counted himself lucky for the opportunity. For him, after studying and working in the field for a few years, this was his big break into film and a chance to make a documentary on his own. His mother was very pleased for him, but his girlfriend, Alix, was not so happy to lose him for three months.

The four of us, together at last and nervously waiting for our flight to Europe, find out that we are going to have to wait even longer – our flight is delayed a couple of hours. So we hole up in the Qantas lounge – David is a Club member and all my years of travel somehow means I qualify for frequent flier earned access to the luxury lounge. We are eating and drinking, and talking excitedly about our plans. Everything is perfect. When we get on that plane and leave Australian shores our adventure will really start!!

# THE ADVENTURE STARTS NOW!

We are late before we even get started. Racing though London's Heathrow airport, having landed a few hours late, we get to the gate for our connecting flight to Amsterdam just in time – but are sent away because we don't have boarding passes. David heads to the connections desk to get a boarding pass for the next available flight, while Troy, Lucas and I arrange the flights from the comfort and solace of the British Airways club lounge. St Christopher is obviously already on the job, but he was about to need overtime.

When we finally get to Amsterdam on the next flight in, my Dutch friends are waiting for us; but sadly our luggage is not. We join the huge queue of disgruntled passengers at the lost luggage window. Because we had missed our first flight, my friends have already been waiting for us for two hours and now we are keeping them waiting even longer while we fill out all the paperwork for our missing bags. The biggest worry is that my 'dry-ice' packed medicine has not made it.

I had originally planned to bring my cold medicine with me on the plane as hand luggage and ask the crew to put it in the fridge – as recommended to me by Qantas. But after months of trying to get clear information about luggage restrictions for the flights to London and Amsterdam, I was told the day before we left that I would only be able to take one piece of hand luggage and was only allowed to carry as much medicine as I was reasonably expected to require to get to my destination. I was advised to pack a suitcase with dry ice to keep my medicine cool. And this meant that I had to complete a 'dangerous goods' declaration in Devonport and label the bag 'dry ice' before I was allowed to check it in.

I need the medicine, but past experience with British Airways and lost luggage has me really concerned. Last year I had helped out a person whose luggage had been lost en route to Amsterdam via Heathrow and also last year BA lost my brother's luggage at Heathrow on his way to Amsterdam.

Disappointed and tired, we eventually make our way to the hotel. We are soon cheered by my friend Martin, who is waiting there proud to show us the beautiful support vehicle that he has prepared for us. It is magnificent – and so are the five wonderful new bicycles that innovative Dutch manufacturer Batavus donated for our trip. My smile is back. I love Amsterdam and can't wait to show it to the team. We are going to have lots of nice Dutch food and pastries, sweets and lollies (lots of liquorice) and they'll meet the friends I grew up with as well as my relatives. I am really looking forward to it.

After finally getting to bed at well past midnight Dutch time, I am woken up by the concierge at 3am to say my medicine suitcase had been found and delivered to the hotel. By this time the valuable medicine is not exactly cool anymore, so before rolling over in bed I immediately put it in the hotel fridge and just hope it will be OK.

The next morning, the only other piece of luggage to arrive at the hotel is David's first aid kit. We are still dressed in the clothes we left Australia in, and so we spend the morning shopping. We keep calling the airline but we often get a recorded message and the calls are costing us a fortune from the hotel - I thought they were local calls.

After one day, the only good news we have is that David's luggage should arrive tonight. British Airways knows we are on a charity ride but still tells it has no idea at what point we can claim damages from them, saying that it is 'reasonable' in their eyes to expect a two- to five-day delay in finding our luggage because it is peak season. To compensate for this they give us one-size-fits-all white T-shirts and basic hygiene kits to bridge the gap and invite us to come back to the airport after 3pm tomorrow to see if we can find our bags in the mountain of as yet unsorted lost luggage that they have stored in a giant warehouse at the airport. I pray that our luck changes as we are meant to leave for Paris the day after.

If our bags stay lost it will be disastrous. We will need to replace our tents, sleeping bags, and hi-tech equipment for filming such as the wireless microphones, hard-disk storage, chargers, data cables – not to mention all the cycle clothing and equipment. Most annoying is the loss of all the awesome clothing that was donated to us by Patagonia. Big money, big loss. I am also distressed that the dozen Lion flags that I had received from the Devonport Lions Club to swap with other Lions Clubs in countries along the way could also be lost. The Lions Clubs would have given us valuable help along the way and without the flags to offer them I feel it would not be right to just call on them for help. Lucas, in charge of the documentary is delighted with all the drama, but I am concerned there might not actually be a ride to film at this rate.

David is reunited with his luggage. It was delivered to the hotel. We know that the rest of our luggage was with it since they had retrieved the first aid kit and my medicine bag, so my hopes are up! But there is another complication developing: team member, Heather Lea, has had to delay her flight because her mother has fallen ill in Canada. Heather, who had only just returned from an African Adventure, had been flat out soliciting support for the COFE trip – even organising a photo night of her Africa photos to raise money   and rushing out the latest edition of Reved, her own quarterly publication in her hometown of Revelstoke in British Columbia, Canada. And now Heather's mother has collapsed with a mysterious illness. I am scared that if Heather's mum does not recover quickly, it could mean she has to cancel – after all, parents are much more important than a bike ride in Europe.

The only good thing at the moment is that we are in Amsterdam and we have a chance to be tourists because of the extra time we have here waiting for our luggage to show up. We get up nice and early for our first run and the streets are pretty well deserted at 7am except for some street sweepers and a few drug pushers.

Freshly showered, we change into the clothes we bought yesterday and eventually find a bakery that's open – Amsterdam is totally shut-down in the mornings – and buy chocolate croissants and coffee, too.

We had intended to camp tonight, but as all our camping gear is still lost we have to spend another night in a hotel. To save money we move to a cheaper hotel and have to find another place to park the car, which is turning out to be very expensive – around €45 a night, it is the going rate and the same as what the first hotel charged us.

Lucas and Troy have been on the phone to their insurance companies back in Australia and are told they will be reimbursed for any replacement gear they have to buy. The insurance agent to whom Troy was speaking was not surprised that British Airways had lost our luggage from Heathrow – we were not the only ones caught up in its summer baggage-handling crisis.

Our last afternoon in Amsterdam and Troy, Lucas and I head back out to Schiphol airport to check the lost luggage rooms filled with a mountain of 'unprocessed' luggage from Heathrow. There are musical instruments, bags and suitcases and duffel bags – all seem to have clearly labelled tags. A few employees seem to be sifting leisurely through some luggage in the corner. We have a seriously sinking feeling. We have been caught up in a desperate situation at the airport. We check all the rooms with luggage but our gear is nowhere to be seen. Our hopes of finding our luggage are dashed.

The lost-luggage-desk gives us some more forms to fill in listing everything we have lost. They tell us that if our gear doesn't turn up by tomorrow, BA will pay us €35 for every day it is delayed and that we should send receipts for anything we have to buy to BA – mind you they couldn't tell us if they would refund the receipt we send them or if there was a limit and didn't have any paperwork to answer our questions. We supply them with the details of our hotel in Paris.

We race back to Amsterdam and go on a wild sweaty shopping spree to buy what we need for the trip before the shops close. We had already purchased lots of essentials such as toiletries underwear, shorts and T-shirts, so we just had to get basic camping and cycling gear. We head to the only sports shop we could find in Amsterdam Central, in the Kalverstraat, and buy duffel bags, tents, sleeping bags, bicycle shorts, rain-gear, and panniers (bicycle bags) for the bikes, cycle underwear and spare socks. We lug heavy bags out the shop as they lock the doors behind us. My American Express card got a hammering but at least we've got gear now.

The replacement gear isn't nearly as good as the stuff BA lost. I guess we half expect our luggage to turn up eventually, but also we simply don't have the money to buy the good gear such as Patagonia gear we had been supplied with. As for the hi-tech equipment required for our filming, we will just have to make do with what we have – the specialised equipment would take weeks of searching to replace. We are really glad we carried our most crucial equipment, such as the video camcorders and cameras, the laptop and my nebuliser, with us in our hand luggage on the plane.

We wonder why David's luggage made it in the end – was it because he changed his flight to Amsterdam at the transfer desk in Heathrow, while we three did it in the BA lounge? Who knows what happened. It's just frustrating to think someone made the effort to look for, and find, my medicine bag and the first aid kit that was part of David's luggage, but just left the rest of our luggage there. Surely it must have all been sitting next to each other. We had big distinctive looking Patagonia duffel bags.

My uncle Bernard has called up a few newspapers and got the publicity ball rolling for us and we get some good press for the big ride ahead. Yesterday morning, while the others had breakfast, I had a phone interview with a journalist and found it difficult to sound positive. We have had a bad start, but we are pushing ahead.

Tomorrow David and Troy will drive off to Paris with all our gear in the support car, while Lucas and I will try to find some crucial computer/camera parts necessary for the documentary before catching our flight to Paris. Lucas is shooting good footage, but we really miss the external microphones as the audio is not so good from the built-in mike.

There is another problem tomorrow, as it turns out. I have accidentally arranged to meet a Dutch press photographer at 10am tomorrow and our flight leaves at 11am. There is no way I can do both. I can't reach the photographer or the reporter who interviewed me yesterday and British Airways is closed for the night. I feel terrible. I am responsible for all of us, and I am stuffing up left right and centre. I just have to hold on to my belief that everything happens for a reason and generally, as long as you keep on trying and ploughing on, things tend to work out one way or the other.

We wake up early and try to do what we need to do prior to making our way to Paris. I start by trying to call the airline to get a later flight, but am unable to reach anyone. I end up printing our boarding passes for the flight using the hotel's computer and walk to the nearby train station before the photographer comes. I pre-purchase our train tickets to the airport, ready for a quick getaway to catch our flight. The photographer turns up nice and early, takes shots of me and my new bike. Lucas and I then left the bike with David and Troy to pack into the support vehicle. We wish them a pleasant drive before making a mad dash to the station.

Puffing and out of breath, we learn that the next train to the airport is leaving in one minute from one of the furthest platforms, but if we wait for the next train we would surely miss our plane. We run like crazy for the train and jump on board as the doors are closing. When I run, or do any exercise at all, I cough copiously, and so coughing and spluttering, paper tissues in my hand, and Lucas filming it all, I am standing in the train, leaning against the wall trying to get my breath back as I cough up chunks of green phlegm which I neatly cough into paper tissues.

Two women, who also just made the train are obviously concerned and can't believe the sight of me, just about to die from coughing while my companion is happily filming me. I explain that I have CF and my companion is filming me for a documentary about our amazing ride to raise awareness of CF. It turns out one of the women works in Istanbul herself. She asks me where I am planning to finish the ride and I mention the historic Pera Palas hotel, which was built for Orient Express passengers. She says she works just 50m from there and if we needed any help to call her. The woman, Laura Bins, turns out to be the Press and Cultural Affairs officer of the Consulate General of the Netherlands in Istanbul, and is travelling with her mother. Can you imagine my luck, getting on the train and meeting her? And my luck doesn't stop there – amazingly we also make our flight to Paris just in time.

# A DROITE? TOUT DROIT!

Driving through France is probably not the best time to discover that the car's navigation system does not speak your language. David and Troy are in the support vehicle heading for Paris and the sat-nav, which speaks German, Dutch and French – but not English – is causing problems. Its built-in system to avoid congestion, is trying to divert them off the main highway – at odds with the directions being given by David's more basic handheld GPS. To make matters worse, as they near the chaos that is Paris, they discover that the car's GPS system only has detailed maps for Benelux and that, beyond a few major highways for France, are now on their own. Probably just as well really as the French voice and language display is already driving them nuts. They turn it off, take a deep breath and enter Paris's ring road using David's trusty GPS.

Lucas and I, thought we had it easy, arriving safely at Charles de Gaulle airport in Paris, we first get the airport-bus into central Paris and then a taxi to our hotel, the Sofitel Paris Porte De Sevres. What seemed like a simple enough exercise, becomes an endurance test for the bus which battles its way through the Parisian traffic for two hours.

Meanwhile, Heather, in Canada, had already emailed me to say that her mother's condition has fortunately proved to be not so serious and that she will be joining us in Paris only one day behind her planned schedule. Our own nightmarish trip from the airport makes us realise, however, that it would be madness to try to collect Heather from the airport by car. After witnessing the crazy traffic and free-for-all driving of the Parisians, none of us were going to volunteer to drive alone (the car only has room for two people) to the airport – especially without any maps in the navigator. She will have to catch the bus into Paris and then a taxi to the hotel, like we did, and so I email her as soon as I get to our hotel with the travel instructions and hope she receives it in time!

It is now Thursday, 26 July, and just two days to go before we set off on the great COFE ride. Heather is now in the air and us men hit the streets wearing 'runners'. It's early and most shops are still closed and roads are empty – a perfect time to exercise, so we set off on a run to the Eiffel Tower. Lucas, whose running shoes are in his lost luggage, decides to run alongside us in his sandals to film the event. Perhaps an indication of how slow a 42-year-old with CF runs. Troy seems to be having a little trouble keeping up with me, even with my coughing – maybe he is just being nice. David, however, says he needs to go harder and says he'll met us under the Eiffel Tower – seems an easy enough meeting point. But when we get there, we can't see David anywhere. We assume he's still on the road getting in some extra miles, so we sit down on the grass and wait. After about 15 minutes we are getting cold and then we finally spot him. Turns out he had been waiting about 15 minutes for us too – also sitting under the Eiffel Tower, not far from us but just out of sight. We realise that we are going to have to be more exact in our plans if we are not going to lose team members along the way.

We all still have chores to do before the big ride, so we split up. I jump on the Paris metro in search of a big computer store to replace IT stuff, such as rechargeable batteries, an external hard disk for our video footage and other necessary gadgets that were lost with our luggage and then head off to the Gard du Nord to pick up my friend Martin who is coming from Holland to see us off and join us for a few days or weeks. Troy and David are looking for bits and pieces for the bikes while Lucas is searching for wireless microphones and a hydraulic tripod.

Calling back at the hotel with Martin in tow, I check my email to see if Heather has replied to mine. Nothing. Had she received my message? Was she going to wait at the airport for us to pick her up? I try everything I can to contact her: leaving messages at the airport, emailing her again, emailing her family and calling British Airways. So when she still doesn't show up at the hotel in a timely fashion after her flight had landed, I start to panic. I'm not even sure now if she knows which hotel we are in, or if she has some way of contacting us.

While I am panicking in the hotel, Heather is left to her own devices at the airport. She somehow finds an internet connection. Surprisingly there is no public internet there, except for the executive business class lounges to which she has no access. A staff member allows her to check her email, she finds my message with details of where we are staying, and makes her own way to the hotel.

In the meantime, panicking frantically I ask the hotel to call the police and ask them to call the airline to see if she has actually arrived on the flight. The airlines are not allowed to give out that kind of passenger information, but can give it to the police. As I am on the phone at the concierge desk downstairs in the hotel,

Heather strolls in. I just about cry from relief! Unfazed, she had made her own way to the hotel. She has already proved herself to be a durable chick before we start riding. Why was I even worried about her?

There are more arrivals; Jenny Busch, the Tasmanian Coordinator from the Hobart adult CF unit arrives in Paris with her Australian friends to see us off. Our fans! We arrange to meet at a cafe. I am still totally wired and frantic from the Heather panic, and need to sit down with a beer! I am in such a state that I can't wait at the table to be served and when I go to the bar, the staff just points me back to the table. I feel desperate for the drink and realise just how much stress I have been under. It has all hit me now. Perhaps when we finally hit the road, it will be some release.

# PARIS, FRANCE. OUR STARTING POINT.

'Walter has been tied up and placed in a closet as a result of buying the stinkiest cheese in all of France. I am Heather and it looks like I'll be stepping in as Blog-updater. Walt's attempt to remove the stinky-cheese smell from our hotel had him carting it around the city, polluting the expensively-perfumed air and attracting small animals along our path to Le Louvre Museum. Unfortunately, our people-watching curiosity and lolly-gagging brought us to the Louvre with only an hour to spare between it and a pre-arranged meeting with David who had done a reconnaissance mission for finding a simple way out of Paris for us. A decision was made and Le Louvre was going to wait until next time for Walter's cheese offerings.

After I arrived in Paris the previous night, and found my way to the hotel we met with Jenny Busch and her friends from London. Jenny had flown in from a meeting in Copenhagen to see us off. Over pizza and red wine, we told her of our luggage mishaps. As it looks for the moment, British Airways has, in theory, located the missing bags of sponsored gear and expensive camera equipment and we are told the luggage is 'at the airport'... which airport, we don't know. It is possible these necessary items are making their way back to the address of origin - Australia. We wait optimistically for its arrival, but haven't got much time left to be hopeful as we prepare to leave at 10am from the Eiffel Tower. Most of the missing camping gear and camera equipment has been replaced during sporadic bursts at the shopping centre across from our hotel - at least convenience is on our side!' – Heather's first blog entry, Friday 27 July 2007.

After a little obligatory sightseeing in Paris on Friday, we prepare the bikes for departure and do some last-minute shopping for bike equipment – basic tools, pumps, tubes, helmets and gloves. Troy's tools are gone with his luggage; he does a good job improvising with what we can buy in the nearby sports shop. David instead spends hours planning our exit from Paris, cycling around Paris with his maps and GPS to make sure we will not get lost on our first day tomorrow.

Saturday, 28 July. We are leaving Paris today. Our luggage is still lost and, although one of the BA numbers that we call has a message to say they are extremely busy and unable to answer any calls, I am certain some of the bags will be found in time and delivered to us before we leave. I like to believe in miracles, and I also believe in Santa Claus. The other team members are not convinced and place their first bets of the trip. At least the search has narrowed and we now believe the luggage is either at Schiphol airport in Amsterdam, Charles De Gaulle in Paris or at Heathrow in London. As we check out of the hotel I let the concierge know that our support vehicle could come back for any luggage delivered to the hotel in the next three days. I gave them our special phone number for the trip.

# WE'RE OFF

Under the Eiffel tower, no pains yet and ready to ride! It's 9am. We are under the Eiffel tower, the drizzling rain is beading on our new raincoats and the remains of a snatched breakfast in our hands. Little Australian flags are being waived by our farewell committee who are all wearing homemade COFE supporter T-shirts and Lucas circles us with a camera, filming every moment.

There are beds and dinner waiting for us in Provins, about 100km south-east of Paris, should we make it by tonight. The president of the Rotary Club there had very kindly arranged hospitality for us after my uncle emailed them. All we have to manage now is to navigate our way out of Paris – surviving the crazy driving techniques we have witnessed already is a scary prospect. Our plan is to find our way out of Paris in four hours. It may be a little optimistic, but we are ready to try.

We look every bit a team with our bicycle jerseys emblazoned with professional-looking COFE logos. The bicycles are also tuned to perfection. We all jumped on for a short test ride yesterday but discovered that Lucas had not been entirely truthful with us – he can hardly ride a bike! He had trouble even getting on his bike and changing gears seemed an advanced move. David showed panic in his eyes. But I told Lucas I was glad he lied about his cycling skills – at least we have a cameraman with us and it shows just how keen he was to join us. David reminded me that learning to ride a bicycle in Paris, with more than 100km ahead of us, was not ideal, and the support vehicle only had room for one passenger. My friend Martin was going to follow us in the support vehicle as much as possible and check up on us regularly. He would rescue Lucas after a few hours.

So, at 10am, as we mount our bikes and ride off into the light Parisian rain to the enthusiastic fanfare of our supporters, Lucas stays behind a while to film us, waiting until no one is looking to clumsily mount his bike and wobble off after us. We took it easy and waited for him to catch up not far from where we started the ride.

Dressed in our new cycling fatigues we leave Paris. I am not used to wearing proper cycling gear, and modestly bought some cycling shorts in Paris to replace the new ones I had lost with my luggage. They were not very comfortable and they seem to be crumbling underneath me. After about 5 kilometres into our ride I could feel the inner bits of these shorts shifting out of the shorts. A little tugging here and there resulted in the padded undy part of these cycle shorts to come out from under my shorts. Maybe I misunderstood something about these shorts. I found a public toilet and realised the cycling shorts were merely cheap cycling undies with a matching pair of shorts that was flimsily buttoned together. Putting them on requires a little more effort and concentration.

We all started out with great enthusiasm, adopting the riding techniques we've copied from watching the Tour de France on TV: riding fast and very close together. We draught off each other and swap position regularly, ensuring we are all riding at maximum speed. All I could think of is how fast we are moving and how fit we are. This ride is going to be easy! We ride smoothly along reasonably flat roads in the light weekend traffic and even stop at a vegetable stand along the road for a break, eating fresh fruit. Life is good!

'Sorry all - we'd love to write about every wonderful thing we saw on our first day of the great COFE ride, but we can't find anyone with enough energy to spell words properly, let alone have them make sense...

Here is the consolidated version, soon to be updated if we ever stop eating ourselves into food-comas every night and can stay awake long enough. Day one of The Great COFE was successful! At 10am Walter, Troy, David, Lucas and Heather left the Eiffel Tower exactly on schedule. We rode through quiet Saturday streets in the drizzling rain that soon stopped and the rest of the way through the suburbs of Paris was in the sun. Leaving the city was a bit tricky at times, and map reading became a frequent activity.

When once we stopped for a map-reading and saw that we were not yet even at our halfway point, the day's objective of Provins seemed dreamy, but at 5.50pm, 10 minutes before schedule, we arrived! Our first day and already 100.01km are behind us! After comparing bum-calluses and using stair-railings as crutches, we were overjoyed to meet Steve and Aline Blackford from the Provins Rotary Club' – Heather's blog entry, Saturday 28 July.

We are welcomed in Provins, by our hosts the Blackfords with open arms and a couple of Guinness's! I am pretty beat after riding 100km – oh, and falling over onto a car stopped at some traffic lights about 100m from our destination. I had my feet firmly clipped into the pedal clips slowly rolling towards the lights hoping not to need to unclip – those clips are tricky – but ended up just toppling over into the car. I will have to make a more concerted effort to stay upright on my bike! Steve Blackford sets us to work helping string the home cultivated beans which form part of our cuisine for the night, but he makes sure we never get thirsty in the meantime. After dinner he shows us to our rooms on the top floor of his house: one room has lots of mattresses; the other, a double bed. Heather and I are assigned the double bed, so I just have to trust her not to have wild dreams. I collapse in a heap after painfully ascending the three flights of stairs to the room. The rest of the team bunk down in the big room for the first snoring contest of the trip. Our hosts have been great and if we are welcomed like this for the whole trip we'll never have cause to complain. It is an excellent start to our trip!

The next morning, after a fantastic breakfast and after a quick group photo with the Rotary Club's President, we head off for Troyes, about 85km of winding roads away. Heather doesn't feel well and returns to the comfortable warm bed at the Blackfords' house – she's had a stressful week, with her mother getting sick and the big flight from Canada to France, and it's probably all caught up with her. It is raining again, but this doesn't deter the affable Steve Blackford, a native-English speaker, to ride along with us on his own bike to give us a personal tour of this charming town. It is the first time Lucas and Troy see a real castle, complete with moat, and the steep narrow cobblestoned roads in the old village are extraordinarily beautiful. To think we probably would have just bypassed this historic village, if Steve hadn't joined us. Unfortunately our host's bike gets a flat tire just before we leave him and his beautiful town but our team mechanic Troy is delighted to have his first job of the trip fixing it. We ride off into the rain, following a road with a large 'NO ENTRY' sign across it, having been assured that it is OK for bikes. Troy dutifully stays behind in the support vehicle, waiting for Heather to recover.

The first few days in France were cold and wet....

# A TASTE OF FRANCE

It all seemed so easy looking at our route on Google Earth. I had plotted the whole ride on the internet after concocting a grand plan based on routes I discovered in the bicycle travel books that I had picked up on my trip to Holland the year before. It had seemed sensible to follow well-documented cycle routes – that way we would have valuable information about the terrain, accommodation and facilities along the way.

I had found a route that crossed France on the Loire River and eventually joined up to the Danube. I figured we could pick up this route at Beaune, about four days riding south-east from Paris. At this point the trail followed the Saône, then the Doubs River on to Germany. That was the plan, but unfortunately the book with all this information was still in my luggage in a lost pile at Heathrow somewhere and we had failed to find another copy of it. So, using place names that I had already posted on the internet, David has been doing his best to keep us on the trail using ordinary maps and his GPS. As we weren't road-fit when we started out, I planned to kick-start us out of Paris with an initial 100km day, then followed by three 80km days followed by a rest day – I figured we were going to be pretty sore by this time – and judging by my aches already, I am going to be right. The next stage of the ride will be uphill as we ride across Switzerland to get to the source of the Danube in Germany, so we are only planning to ride about 50km a day. After that the ride should be all downhill and a lot easier going, plus I have scheduled in rest days for the capital cities and other significant places along the route so we can get in some sightseeing as well.

The next day it rains on us for the entire 80 painful kilometres south from Troyes to Verdonnet, we begin to realise the ride is going to challenge us all. Drenched, muddy and exhausted we try to find rooms in the centre of Verdonnet, but the few that are open are just too expensive. Troy and Martin find a two-star hotel a few kilometres from the town centre but it costs as much as the four-star hotel we had in Paris – and breakfast is extra! We realise that we have little choice, so we take the three cheapest double rooms and spread our wet and muddy gear under a covered walkway outside the rooms.

Our food supplies are all but depleted, so Heather – now recovered – and I forage for supplies in the town, but the grocery shops are all closed and we return with just some beers that we found for sale in a petrol station. We vote to eat out. Heather wants to drive and I can't see a problem since, as a Canadian, she is used to driving on the right-hand side of the road. Martin, understandably still possessive about his car, does not seem happy about relinquishing the wheel so he sits up front with Heather. David, Troy, Lucas and I pile into the back of the van which, being designed purely to carry cargo, has no seats, no ventilation and no way to communicate with the front. Through the small window between the cargo area and the driver's cabin, we can see Heather and Martin laughing hysterically as she tears around the empty streets, driving the wrong way up one way streets and down bicycle paths in her manic search for a restaurant. Everything appears to be closed and then she spots a McDonald's. She peers back at us through the glass for approval and sees David gesturing wildly to pull over. This is not because he is enthusiastic about eating McDonald's, but because he is scared for his life.

McDonald's is not such a bad choice for me. A high calorie, high fat and high salt diet is exactly what people with CF need, so if we can fit in a burger in between meals we should. I am even advised to order deep fried dishes when I'm out at restaurants.

While my diet may sound sinful to most, people with CF do not digest fats very well and hence suffer from a deficiency of fat soluble vitamins and minerals, and therefore fatty foods are a necessity – supplemented with ample pancreatic enzymes to help digest the fat. It's the same with salt: we have a salt imbalance of sorts which makes us sweat salt out, so we require a greater salt intake. My cholesterol levels are generally extremely low because of this, and I have little fat under my skin. Many people with CF drink hospital-strength meal replacement drinks in between meals to try put on, or just to maintain their weight.

McDonald's seemed to be one of the few open restaurants in town, and it was extremely crowded. Troy and I queued up to order the food, which had to be done in French. Needless to say the orders were stuffed up and not all of us got what we had ordered. The pain was lessened by the fact that McDonald's in this part of the woods serves beer. On our way back from McDonald's we drive past a kebab restaurant. Surprisingly this little café is also open and David, Martin and Troy jump out to take advantage of their luck.

Back at the hotel, Martin tells me he approves of Heather's driving and, as far as he's concerned, she can drive whenever required. He must be drunk! David has decided, however, that Heather is only going to drive again in an extreme emergency – and only if we are all already dead.

# ON THE MAP IT LOOKS SO EASY!

'We are averaging close to 100km per day and everyone seems to be doing remarkably well, if you don't count the fact that Troy needs hip-replacement surgery and I'm starting to wonder why the hell I trashed my knees so much skiing all those years. Then there's the absolute side-splittingly funny times when Walter, David and Troy fall off their bikes because they've chosen clip pedals, which means you are at the mercy of your motor-skills which have to coincide with getting your toes unclipped from their 'locked-in' position on the pedals before falling-momentum takes over.

Why do this, you might ask...well, supposedly it gets you up the hills easier as you can pull up as well as push down, but if you've had a few too many beers, or eaten too much cheese, you simply look like an awkward turtle thrashing around on the pavement trying to kick a bike off your heels and swearing violently – I'm laughing just thinking about it... We have been spending some time in hotels, but some of us poorer folks try to convince the more affluent of our group to suck it up and sleep in campgrounds – that's why God gave us tents! We spend about €100 a day on food! That's almost $200...

We are starting to notice some of us feeling the pain. I've wondered at times if Walter even has CF at all, the way he's been carrying on with hardly a cough or two during the ride! Only on the really steep bits can you tell.

We all have our jobs on this trip: David is navigator/medic and injury fixer (though in true-life, he plays a policeman, which becomes apparent when a person might, for example, drive down a bicycle path to get to McDonald's quicker).

The support vehicle was donated by Martin, who is joining us for two weeks and helps trade-off being the driver with Troy, whose job it is to fix anything mechanical or otherwise that is broken. Troy also has the important job as support vehicle driver. After stopping whenever Lucas, our filmmaker, sees a good shot several times a day, the support vehicle driver must also prepare lunch stops and arrange sleeping spots for that evening – not easy when you don't speak the language.

Lucas is still getting used to the bike, but is doing great. It isn't easy filming and biking at the same time – I tried it and ran into cows. Lucas is definitely more elegant at it.

My job is to sit around and demand people do things for me, like rub my feet, but this doesn't seem to work. At all. Lest someone start inquiring, 'why is Heather even here at all?' I think the least I can do is keep you all updated on the tom-foolery that is COFE. Least, but not last - even when there IS a hill - we have the star of our program – Valta.

*Walter's job is to finish in Istanbul. Of course, he has already done most of the work to plan this whole thing, so now it's just a matter of ticking off those kilometres.' -* Heather's blog, 2 August 2007 .

# BUDGIE SMUGGLING

Our first hotel on the road, no concessions for us, full rate and no breakfast! It was much  too wet to camp and this was the cheapest we found.

After three days on the road, and another 100km under our belts, we have our first official rest day on 31 July. Martin's brother, Paul, sister-in-law, Monique, and their five-year-old son Marc, who were on their way back from a holiday in Italy, are going to join us today at the comfortable campsite we found in Verdonnet. Both Paul and Monique have been very enthusiastic about the ride and even donated money online, so they thought they would drop in to meet us. Paul and Martin's late uncle, Doctor David Lawson, from England, who had a daughter who died from CF, was one of the founders of the CF Trust in the UK. He was also one of the first doctors to specialise in Cystic Fibrosis and ran a CF Centre at the Queen Mary's Hospital for Children in London in the late 1960s.

*'Although most days we have had a lot of rain, the two days we camp with Paul, Monique and Marc are wonderfully sunny days. Martin tries to go swimming with his brother's family at the aquatic centre next to the campsite, but, as is customary in France, they don't allow him in the pool because he's not wearing Speedo-like brief swimmers – shorts are a no-no. Europe is full of the teeniest swathes of fabric just barely covering the male genitalia. If you're really lucky, some men might opt out of the swimming briefs entirely and just parade around the campsite in their tight, see-through whities. Some hotel pools only accept the Speedo-style swimming briefs – as we found out at our Paris hotel, where Walter was actually kicked out of the pool for wearing baggy shorts. He had to go to a nearby sports store to buy a skimpy 'banana hammock' before they would allow him back in. We won't let him wear it again, even though he tries to ride in it from time to time.' -* Heather's blog, 1 August.

My 'budgie smugglers' (Speedos) come in handy. I obtained them in Paris when I was refused entry into the hotel pool wearing my regular swimming shorts. The same rule applies here in Verdonnet and Martin borrows the Speedos to get into the pool with his brother's family. I am not too interested in swimming in any public pool as swimming tends to induce coughing, and coughing tends to induce mucous. And mucous turns off a lot of swimmers.

While Martin spends time with his family, Lucas and David cycle out to the Fontenay Abbey, one of the oldest Cistercian monasteries in Europe dating back to 1118. It is a collection of really magnificent buildings, which have been restored and are World Heritage listed. Troy and I drive out later as well and walk around just soaking up the history of the place. Troy has never seen anything like it before – Tasmania was a pristine wilderness with Aborigines when this monastery was built! I decided not to ride up to the abbey as I have been coughing a fair bit lately and was feeling on the verge of a lung infection. I was so pumped on antibiotics up till Paris that I hardly coughed, but now I had to cough each morning for the first couple of hours on the bike and riding up any hill would make me cough. Ten days before we left for Europe, I had started taking oral and inhaled antibiotics and continued until a few days into the ride itself. I then reduced it to nebulised antibiotics for a while before going off them all together. Right now I am just on my usual cocktail of vitamins and the usual CF drugs minus the antibiotics.

The wet weather hasn't helped. Camping out has been a little moist in our cheap sweaty sleeping bags. In fact we are really missing all the good quality gear that was in our lost luggage. We have given up on chasing our luggage now; our experience of British Airways makes us think it is not worth the time and cost of the constant calls. BA has all our contact details, but none of us really expect to see our luggage again.

My GPS navigator/PDA gadget is a particularly painful loss and we still might have to buy one soon before we head into the wilderness. David's Garmin GPS is doing well, but the support car has nothing to locate us with now. All my notes on contacts along the way were in the PDA too with handy information like where and when the Rotary and Lions Clubs meet as well as their contact details. It is so convenient to have all that information at a glance. Thankfully, we had printed out some of the information that I had put on the internet. The great Patagonia outdoor gear that was in our luggage would have made life much better too. The new gear has been tested by the wet weather we've struck in our first few days on the road and is proving pretty inadequate. Only David, who has his Patagonia gear, is as snug as a bug in a waterproof rug. We cope by cycling hard and changing into dry gear at the end of the day.

The clothing I bought in a hurry is mostly ill-fitting (whose fault was that?) and uncomfortable and the replacement equipment is well below par – especially the sleeping bags. But once we are out riding on our fabulous bikes everything is perfect, hills or no hills, tail or head wind, no matter! Just riding in the forests, the hills, the big outdoors – it is just so wonderful to be riding. Riding in France is very scenic in August. We see lots of colourful wildflowers growing everywhere, decorating the sides of roads and entire fields. If only I had a better sense of smell I could enjoy the scent. One of the scents I might have picked up would have been the marihuana which freely grows in many fields amongst the other weeds and wild flowers. This is not surprising considering we have ridden past several large commercial hemp crops.

The hemp is tall and thick, and stands metres tall on the side of the road. Apparently it is not a smoke-able variety, it is grown for fibre, and none of us are keen to try it out. Me and smoking, even passive smoking, are totally incompatible. I have experimented with tobacco and the likes when I was young and at university and learned the hard way that I should not indulge in anything that involves smoke.

Another common sight in France is the many nuclear power stations with steam bilging out of them. Impressive to see these nuclear reactors, I just hope none of them will melt down as we ride past. France has 59 of these power plants, and they provide over 99% of France's energy needs. France even exports energy to nearby countries, and they have some of the cheapest electricity prices in Europe.

Whatever prejudices we might have against nuclear energy I must admire France for their commitment to phasing out the polluting coal powered power stations. They do make for an interesting backdrop to the sheep grazing nearby.

With all the exercise that I'm getting on the bike every day, my food requirements have gone into overdrive. But when we arrive in Dole, eastern France, near the Swiss border, even my eating stamina is put to the test. Health-wise I was pumping on the first few days of the ride. I had been on strong antibiotics for almost a month and my lungs were very clean. David had never seen me so fit, but slowly my lungs were filling up again!

After a few damp nights on hard ground in our tents, we are all suffering and we like to have a break from camping in the wet. One of our tent poles has snapped in half and has kept Troy busy and annoyed, and my moist sleeping bag is not doing me much good either. Nothing is drying out either, even though the support vehicle sometimes waits for the tents to dry a bit before packing them up.

Fortunate for us the Rotary Club of Dole comes to our rescue and organises accommodation and meals for the team. We are given their number via my uncle and when we get to old town of Dole, a small city on the river Doubs, with a population of perhaps 25000 we make ourselves comfortable in a café within sight of where we are to meet our hosts at 4pm, on Place Jules Grevy. Two shiny cars arrive at the square and they easily spot the pile of bikes against a tree next to the adjoining café. We are split up into two groups: Troy, Lucas, Heather and I stay in the 18th century château of Andre and Annie Leclere; and David and Martin in a farm house a few miles out of town with Etienne and Annie. Andre Leclere we discover is an inventor: two of his creations are the PVC gnome and the non-exploding gas tank, which is now used in all cars. I surprise his wife, Annie, when I take over the chore of pitting home-grown Mirabelle plums, a specialty of France. The small dark-yellow plums, about 2cm in diameter, have stones like cherries inside and preparing them certainly is a tedious job. The Mirabelles were picked from her backyard for a dessert she is making for our dinner tonight. She has never seen a man do this kind of work in all her 80 years on this planet. I am an instant hit! She later drives us to the farm house of Etienne and Annie (No. 2) where the other guys are staying for a memorable meal. It seems Heather's driving style is not so out of place in France after all. Troy was scared for his life this time.

'The dinner at the home of Annie (No. 2) and Etienne is one of the longest, most elaborate meals I have ever had. We start with liver pâté, then ham and pea rolls, wine from Andre's brother's estate and, of course, bread. Then the barbecued sausages are brought in, and more peas and ham, more wine, more bread. I am absolutely stuffed by this point, but no! Now comes the main course - barbecued pork and shredded carrots, more wine, more bread, then more pork! Then the cheese platter, before dessert, which is fruit flan and peaches and more wine

While I waver in my seat, trying to focus on anything besides my wine glass, the rest of the team try to fit more food into already packed stomachs. The feast went till past midnight. The next morning we stuff ourselves with croissants and homemade plum jam, then visit the house of one of Dole's most famous past residents – Louis Pasteur. Afterwards we return to our lodgings where the local press is waiting for us for pictures and a brief interview. We are very happy with our progress and with each other's company (so far!) and are thinking of all our friends and family as we ride along.' - Heather's blog, 5 August 2007

We ride along lovely wooded tracks and paths, pretty much following the Doubs River east out of Dole. The river trail is signposted as EuroVelo 6, and is part of a proposed bicycle route from the west coast of France to Eastern Europe not due for completion till 2010. It mostly snakes alongside rivers, joining the Danube in Germany and following it to the Black Sea. Considering it is still a 'proposed route' I am very impressed to already see signposting for it here in France! I had tried really hard during my preparation to contact anyone involved with the EuroVelo 6 project to get more detailed route information, but the language barrier proved too difficult. Some of the people involved thought I was contacting them because I was interested in helping built the infrastructure for it. I had similar babelonic issues with my efforts to communicate with Rotarians and Lions along the route.

After covering 20 fast kilometres in an easy hour through a beautiful forest, we stop for lunch – something that we would not normally do after a mere one-hour ride, but this has been arranged by the friendly Dole Rotary Club at the house of a friend of Andre and Annie's. We are treated to another giant lunch, with more wine and bread, and some surprise gifts from Annie (No. 2) – T-shirts, jumpers, a collection of French mustards and a box of French perfume for Heather. The lunch lasts three hours and at 3pm, we go our merry way, loaded with full stomachs and presents. We barely make our destination for the night – Besançon, 60km away. We set-up our tents in darkness, while Lucas cooks up a storm for us. It is wet and dreary and we long for the feather doonas that we were sleeping in at our Rotarian hosts last night. We are all a bit stressed and tired and we end up bickering about who should wash the dinner dishes. The rain is relentless and we are recharging our electrical devices under a makeshift tarpaulin made out of plastic bags – an accident waiting to happen. The campsite office and adjoining cafe are closed so I can't ask them to put my medicine in the fridge overnight, but fortunately some curious Dutch campers, having seen our bikes and the support vehicle, get chatting with us and offer to put the medicine in their caravan fridge nearby. It comes in handy that we draw a bit of interest with our bikes and support vehicle!

After a miserable night, we cheer ourselves up with a proper breakfast at the campground's café but Heather thinks the food is seriously overpriced and refuses to join us. After eating our fill of croissants, we take on the puzzle of roads that lead out of Besançon and head east toward the Swiss border.

# OUCH!

Riding the bikes seems simple enough, but when we stop for the night, matters become very complicated. First we have to arrange for power, mainly to keep the AC/DC 12-volt fridge for my medicines going, but also to recharge our mountain of telephones, GPS batteries, laptops and cameras. This is tricky in campsites, especially when it rains as we can't leave the electronic equipment plugged in to charge overnight, and besides there is always a risk of theft even if there is no rain.

The little portable fridge can only keep the most critical medicine cool, but is too small for anything else and so every night we need to locate a freezer to freeze the blue plastic ice packs for the Esky (ice-box), in which we keep our food and the other medicines cool during the day. If we fail to freeze our little bricks then the Esky gets very warm during the day and our food goes off and we run the risk of spoiling my medicine. We feel it is mission critical to keep the blue bricks frozen. And if we do manage to find a freezer – never an easy task  we then have to remember to pick up the frozen packs in the morning!

We are also becoming expert at putting up and dismantling our campsite and learn that it's better to pack up what we can at night – including washing the dishes straight after dinner – because there is little time to mess about in the morning before we hit the road. Although this sounds obvious, when you have an exhausted group of sore cyclist and an equally exhausted support driver and navigator we sometimes fall over from sleep shortly after and sometimes almost during dinner. Times like that we easily convince ourselves that we can do cleaning in the morning when perhaps it might not be raining, and when we are fresh again. This is not the case; Rain does not always stop and sometimes we do not feel fresh in the morning after camping in the rain, after sweating in our condensed sleeping bags all night.

Our target of riding to the intended destination every day proved quite hard this first week and the weather – some rainy days and some really hot days – has not helped. I am the slowest rider on the trip after Lucas, but Lucas rides in the support vehicle a lot to help him film the ride. Apart from David, I am the only one riding every day. I am not the only one suffering, however, and we all have aches and pains – some of us even doubt if we can make it to Istanbul. Although we have all trained for the ride, none of us covered anywhere near 100km a day in training, let alone consecutive days. Heather's knees are giving her trouble – so much so that David is worried about her continuing to ride. He is also worried about our dwindling first aid supplies. You can only strap so many knees and use so much ointment before you need to visit a pharmacy. But that's easier said than done. Not only are we all suffering from the riding and exhausted by the time we get to a town, but many shops in France seem to be closed for the summer holidays.

I added to my own woes by deciding to use the darn bicycle pedal clips which I bought in Paris when I had to buy cycling shoes to replace the non-clip ones that were in my lost luggage. The shoes I had could be ridden with or without clips and I bought the matching clips for them. Unfortunately my unclipping is still not perfected – so I still end up falling over a few times a day. The clips also keep your feet exactly in the same position at all times. I suspect that this might be contributing, if not the sole cause, of my sore knees. Just above my left knee a tendon of sorts has become especially painful and my left leg is now really stiff. I started taking a soluble aspirin in the mornings to reduce the inflammation and decide to ditch the clip pedals and resort back to the original bike pedals.

My knee aches are starting to go away now – but also the daily distances we are covering have shortened. David thinks my problem was RSI-related, caused by the continuous rubbing of tendon over the bone above my knee, held in the same position because of the clips. I am not sure how much the other members of the team are prepared to put up with aches and pains, but I am certainly prepared to suffer. I don't want to give up.

People with CF often suffer from joint discomfort – and I certainly have suffered from it in the past– but my wife Katherine got me (and my arthritic dog) on to glucosamine-chondroitin tablets, which I have been taking pretty much every day since, and it has kept knee aches and stiff backs away – until now. Glucosamine, apparently derived from New Zealand mussels, is supposed to help rebuild cartilage and treat arthritis. It is usually combined with chondroitin sulfate ('a chain of alternating sugars' according to Wikipedia!) for the treatment of osteoarthritis. Ten years ago, after setting out on a 10-day cross-country bike ride in the Kosciusko National Park in the Australia Alps with friends, one of my knees got so sore I felt I would have to abort the trip and hitch a ride home. But somehow, miraculously, my knee came good again, and I was able to finish the trip. My friends call this 'Wally luck'. I am now hoping that a similar miracle will get me all the way to Istanbul.

We are now riding next to fast flowing streams, along forest paths, farm roads and a few busier roads. With only some maps and the GPS (none of which showed contours) to guide us along the route that I had planned back home in Tasmania, David is trying his best to avoid main roads – the pollution is hard on my lungs, not to mention the dangers of traffic – David manages to get us on to some amazingly small side roads, some of which we are sure would lead nowhere. We are surprised some of these roads are mentioned on any map, let alone the GPS. Putting enormous faith in the GPS and David's capabilities we follow his suggestions. Occasionally we have to make detours, choosing an alternative destination for the night or deciding to ride 10 to 20km on a highway in order to avoid 50km of possibly hilly minor roads. Once the village I had scheduled back in Tasmania as a place to stop for the night turned out in reality to be so small that it didn't even have room for the obligatory one horse. It didn't even rate a mention on David's GPS, so we decided to push on. The sun was finally shining – and with a vengeance – so it is lucky we brought a lot of sunscreen.

I also learned to always carry tissues with me on the road (or a wad of toilet paper!) after one morning when my Number 2 arrived mid morning. I borrowed some toilet paper from Heather and found a nice paddock on the side of the road to have a big mid-morning dump. We all carry a spare wad of paper or tissues just in case.

Another day, we noticed a patch of green/brown in our path on the map (not in the paddock). David guessed correctly that it was bound to be hilly, so we decide to go on the highway, assuming that it would have the least steep gradient for us to cycle on. But now that we are cycling along the highway we realise that it too climbs steeply, and the traffic flies past us at great speeds as we struggle up the long slow hills. Crawling along a rough edge of almost 30cm, trying to stay well away from a big truck approaching from the rear, I fall off the side of the road. Unfortunately, this is when I was still wearing my pedal clips, so I end up lying there like a tied chicken on the side of the road. My upper body still on the road and traffic whizzing past as I struggle to get free of the clips. But my feet are jammed somehow and I cannot twist out easily. Meanwhile, a nice French lady who had noticed my plight as she drove past, yells out at David and Martin cycling further up ahead: 'Ton ami il tombe!' (Your friend has fallen over). Martin understands that 'tombe' means 'falling' in French and turns around in a hurry to cycle down the hill to rescue me.

But in the mean time I manage to free myself and he discovers me, safely and slowly – and slightly shaken – cycling up the hill again. Lucas, who is a cycling novice still, is keen to ride but not brave enough yet to attempt a full day. So he has been riding small distances, sometimes the last 10 to 20km before we reach our destination for the night. Sometimes we lose sight of him and worry, and other times we fear for his life as he weaves too much into the middle of the road. Nevertheless, he is improving greatly every day.

On one of the first few days of the ride, Lucas attempted to ride with us. Martin and I were cycling ahead, going as slow as we could possibly go with a strong tail-wind pushing us along at walking pace. We would have had to apply the brakes to go any slower. David was 100m behind us whipping Lucas into shape. And floating on the wind, we could hear David yelling sound advice: 'You have to push on the pedals Lucas!'

It is August 5, Day 9. We are now nearing Altkirch, our last French town before the Swiss border after what we considered a hard week of cycling. The landscape is changing: the crops and pastures of rural France are giving way to forests. The villages are becoming smaller and more numerous as we head towards the border – and all have long and unpronounceable names such as Michelbach-Le-Haut and Ranspach-le-Bas which, according to Heather, contain more syllables than the number of residents living there. 'Trying to pronounce some of the names of these places is like clearing phlegm from your throat; you can practically see the wet SPLAT at the end of the word,' she says. The hills are certainly getting bigger too as we approach Altkirch, the last French town on our route. We schedule a rest day here and find a nice campground in the hills above the cobblestoned town. An English man, who suffers from asthma, and his family wander over to visit us at the campsite and offer a donation – these are greatly appreciated gestures, as are the donations we keep on receiving on-line. Heather, who had gone ahead in the support vehicle, told us she had found a cafe which had a computer we could use. So after setting up camp, Martin and I ride down to the town to look for her. We find her happily sitting at a computer in a Turkish café, staffed by friendly Turkish people and well equipped with their favourite smoking implement; the water pipe. Unlike Australia, in Europe it seems like everyone smokes. You are hard-pressed to find a non-smoking establishment. In this quiet little Turkish cafe, nearly everyone is smoking. While I spend an hour answering my emails, Martin finds a soul mate in the cafe who has an interest in African safaris and they share a water pipe. Martin smoking a water-pipe in a Turkish internet cafe in France!

The team meets up later to mark our last day in France with a meal in a real French restaurant. It is a little too real for me: while the others try snails and frogs legs, I have onion soup and schnitzel with potatoes.

# BLOOD, SWEAT AND GEEKS

Coughing up blood is something that does not sound nice, but it is to be expected with all the coughing I do. I don't normally cough up blood, but it happens sometimes when I hit polluted areas or spend hours, for example, in a smoky internet café or ride into the pollution of a big city – like that of the chemical capital of Switzerland, Basel, as we did today. Basel is a major industrial centre for chemical and pharmaceutical industries, and its location on the Rhine, connecting it to the North Sea, and situated on the border with Germany and France makes it a perfect hub for any industry.

Heading down a hill, we can make out Basel airport ahead in the distance. Adrenaline is rushing through my veins with the excitement of knowing we will soon be leaving the first of the countries on our itinerary and crossing into Switzerland, and my coughing gets worse. I'm soon coughing up streaky phlegm and as we turn on to a minor road close to the small town of Hésingue, I'm spitting my increasingly reddening spit off the track into the bushes so as not to freak out the other cyclist passing by.

I stop to tell David what's happening, but I'm now coughing up and spitting out bright red puddles of blood. It looks worrying. David is concerned and I am worried too. It's not that coughing up blood hurts – it feels rather good to get it out of your system as the blood-mixed mucous is thinner than I am used to which makes it easier to cough out – but when you rupture a capillary in your lungs from coughing hard, it provides a pathway for infection to get into your blood. It can also lead to infection of the heart's lining which, with my infections being mostly penicillin resistant, can make you really sick. David and I agree that I should go back immediately on a full complement of antibiotics, start doing extra nebulisations with the various drugs at my disposal, and lots of hypertonic saline, which helps break up the mucous in the lungs so I can cough it up more easily. I hope I am able to get back to my healthy status-quo quickly.

Following the advice of Martin's new water-pipe friend at the Turkish cafe, Martin drives the support car to Saint Louis, a French town just before the Swiss border to book us into a hotel – apparently much cheaper and quieter than Basel itself, which bumps right up to the border. Saint Louis feels like just another part of Basel, except there is a border crossing about a kilometre down the road from our hotel. Although we are technically still sleeping in France, tonight is meant to be our first night in Switzerland, and so we decide to do the decent thing and take the tram across the border into Basel to experience a fondue dinner. We walk down to the tram terminal, which is just across the Swiss border, but have to exchange some Euro for Swiss francs before we can buy a ticket to board.

To add to the confusion, the people in Saint Louis speak French whereas those in Basel speak mostly German. After much searching we find a hidden away upstairs restaurant that is actually serving a traditional cheese fondue (it is a winter dish). Lucas can't imagine surviving a dinner that just consists of cheese, so he orders something else. The rest of us dip bits of bread into the hot cheese sauce – kept gooey in a terracotta pot with a little flame underneath it. The fondue is traditionally made from Raclette cheese, a salted cheese made from cow's milk, and has wine it – totally delicious. We are advised to accompany the fondue with wine rather than a beer since the cold beer can turn the soft cheese into hard cheese balls in your stomach. Digesting a huge quantity of cheese in one sitting is a challenge even without complications like that!

We have a rest day at the hotel which is so quaintly old-fashioned it even has an ancient lift that has metal bar doors that you need to pull aside to get in and out.

'Lounging in the dining room of a Hotel de l'Europe in St Louis. For a luxury day of doing nothing, we managed to keep quite busy, what with eating, laundry, eating, emailing, eating, drinking...as you can imagine, life's tough' - Heather's blog 7 August 2007.

It is not only a chance to do the laundry, but also to recover from sore knees, shoulders and other aches and pains. Heather is really feeling it; her knees are so bad that we really don't think she is going to ride the distance. She always bravely gets on to the bikes in the morning, and then treadles in low gear for the first hour to warm up her knees before disappearing ahead of us into the distance. We head back into Basel, this time hoping to find maps and route books, as well as some extra camping and cycling gear. After travelling through rural France, which appeared to be closed down for the summer holidays, cosmopolitan Basel is bustling. It is a shock to our system to see all this activity. And I am extremely pleased to be in a country where I can understand a little of what people are saying. Dutch is somewhat similar to German, and hence I seem to remember more of my high-school German than I do of my high-school French. I haven't had much call in Tasmania to practice any foreign language, so I am surprised that my German is good enough to ask directions and order food from German menus with confidence. We try specialties such as glühwein, a treat for me and a surprise for the others. Glühwein is wine served hot with honey and spices which helps to warm you up. It makes us positively glow.

Everything in Basel appears clean and open, friendly and teeming with people. We find a massive sports store where Lucas, to our amazement, invests in a compass, while David, Troy and I get an assortment of goodies for our bikes that are meant to make our lives on the road more comfortable. We are particularly excited to find good bookshops where we easily find maps and riding books to replace those lost with our luggage. We also buy duplicate copies so that the support vehicle and the riders can have the same set of maps. This, we find, is particularly important as, despite having mobile phones, on a few occasions we have had trouble finding each other. It would be nice to have lengthy discussions to describe our precise locations over the phone, but none of us really want to use the mobile phones that extensively because of the outrageous costs – David and Troy have Australian mobiles and Martin a Dutch one and it costs us almost $3 a minute (depending on where we are) on global roaming to receive calls as well as to make calls, meaning that each call is worth more than $5 per minute in total.

I personally am obsessed with tracking down a local prepaid SIM card for my mobile phone in each country that we pass through, which is a challenge in itself. Finding out where to buy the prepaid SIMs is one thing, registering them is another and in some countries this requires 129 forms of identification and then you still have to wait another 24 hours for it to be activated. Once I have the local number working, I then have to find an internet connection, sign on to my internet telephony account with Skype and forward my Skype number – a USA phone number which I gave to everyone –to my new local mobile phone number. All this hassle means that I avoid the $3 per minute global roaming charge and we can call local numbers more easily. The others still pay $3 per minute to call me, but I do not pay the $3 per minute to receive the calls. It is a convoluted way of doing it, and by the time I have actually gone through the process we leave that particular country and I need to do it all over again.

The rest of the team think I am making life too complicated with my SIM panic in every country and are frustrated that I want to look for phone shops when we ride through towns. They are right. I thought I'd be making and receiving a lot more calls along the way to try to get support from local organisations to arrange talks, dinners and accommodation, but we are just too busy sticking to our schedule and getting from A to B to bother about struggling with language barriers to set up hospitality.

The fact that my Skype account has a US number also puts most people off calling it at all as they, mistakenly, believe it will cost them a bundle. In Australia it is sometimes cheaper to call a USA number than to dial an Australian mobile number. Another draw-back is that prepaid mobile rates in general are ridiculously high, meaning that even making local calls is not that cheap in the end, and recharging prepaid phones in foreign languages is another drawback.

Sometimes we leave countries with a lot of remaining credit, or the credits I think I am getting when I buy the SIM can only be received by mail after registering with a form in a foreign language… impossible! It is only in Bulgaria, our last country, that I realise that I needed to buy two local SIMS, so that the support vehicle and the riders can communicate easily and cheaply with each other. David and Troy use their Australian phones for the entire trip but their bills are astronomical. My phone bill is not too bad in the end, but if I add on $5 for every hour I wasted in my SIM hunt, I think the guys actually got a good deal.

As you gather from reading about my phone routine, I am a geek. But thankfully, so is Lucas. We share a special geek-bag full of twisted cables and wires and computer bits and pieces and, for this reason, are often paired in the same room at hotels. We create a recharging hub – an Australian plug extension board which is plugged into the wall using a Europe adaptor. We have generic cables plugged into it that serves most of the equipment that we carry around – to try to cut down on the number of cables we have to get out of the bag each day. For example, pulling out my camera battery charger and its power cable from the bag would take 10 minutes to untangle, but just grabbing the charger without the original lead is quick and then you can just plug it into any one of the generic cords on the board.

David is not convinced and insists on keeping the correct and original lead with each electrical item he has and, cleverly, stores them separately, far away from the chaotic geek-bag. We geeks are also in charge of the medicine supply, so we have the portable fridge and a few days' supply of my medicines that don't need refrigeration also stuffed into the geek bag.

Sometimes geek bits are left behind when we pack up or bits disappear in a dark corner of a hotel room. One or two close calls and a rescue mission or two were executed at times during the trip to look for crucial lost bits, such as a battery charger that got left under a bed, or an Australian/European power plug adapter. It is not easy being a geek on the road. The team has three laptop computers: mine is primarily used for Skype Communications, blogging, storing photos and transferring digital video film footage from the SD chips to the portable drives; Troy and Lucas use theirs mainly for accessing the internet and maintaining their diaries.

It's not often that we have wireless internet, but on our first night in Austria we find it at a camping, for free! More often than not Heather goes in search of an internet café to download her blog entry from a memory stick she carries with her. The blog turns out to be quite a responsibility and sometimes, exhausted and holed up in a wet camping spot, we have no way of updating it, leaving our faithful readers in suspense. My wife, Katherine, back in Tasmania, sometimes makes the odd emergency entry for us:

'Just wanted to let everyone know that the team is doing great, I just spoke to them on the phone as they stopped for lunch. They have not been able to access the internet. I complained strongly about the lack of updates, comparing it to having my favourite soap opera pulled from daily TV line up! The team has been doing big days and do have some sore bits but that is to be expected. They all seem to be getting along but it is still early days. I did hear profanities in the back ground while speaking to Heather. I am not sure who they were directed at.' – Katherine's blog entry 1 August 2007.

# RIVER DANCE

The Danube River officially starts in Donaueschingen in the south-western corner of Germany – the point at which two smaller rivers, the Brigach and Breg come together. In order for a river to flow it needs to start high up in the mountains, and the Danube is no exception. In the 150km from Basel in Switzerland to Donaueschingen in Germany, we have some excellent climbs as we ride across the width of the Black Forest. My strategy is to pedal slowly and stop occasionally to cough before getting back on the bike to continue the two-day ascent. Walking along with the bike is not an option as it seems more difficult than riding in tree-climbing gear at speeds as slow as 3km/h. I can't imagine how we would have carried our gear up these hills if we didn't have the support vehicle.

I learnt my lesson in that respect a few years ago on a bicycle ride across Tasmania with my wife Katherine when we tried to carry all our gear up on to a high plateau after many days of hard riding. After a good three hours to get to the top, we were so exhausted we had to find an emergency place to pitch our tent and we had to stay there for two nights to recover. The huge (head) winds we could hear blowing over the edge of the plateau discouraging us from continuing on.

The scenery is spectacular as we head into the pine-tree covered mountains and at over 800 metres above sea level we see our first 'Swiss' village (though, it is actually German), Todtmoos. The houses all have steep pitched roofs and the church steeples point high into the sky as if they are trying to overcome the fact they are dwarfed by the hills surrounding them. We ride on to an equally impressive town of about 4,000 inhabitants, called Sankt Blasien, where Troy has found us a most traditional gasthaus called Kurgarten Hotel Garni for the night. I immediately order glühwein to get over the ride while the others have a few beers. The only other person in the lounge is proudly introduced to us as being a German war hero. Struggling to understand the thick accents of this region, I am not entirely sure which side the hero had been fighting for in the war, or indeed why he was a hero, though he clearly impressed the gasthaus owners who fetch a tome from their bookshelves to show us that the picture of the author on the back cover is the man seated in front of us.

The book appears to be an autobiography, but after a long day of hard cycling through the Black Forest I haven't got the energy to keep struggling to understand. We thank them for their interesting tale and turn our interests to something we could understand – the locally fermented wine and beer. After we had recovered from the mountainous ride and sorted out our rooms we left for a walk through the town. We walk past the awe-inspiring Benedictine abbey, Saint Blaise's, which is pretty much next-door to our guest house. The abbey, whose history dates back to the ninth century, has a large cathedral at its heart and a huge town square stretching out before it.

Tents are being set up in the square in preparation for the town's annual Domfestspiele festival on the weekend coming, which the locals urge us to stay for. The festival includes a light show to re-enact when the original abbey church burnt down in the 18th century and a performance of Mozart's Requiem performed by 150 people in the cathedral. It sounds like a spectacular worth waiting for but sadly we can't – we still have countries to cross and rivers to find. We stroll over the majestic bridge in front of the Abbey that crosses the Rhine to seek out the restaurant which was recommended to us by the nice people from our guest house for having traditional no nonsense food. The traditional German schnitzels we order are served by a young voluptuous waitress in traditional clothes who brings us amply sized beers to match. Lucas is particularly impressed by the size of the beers and Troy is equally impressed by the serving fräulein.

The next day we ride through Bonndorf Im Schwarzwald ('Bonndorf in the Black Forest') and Hausen vor Wald ('Houses in front of the forest') on winding roads in never ending rain. But the scenery is absolutely magnificent: Lush, forested hills and old fashioned villages, small palaces, traditional wooden houses with massive solar panels on them, beautifully maintained gardens and village squares. The beer is consistently great in all these places and, if I could just keep my mouth shut, I'm sure the coffee would also be great. In my rush to order a plain white coffee on quick coffee stops, and using my dodgy multi-lingual ordering technique, I often cause waiters to think, mistakenly, that we all want the same thing and they proudly bring us a concoction that has coffee and probably milk in it but is nothing like coffee with milk. Poor David, all he wants is a shot of espresso! He resorts to the more exact science of ordering that involves just pointing at what he wants on the menu, and discourages me from opening my mouth in fear of messing up his order. Maybe when I start ordering my coffee and David senses that the waiter might include the others in my order David might try to again point to his item on the menu 'espresso' and gestures to the waiter to ensure his order is not affected by my antics. I often manage to affect everybody's orders. All I want is a cup of regular black coffee with a dash of regular milk in it. This appears to be a tall order. Nothing worse than ending up with a huge serve of hot milk with a hint of coffee flavour.

# LUCAS TAKES THE LEAD

Five kilometres away from Donaueschingen, Lucas flies past us at an intersection where David, Martin and I have stopped to study the map. While Donaueschingen is our destination for the night, we don't want to end up on the autobahn and the sign above us at the intersection indicates that is exactly where Lucas is now headed. David asks Martin if he would chase after Lucas and bring him back, while we work out an alternative route. David and I wait and wait for Lucas and Martin to come back. It's not the best place to be waiting; heavy traffic, lots of noise and pollution. We have no idea why Martin and Lucas have not returned so after 15 minutes we head off in the same direction they took – downhill along a busy road where we are not actually allowed to cycle. Nobody in their right mind would want to cycle there.

After going a few kilometres, with every passing car beeping at us, we come to the real autobahn, and wonder if Lucas and Martin have actually risked life and limb by heading down there. We are now very worried about them. It is too dangerous for us to turn onto the autobahn, so we wait a while until we can scramble across the busy road and head back up the hill we just came down on, with heavy traffic flying past us at high speed and only a narrow soft edge for us to cycle on.

We continue into Donaueschingen on the back roads and call ahead to Troy in the support vehicle. He has found a camping ground, the Riedsee, a few kilometres out of town and sends us the directions. It takes us another 20 minutes to get there, and exhausted and frustrated at having lost half our team, we settle into another wet and soggy campground. To ease the tension, Heather and I go shopping and come back with a collection of strange alcoholic potions, including a mini-bottle of Jägermeister, an herb-flavoured liqueur.

By the time we get back from the shop, Lucas and Martin have turned up and all is revealed. Lucas didn't stop at the intersection as he thought one of us was peeing – which is entirely possible – and basically, feeling a little embarrassed, he was trying to avoid looking at us. He then powered down the hill, knowing that he is generally slower than the rest of us and grabbing his chance to get ahead. There was a clear sign to our destination, Donaueschingen so he did not hesitate. By the time Martin caught up to him they decided it was too dangerous to cross the busy road to ride back up the hill so they took an alternative route back to the crossroads – I later saw pictures of them lifting their bikes over fences, so they really did do their best to avoid that rotten road. By the time they got back to the intersection, we had already left to go looking for them. The alcohol in the wet campground doesn't make us feel much better, sitting around on wet grass with the drizzle keeping us nice and moist, but the dinner Heather makes us on the gas stove does and all is forgotten until we notice that another one of the tent poles has snapped in half (the second so far in the trip).

The rain and our late arrival also means we don't get to explore the town. It would have been nice to see some of Donaueschingen, but when you are camping out of town and your transport is a bicycle, you sometimes have to make some sacrifices. On the bright side, we do get to see the Danube River for the first time and it really is a great relief. This means the start of some easier riding. We will now be following a major river on an established and clearly sign-posted bicycle route for 1,500km to Vienna in Austria. Cycling downstream along the Danube is a piece of cake. The route is incredibly well marked and is mostly off the main road and on bicycle paths. Retired Dutch people appear to be the most common cyclists along the route now – or perhaps they are just drawn to us by our Dutch branded Batavus bikes, which they all recognise.

Most of these Dutch tourists have travelled from Holland in buses or campervans, but a few have cycled all the way. The other cyclists we meet, including many young families, are all tourists – this is not, it seems, a serious cyclist's route. Maintaining my goal of an average speed of about 20km/hr means we overtake

most other cyclists on the way. I begin to fancy that I am becoming an elite cyclist with all the kilometres now under my belt but then an old local man, perhaps in his seventies, on a pushbike with a basket – complete with an umbrella in it – passes me. And this is at a moment when I think I am going quite fast. I try hard to keep up with him, which is proving difficult, when, fortunately, he turns off quickly into a small village. I slow down and cough for about 10 minutes before resuming, rather humbled, at my own comfortable pace again.

'Day 14, 921km: We had a gorgeous ride today! Sadly, Walter and I are barely awake here at the internet cafe and neither of us can remember the name of the town we are staying in. Sigmaringen is where we are for our internet, which is a town 8km from our gasthaus (hotel).

The last 4 or 5 days it has been raining and we are consistently wet, but it doesn't seem to be too cold, so we aren't too badly off. Well, I guess we should be honest - Walter is feeling it. He had little energy today and feels like his lungs are having a hard time keeping up. Our chilly, wet night spent in a crappy, overpriced campground last night didn't help liven our moods much.

Tonight we have splurged on beds in a gasthaus, sort of like a bed & breakfast, which are popping up everywhere, now that we are on a very popular bike route following the river Danube...

This has been the most scenic part yet! Giant old castle-like mansions perched on cliff tops; beautiful green pastures with sheep; fingers of rock pushing up through green farmers fields....the going was fairly flat today, while riding along river valleys. But not the last two days - oh no! Extreme uphill, anyone? Day 12 was the longest stretch (20 plus km) of straight uphill as we left the low-lands of Switzerland and headed into Germany. That day was hard and mostly in the rain. We are toughening up at times, but then it all seems to go to hell and we whine and whimper and complain. But we have been having a great time and are seeing lots of beautiful scenery and smiling faces.' - Heather's blog, 11 August 2007.

Our map failed to mention the Black Forest east of Basel, it was scenic but straight up! The Danube officially starts in Donaueschingen.

My original itinerary for this ride was planned to get out of Paris and away from the traffic quickly, really putting in the pace for the first few days. It got us sore but hardened! It was a wake-up call for our bodies to get into gear. The distances were technically not that long, ranging up to 100km per day, across moderately hilly terrain. The next week we covered shorter distances, along the rivers and valleys and up hills to get to Donaueschingen. For experienced cyclists, the distances we are covering are pretty small, but this schedule certainly has us hurting good, and I expected that. So for the next month I have scheduled very easy and short days so we can all recover, but stay fit by riding every day. I also figure that we will now be on the tourist trail so we are sure to come across interesting places such as monasteries and castles to visit and we will have more opportunity to sample the local cuisine and the local refreshments.

The hardest thing now that we are on 'easy street' is staying together. Because the Danube bike path is particularly well signposted, the team members are getting a bit overly confident – slacking off or speeding up – and we start to lose each other. David, as a trained policeman, is professionally trained to keep an eye on people and has to be observant for his job. Although his mission, given to him by my wife, is specifically to deliver me alive and in one piece to Istanbul – bike or no bike – he feels very responsible for the entire team and does his utmost to keep us together. We have no exact route, just destinations to reach each night; and David, as our navigator, has the only map for the riders – the support vehicle has another – so we have to stay with David.

How hard can that be? It sounds so simple: stay within sight; yell when you need to pee; yell when you need to take a photo; yell when you fall off; yell when you lag behind, etc. But there is only so much you can do when the distance between one cyclist and another becomes a kilometre or more, or somebody has disappeared off the back and the front rider keeps on cycling. Lucas sometimes stops to film something, then races to catch up only to take a wrong turn, while Heather, who likes to ride whilst listening to music through headphones, ends up riding the wrong way as she can't hear us. Even if we know the name of the town where we're headed, it doesn't help. We are sure to forget it immediately (OK we could write them down) or in case we remember there is no obvious spot to meet there, and there might be a number of cycle paths into the town, the town is bigger than we thought, or the bike path bypasses the town. We do not all carry a mobile phone. My suggestion is that if you end up lost, you should go back to the place you last saw the team and wait 10 minutes. If no one shows, you should go on to the next town, find the first café, sit down and have a cup of coffee for half and hour, then ride on to the proposed destination for the day. It is a terrible idea as often there are many possible bike routes in and out of towns and many obvious 'first' cafes, but at least you get some coffee. David rationally decides that the most feasible plan is for us just to keep an eye on each other.

The first week of cycling along the Danube!

# SPIN CYCLE

'Day 15, Ulm, Germany, 1,050km. I was all excited to have a photo for you all of us toasting our first 1,000km milestone with Champagne, but after trying unsuccessfully to order a bottle again and again from the nice old Spanish German lady that runs our hotel and the restaurant underneath, we gave up. David kept asking and she kept nodding and smiling, but we never got it.

Before retiring to bed that night I had to go and check what exactly the matter was, and why we did not get our Champagne. Turned out that she had no Champagne cooled, but had put some in the fridge for us. Every time we asked she checked on its temperature to see if it was cold enough to serve. Anyway, who needs Champagne to celebrate! We are a quarter of the way! It's going so fast.

We ended up doing two days in one today, as we were done with our planned 40km before noon, so we kept on going towards Ulm, a giant city. As is always the case in cities, it was hard to find arrangements for the night. We have ended up in a very nice hotel in the town centre, right across from what seems the highest church tower in the world - at this point, the scaffolding mounted to the side of the church for some repair work is what captures our interest the most – it is quite amazing, but the tower itself is gorgeous.

The rain has been following us for days on end; however, today we did have the whole afternoon in the hot sun but it´s pouring rain again now.

We are eating insane amounts of really great food and the only one who feels moderately guilty about the quantities is Troy, who as the support driver doesn't get much exercise. He has decided to start pulling the car to even things up a bit. The guys also drink an impressive amount of beer and most of our late afternoons involve lumbering from one outdoor patio to the next to taste all the possibilities. I, of course, rarely partake in such tomfoolery - oops, gotta go, my beer has arrived...' – Heather's blog, 14 August 2007.

Although team geeks, Lucas and I, often end up sharing a room, the allocation process is pretty random and very spontaneous. This keeps a certain amount of sanity in the group as we regularly change configurations. For some strange reason, our rooms are rarely ever next to each other, and are typically floors apart. We never get to the bottom of this, but it probably is our own fault – you try asking the hotel reception for adjoining rooms in a foreign tongue: 'We like to kindly request adjoining suites on one of your lower floors please, oh and if we could have single beds we would appreciate that very much.' Troy, who always arrives way before us in the support vehicle, gets as far as to try: 'Ja, bitte, we are hier, wir needing room, seven mensch thanks.'

Lugging the bags up to our hotel rooms is not something we expect Troy and his navigator to do, but still he usually does it. Not only does he have to guess who will be in each room, but often he has to carry the bags up three or four flights of wooden stairs and all over the hotel. Personally, I am totally puffed just walking up the stairs with my little bags from the bike! How other people can run up and down stairs certainly makes me realise my lungs are not working properly.

There was a time when I could climb 100+ flights of stairs: Many years ago when the World Trade Centre towers in New York were still standing, I felt it wasn't worth paying $10 or so to catch the elevator up to see the smog so I decided to run up the emergency stairs to the top of the towers – I needed the exercise anyway. I coughed the whole way up in about an hour but was met by some serious-looking security officers who promptly put me back into the lift. I tried getting out of the lift a few levels further down to go back to the stairs again but that did not work either, – the security was on to me! They even stopped me from running back down the stairs. Perhaps they had monitored me on a candid camera, watching me coughing and gagging on the way up and were more worried about getting me out of their building before I died on their shift.

Sharing rooms with other people is one thing, sharing a bathroom is a real trick. Heather, for example, loves her shower, but showers don't seem to love her back! Especially those at the older hotels, where the bedroom carpet always ends up soaking from the water spilling out from under the bathroom door. Heather comes out looking all surprised and saying something like "it's not me, it's the bathroom!" I, on the other hand, am not much fun to share a bathroom with because, with CF, I can leave it not smelling so fragrant.

The bathrooms also become our laundry, with most of us washing our clothes at the same time as having a shower. It takes me a while to realise that it is not a hygienic idea to stamp my feet on my bicycle shorts and undies in the shower in order to clean them. I even manage to get a mysterious rash this way! Fortunately it goes away very quickly after my wife Katherine gives me clear instructions over the phone on how to do my laundry in the shower, which specifically involves not washing my undies on the floor of a public shower.

David, with his mountain of experience in these things, always does his laundry in the shower and wrings it out in a towel and it is nearly always dry in the morning. I learnt the same technique when I was in the Australian Reserve Army in Canberra many years ago (I somehow slipped through the mandatory health check-up and was accepted!), but it still took me a couple of weeks to catch on that I should be doing it that way. Troy catches on earlier and has less of a need for the Laundromat than Lucas, Heather and I do. Although I am now successfully drying my daily wash with a towel I still feel compelled to run all my stuff through a machine at any opportunity we are presented with. Washing our clothes at a Laundromat is a huge challenge, with one of us collecting dirty laundry from the others then carrying it all around town in trains and buses when the Laundromat usually ends up just being a few bus stops away. Then you have the hassle of getting enough coins to get everything washed and dried and the boredom of waiting for it all to finish. We all convert to become disciples of David's shower routine.

'Meanwhile at home in Australia, the latest issue of cycling magazine Australian Cyclist hits the newsstands with a special feature introducing 20 of Australian's most interesting, inspiring, and intriguing cyclists of 2007 – and Walter is one of them. Wow! The 20 also includes professional sportsmen and the Federal Minister for Health and Aging, Tony Abbott. My husband continues to impress, inspire and enlighten and I love him for all his effort…and I miss him too!" – Katherine's blog entry, 9 August 2007.

# THEN THERE WERE EIGHT

One of the best things about the digital age is that you can take a trillion photos on holiday and it doesn't cost you a fortune to get them developed. Which is just as well as Europe seems to be a non-stop photo opportunity. There are a lot of distractions for us along the way. We have drifted off into the Middle Ages riding past castles and stray well into the future riding past all the solar, wind and water power stations. The fields are fascinating us too: we see lots of wildflowers, the ubiquitous cornfields and sunflower crops and plenty of green grass with mist magically floating above it. We can't imagine why they need so many corn and sunflower crops in Europe but they are lovely to look at. I really have to restrain myself from stopping to take photos every five minutes and remember that we have an itinerary to stick to.

Sightseeing is usually restricted to the places we stop at for the night and is on foot – once we arrive at our destination each afternoon, the first thing we do is locate a secure place where we can lock up the bikes overnight. Enthusiastic hotel staff generally helps us tidy the bikes away quick smart, not to be seen till the morning.

*'Day 18, Rest day in Donauwörth, 1,121km*
*We had a long, but easy day of riding yesterday (over 100km). The riding was flat and not one of our more scenic routes (farmer's fields freshly manured up for planting), but nice, nonetheless, to follow what seems to be a normality in Germany – exceptional bike paths along the Danube River.*

*These mostly paved paths lead to over-confidence and we are trying to impress each other with what sort of activities we can do while riding. David can take off his shirt, more difficult than you'd think as he first has to remove his man-purse that straps over his shoulder-blades, and then he must secure the shirt – all while riding no-hands. I can eat a schnitzel sandwich, but it was already prepared, so I lost points. However, I can also get my MP3 player going.*

*Lucas can film while on the move – sort of. A few days ago, while trying to film a high speed downhill, he met with some unfortunately placed gravel and subsequently filmed his incredible wipe-out. He showed us the clip later, but said he wasn't turning on the sound as he may have screamed like a girl when he went down.'* Heather's blog, 14 August 2007

I am still the slowest of the team and David makes sure he keeps me in sight. Lucas is typically behind me because he needs to film and wants to be there when I cough, spit, vomit or pass out. Heather on the other hand is fit as a fiddle and, despite her knee problems, often pedals ahead comfortably, enjoying the nice new Batavus bike, thinking about green hills in Canada and listening to her MP3 player.

We are supposed to be getting fit and strong by now, but some of us have actually managed to gain weight – I blame the schnitzels. One of us who is getting much stronger cycling is my friend Martin, who originally was coming along with us for a week or two, but now he is enjoying himself so much he wants to stay as long as his other commitments would allow, but he will not grace us with his presence for much longer.

Day 17. We set up the tents at a campsite near a tiny town called Eggelstetten, about 10km out of Donauwörth and our first stop in the German state of Bavaria. The sun is finally coming out and we have a planned rest day. Brent Reynolds, the Mad Bomber, another old mate of mine – and one of the ride's sponsors – is coming to join us for three days with his seven-year-old son, Niki. We're not sure exactly how it's going to work with a young boy on the ride, but but we'll soon find out! I'm glad Martin is staying a little longer because I want him to catch up with Brent, who he hasn't seen since the three of us scammed a trip together on the

Trans-Siberian Railway 20 years ago. Back then I had convinced Martin, whom I had met in Holland whilst we both worked at the same bank, to take the train across the then USSR en-route to Australia. It was during this trip we met Brent in Budapest and we joined forces on the legs to Moscow, Harbin and Beijing in China, and on to Hong Kong. We had a great adventure, doing all sorts of things that I never regretted but would never ever do again, or recommend that others repeat – including travelling with some pretty dodgy visas and ID. We also discovered that the cheap digital watches, chewing gum and plastic carrier bags that we had brought along with us would buy our way out of quite a few scrapes.

Brent (The Mad Bomber), Martin and Walter. We have not been seen together since the 1980s!

Brent and Niki join us late that night after a harrowing trip from Paris that should have taken three or four hours, but took 11 after their rental car broke down. I discover that my sleeping bag is still drenched from the condensation and sweat from camping out in the rain the previous night and Brent had shown up without any camping gear so I ask Brent if I can spend the next two nights with him and Niki. At around 10:30pm, when Brent and Niki walk to their car to find a hotel, I casually grab my gear and head off with them. The rest of the group looks a little bit surprised, but I just smile and say: 'see you in the morning, dudes.' I feel a twang of guilt leaving them there.

Now setting off to find a place to stay with a child in tow after 10pm on a weeknight in a foreign country, in a small town, is not generally an easy task. My experience in France to date is that towns seem to be mostly closed for the summer, and even finding milk in the morning, let alone croissants and coffee was next to impossible, so I am a little worried now. But with combined Brent and Wally luck we have no trouble. We stop at the first hotel that was open this late at night, the Posthotel which dates back to the 1600s and whose guests have included Goethe and Mozart. Brent manages to negotiate a good price for a fantastic suite which is not much short of palatial. It even has wireless internet, a separate bedroom for me and includes breakfast.

The team is always concerned about spending the donated funds wisely and not 'blowing it away' on luxuries, such as a dry bed, insisting on camping whenever possible. I love camping and the fresh air is great for me, but I can't risk my health for a few Euros. I have no qualms about staying in the hotel. Although I am feeling much better now I am still on antibiotic pills and inhalations and not back to my usual 110 per cent. I am still coughing up a little blood with my morning and night airway clearance sessions and I am sweating badly at night, waking up wet. Unfortunately, I have a bad habit of convincing myself I feel well even when I am obviously not well. My wife, Katherine, can tell when I am getting sick at home when my appetite goes – other symptoms are more obvious such as my face turning grey, my fingers going blue, and my breathing at night becoming so short that she gets freaked out and decides to sleep on the couch. On this trip, without Katherine to tell me that, yes, I am sick, I am trying really hard not to fool myself or take chances that could lead to medical complications. After all, this ride is all about showing people how CF can be managed on the road, not how you can really get sick with CF by living on the edge!

I still cannot help feeling bad for the others though: I know Troy is sleeping in a wet sleeping bag and he is really not very comfortable camping anyway. David would always prefer a bed to a tent – so much so in fact that he has made it known that he would gladly subsidise the others if it would convince them to stay in a hotel. But the rest of us do want to camp wherever possible. I am conscious of the cost of accommodation and also of the need for the team to stay together. We tried youth hostels, but found the day curfew inconvenient and they still are about the same price as a modest two-star hotel – about €25 per person. The hidden cost of a hotel is that we are unable to cook for ourselves and end up eating out in restaurants. Even the most simple set menu costs about €10 a head and it all adds up. On the plus side, we are dry and comfortable and benefit from the good meals that help build up our reserves and keep us healthy! Camping in Europe is also not cheap, sometimes as much as a hotel, and buying food for meals does not always work out cheap either. Katherine, back in Tasmania, manages to clear some more funds for us so we can pay for a bed more often.

The next morning Brent and I get lost trying to find the campsite – we have lousy memories – but there is no hurry anyway as, being a rest day, all we have to do is hang around and give our muscles a break. We find the campground and supply the happy campers with fresh bread and some milk for breakfast. We tried not to brag about our included hotel breakfast. Today we all want to go into town and pretend to be tourists. David, with an eye on security, is not so keen to leave all our gear unattended at the campground, and he and Troy volunteer to spend the day there, soaking up the sun. Just as well really as the team also suffers from exploding pack syndrome, which means that the minute we arrive anywhere all our belongings are spread everywhere within minutes, and it probably would have taken the day just to pack everything up neatly.

Heather and Lucas come to the Posthotel and chill out in our hotel room, setting up their computers to write blogs, download photos and film footage, and send emails. Martin, Brent, Niki and I go for a walk around Donauwörth. I buy new socks and underwear – top German quality – then after sampling local sausages and cheeses at the market stalls we finally succumb to good coffee and pizza in the old town next to an historic bridge that has been destroyed 30-odd times in its turbulent past! We return to the campsite with a kebab dinner for our tent guards, David and Troy, and join them for a few beers and a late afternoon swim in the lake next to the campsite.

Niki has brought his own bike along for the trip and Martin kindly offers to drive Brent's car, meaning that Brent is also able to ride the 30 easy kilometres that were planned for the day. Lucas and Niki get on fabulously well and are putting more effort into talking than cycling, meaning that we are making very slow progress at first. In the end we decide to separate the two new buddies and pair Niki with his dad. – nothing like a little father and son competition! As we make our way through the beautiful countryside, past a deserted castle (one you would just love to buy and renovate), fields with obscure crops, tall pine forests and some industrial terrain, the sunshine gives in to the rain again, and we enjoy a slight drizzle that keeps us cool while we ride our bicycles along the Danube. Niki has no trouble doing the distance and looks fresh as a daisy when we finally stop for lunch 30km along the Danube in Neuberg an der Donau. We find a hotel near a campsite on the river and call it a day. The sun makes a strong comeback and we all go for a swim in the Danube. The water is cold, murky and very fast flowing, but we are really happy to finally be baptised by the Danube. Not often we see a sunny day! David wants to swim right across, but the rest of us are just jumping in, swimming along with the strong current and scrambling to safety at the next opportunity. Niki is issued with an inflated bicycle inner tube and Brent keeps a watchful eye on him at all times.

The next morning the sun had left us again but this did not deter Niki and Brent from bravely mounting their bikes again to ride with us to the next town, Ingolstadt, where we have a last supper – lunch – for our extended family in a smoky restaurant near the train station. After the meal we say goodbye to Martin, who boards a train to the Mosel River in Germany, where he is meeting another friend to go kayaking. Brent and Niki also bid their farewells and drive off in their rental car to Paris, where they will catch a flight home to the USA. Brent brought the sun with him, and now as he disappears in the distance, the rain begins to fall on us again as we ride another hour or two from Ingolstadt to Neustadt an der Donau.

# PROMISES AND PINS

'I just spent the nicest three days of vacation biking through the German countryside along the Danube with Niki (my seven-year old) and six interesting and fun people including our favourite wandering Dutch-Australian; Jonas Jacob Walter van Praag. As many of you know Walter has Cystic Fibrosis and should not be capable of biking any distance. Yet, he is biking from Paris to Istanbul to raise awareness and funding for Cystic Fibrosis and to create a documentary to encourage kids with CF to explore and enjoy the world.

I would consider it a personal favour if you would visit their website and make a donation to this fine group's efforts. They are going to end up helping 10,000's of CF kids improve their outlook on life.

Ten entertaining minutes on line and $10 in donations will go a long way to keep this expedition and documentary moving forward.

Many thanks to Walter, Martin (last seen in 1984 on the Trans-Siberian railroad), Troy (mechanic extraordinaire from Tasmania), David (when your boat is floundering in 20ft seas, this is the man to call), Heather (oops! dropped your rope at 22,000ft on Everest? Heather can help), and Lucas (future famous filmmaker and all around nice guy); - Brent Reynolds the Mad Bomber in a mass email to his countless associates and partners in crime, 16 August 2007.

To entice the team members to join up to the trip I had promised that the entire bike ride would be flat or downhill, tailwind, and sunshine, bicycle path, more sunshine, and that we would also soon have world peace and an ocean full of whales as a bonus if we were nice to each other. They never believed me, and the last piece of credibility I had disappeared in the first week of gruelling rides in drizzling rain. But now, cruising along the Danube on fantastically flat paths, I see my chance to make them some more promises. Since Martin, Brent and Niki left us, we have realised that five really isn't enough people for a team. Two of us generally need to be in the support vehicle, so that only leaves three to ride. David is riding the entire distance to Istanbul with me as he was not only needed to navigate with his GPS, but also he has to be there in case I keel over! So that means Lucas and Heather have to take turns to join us and Troy is stuck driving every day. With only three riding it seems a different experience, if anything it is faster and easier to stay together, but also more competitive. David is as equally determined as I am to ride the whole way and nothing less.

So, facing the trials of a small team, I now see fit to promise them that all will be better once we reach Vienna in Austria in just over a week when my friend Cindy Brazendale, a hairdresser from Forth in Tasmania, is going to meet us in the city and from then on she will help drive the car, navigate, give us massages, entertain us and cut our hair as well!

Actually, I still am not 100 per cent sure if Cindy is going to show up. She is currently somewhere in Europe – she decided she needed something exciting to do and set off travelling. I have her basic itinerary and she said she would be able to join us in Vienna. She left for Europe before we did and, although she has my magic USA Skype phone number, I haven't yet heard from her. I know Cindy, better known to me by her Hash-name 'Thrust', from the Devonport Hash House Harriers, a running group of middle aged people who like to go for a beer and a meal after an hour's run.

Of course I am advertising her to the team as the bee's knees. Now that we are beaming along nicely on the bikes, the weather clearing, the tailwinds picking up, we get some nice downhills and we are even getting ahead of schedule, I am silently praying that my promise to the team will be fulfilled and Cindy will actually meet us in Vienna.

There is a lot of praying going on at the moment, but if one of my prayers is not answered the result will be disastrous. I am running out of money. Having to replace the lost luggage was not an expense we had budgeted for and with my credit cards pushed to their limit I am really concerned about how we can keep going. I call American Express from Germany and they tell me I am running close to my credit limit and tell me that the best way to solve this is by immediately depositing more dollars. I explain about the lost luggage and having to buy replacement gear and even added that I have the American Express travel insurance. Yet they stand fast: they cannot help me at all, they cannot extend my credit limit – not even a little – nor could they arrange for a cash advance facility, which would have to be done on the correct application form and be posted or faxed and would take several weeks to process.

Not only that but my travel insurance would really only be of use to me once I get back home. I am particularly annoyed because I contacted American Express in Australia before leaving to discuss the procedure and the cost involved when withdrawing cash from an ATM. At no time did they tell me I would need to apply for a cash advance facility separately. In any case, the card has hardly ever been accepted, and even Visa and MasterCard have been troublesome at times. For a start, the Europeans have a chip in their credit cards which requires a pin number at the point of purchase. As our cards don't have chips they are often rejected by salespeople. Although the chip machines often have the ability to swipe the card's magnetic strip as well trying to explain this to a sales assistant in French or German is just too difficult. This is another thing that American Express failed to mention to me. Not happy.

My Australian bank, ANZ, tell me I can use my debit card at any machine with the Cirrus sticker on it, but this doesn't work for me at all in Germany.

In the end, Katherine arranges for her parents in the USA to send us US$2000 by Western Union funds transfer to Vienna. This is not the most economical way of getting money, but it is fast and convenient. When it is converted to Euros we still end up with just over €1400. As hotels so far are costing at least €100 per night for all six of us, we hope this cash with the credit cards and the other's money will see us through the final 40 days of the ride after Vienna. I find carrying this much cash scary and give half to David for safe keeping, and hide my stash in my luggage.

People with CF do not often get a chance to handle hard cash like that! Fortunately the other team members are also helping pay many of the bills, but I feel responsible when we have to stay in hotels because of my poor health. Up till now I would pay for hotels with my card, and if the card was not accepted look around the team for cash. At least now I will have some cash again. After all the trouble with credit cards in Western Europe, what is it going to be like in the East?

# BAD MOJO

After a couple of days with just the five of us, we are excited to have another visitor – Mark Litterick, an old climbing buddy of Heather's this time – who meets us at our campsite, Camp Denn, a campground in Deggendorf where we camped virtually under the railway bridge over the Danube river . Heather and Mark take the support vehicle for the day to do some sightseeing together, which means Troy gets to ride a bike – and they arrange to meet us at the end of the day in Passau, about a kilometre from the Austrian border. Passau is a university city which was one of ancient Rome's northern border forts around 80AD. Three rivers – the Inn, the Ilz and our guide, the Danube – meet in this busy German city with an imposing old fortress built by a bishop, winding cobblestone streets and terrace houses.

All the small hotels we find in the city are fully booked or don't accept American Express, so I find an internet cafe and book nice rooms online at a Holiday Inn that we had passed on the way into town.

As we have tried, unsuccessfully, to celebrate our 1,000th kilometre with a champagne toast at every pit stop we've had, I decide to take advantage of the hotel's restaurant, which looks promising, to book us a special dinner. We finally get out champagne – although it was a little warm – after a rather ordinary meal but nothing was going to stop us from celebrating our success so far. Even less successful was David's attempts at getting another bottle. We end up in the bar downstairs which apparently has a happy hour after 11pm. The bartender tells us it has never been a great success as most people leave before it starts, but kindly offers to start the happiness 15 minutes earlier for our benefit. We decide the drinks are too expensive and opt for an early night. Troy is excited to see our floor has a drink vending machine with beer in it, but his joy does not last long as there are only two beers in the machine, and all the other machines he can find have also run out. We can't stay awake long enough to make happy hour in the bar, and most of us are in bed by 10pm.

Having purchased internet access for my laptop, everybody has a turn sending emails and to contact family. As a night person, I take last turn and by the time I have spoken to my wife on Skype, put up a slide show on the blog, checked my email and then finished my nebulising (read: coughing) it is 1am . Lucas manages to crash, but poor Heather in my room has been trying to sleep since 9.30pm. and is kept awake by my night-time activities. The following morning she is understandably grumpy with me for being up till 1am at night. She is also probably sad to part with her friend Mark who drove back to his temporary home in Munich. Heather is eventually cheered by the hearty buffet breakfast, which I am assured is included in the price of the rooms.

'We were especially entertained at breakfast by a woman who got her toast stuck in the toaster. A chef came along and stuck a fork right in there and then all the lights went out. The chef appeared to be fine. Can you have delayed electric shock? Maybe someone should check on her....' - Heather's blog.

Monday 20 August, Day 23, a rest day in Passau. I jump on my bike and head into the city to buy computer bits and pieces that we really need. I find a huge store about three kilometres away that has nearly everything on our list but when I get to the check-out I discover that they don't accept American Express; my MasterCard doesn't have enough funds left and, although I see the Cirrus sign, my ANZ card doesn't work either. I try to get some help by calling the American Express travel insurance people, who I think may be able to arrange to pay some of the compensation money for our lost luggage. I spend almost an hour trying to get some help from them then give up and am forced to spend my last Euros on the hard disk drive that we need to store our digital camcorder footage and I leave the GPS I had wanted to buy. Hopefully the power cable for the external disk drive will also fit on Lucas' disk drive, the power cable for which is lost with our luggage. On the way back to the hotel I also pick up extra pancreatic enzymes and antibiotics that I had ordered from a nearby pharmacy that accepted my MasterCard - which had sufficient funds to pay for that.

It is raining and miserable and nothing has really gone according to plan. I'm feeling stressed and depressed and resent the others who have headed off to visit the bishop's fortress, Veste Oberhaus, on the hill which I had really wanted to visit it too. I also resent British Airway's failure to find our luggage, which means that instead of resting and having a chance to be a tourist as well, I have to race around looking for replacements for our lost equipment every time we come to a good-sized town.

When I get back to the hotel, I show Lucas the external hard drive. We test the power cable on his external disk that we have and it doesn't fit although it is the same brand. Lucas wants to come with me to the store to return it. I get my money back and we ride off in the rain back to the hotel again. To avoid road-works along the way we have to get on and off the kerb. Lucas slips and falls off his bike. This is the last straw. The doom and gloom really hits me and I freak out. The others are out there playing tourist (and buying much needed maps, actually!), and I am stressing out. It is raining. I know it wasn't Lucas' fault. I was riding too fast ahead of him, jumping up and down the curbs quickly in my bad mood and he did his best to keep up. I think I should probably just go to bed and hopefully wake up in a better frame of mind but I decide instead that I should just stop rushing about and sit down out of the rain in the Thai restaurant in front of where Lucas has fallen off and have a nice bowl of hot and sour soup. Lucas, sore and sorry from his fall, is freaked out by this. He cannot be persuaded of the joys of soup and simply wants to get home to the hotel – he is not comfortable about separating the group, especially not for dinner, and especially because the others would likely be waiting for us to go to dinner.

Without the calming effects of the soup I am still grumpy by the time we get back at the hotel. I am in no mood to meet the 'tourists' and decide to go out alone to find a McDonald's. I don't have keys for the room, so I knock on the door. I can hear Heather is in there, but there's no reply. I thump the door louder and louder and eventually I hear some muffled reply and the shower being turned on. I storm over to Troy and David's room, knocked loudly, and tell them I am in a terrible mood and will be having McDonald's and beer on my own tonight. They decide on the spot to come too, so they chase after me. We run into Lucas downstairs in the lobby and he comes too.

My McDonald's plan and my bad mood are forgotten after we stumble upon a noodle house with good beer and fresh noodles with extra chillies. It is nice to have some men-time too but I do feel guilty when we get back to the hotel to find Heather all showered and dressed up, ready to go for dinner and wondering where we had gone. Lucas, always a perfect gentleman, goes out with her for a second dinner. I blame the bad mood and bad luck on the hotel mojo. It continues the next morning when we check out and they try to charge us for the breakfasts we had during our two nights stay – about A$35 for each person – a total of A$350. I argue that I was assured several times that the breakfast was included in the price. Eventually I have to pay the whole amount, but they gave us a free picnic lunch for two to take with us. I am just glad to be back on the road and feel the stress wash away as I ride my trusted Batavus out of town. Back on the bike, thoughts revert back to the relaxing rhythm of my legs, my lungs, my breathing – of life on the road with fresh air to breath.

'It's day 24 and we are at 1,452km. We are just about to leave Germany: land of fantastic food and service, scary castles, lederhosen sold off-the-rack and gender-specific parking spots – I went to park the support vehicle yesterday and to my surprise, the Frauen (German word for women) name was written on the wall in front of the car-parking.

Germany has been great! We had great service from day one in most restaurants, stores and hotels. But one hotel that stood out from the rest was Gasthof Gigl, a super friendly, family-run guesthouse in Neustadt. They were happy to go to extra effort necessary to bring David his iced coffee with a twist – although they had never heard of Kahlua, they did come up with a fine tasting whiskey. At another hotel in Wörth, the owners brought their own box of muesli from their house for my breakfast because I'd mentioned liking it - what a bunch of brats we are!

Our filmmaker Lucas had a revelation. An inexperienced rider who had been juggling riding his bike at the same time as filming us, Lucas' learning curve was on a steep incline and he was doing great. So great that, while experiencing a sudden burst of energy and busting out into a speed of 29km an hour, he suddenly yelled: "Hang on, what's making me wet?" To which Dr. David replied: "That's sweat, mate."

When we weren't riding or teasing Lucas, we were making bets, er... mostly on Lucas. The other evening after we'd finished a day of riding, Lucas, having been Troy's co-pilot all day, asked if he could take a bike and a map and go back to where we had stopped for lunch – about 20km away – to visit a castle he had spotted. Once he had set off, we quickly placed bets: Would he return before dark? Would he have the map or have lost it? Would he call for a pick-up or get lost or have found the castle closed? By the way, Lucas returned smiling, with the map and the bike and having seen the castle. Just slightly after dusk.

We happily rode on for a few more days, feeling fit, strong and happy. David's birthday came along and we celebrated by proving our fitness levels. There was a castle on a hill and we had to get to it – on the bikes. We climbed 375m over 4km – that's steep! David was first to the top (we let him get ahead because it was his birthday). Yet impressive that even the bike-virgin, the girl and, oh yeah, that guy with CF, made it up there. Walter hardly even coughed. He imagines people watching the documentary later might see him riding up (well, walking the bits with a 20 per cent incline) with nary a cough and think: "Well, he doesn't have CF as bad as I do..." Actually, Walter's coughing is mostly done in the first 60km of the day, complete with the expulsion of bits of 'lung', coffee and other random bits of breakfast!' - Heather's blog, 21 August 2007.

The castle on the hill is Aggstein, a very well preserved medieval ruin with a strange history. The castle was built in 1100AD to protect merchants travelling through the Danube Valley, and the story goes that the tables turned in the 1430s, when the resident baron, Jörg Scheck vom Wald, took to robbing merchants sailing down the river on barges. He would take them as prisoners and give them the choice to die of starvation or voluntarily jump to their deaths on to a rocky outcrop, known as the 'rose garden' because it was often stained red with blood. While it seems that historians differ on the veracity of this gory story, it does add to wonder of the castle. It is a huge ride to reach it, but there is a great pay off: views, history, and a good lunch in a café. Plus the downhill ride back to the Danube is excellent. Troy hits a record 82km an hour, according to his bicycle computer, a speed record that none of us manage to beat. I suspect that his new extreme 'number 1 buzz' haircut may have helped.

# OH VIENNA

We soon realise that Austria is going to be different: murderous aristocracy, Wi-Fi in tents, a castle for a home, and naked people strolling across the bike path in front of us. Our first night in Austria we find a campsite in the industrial city of Linz, Camping Pleschinger See, which has free wireless internet that we can access. In the morning I update my blog right out of my tent, typing one-handed while nebulising. The next day we ride to a quaint town called Sankt Nikola an der Donau. We notice a little old castle on a nearby hill so we all pile into the support vehicle to investigate. The gardens are heavily overgrown, but we decide to walk up the path. The castle appears to be a private residence. There is a rope attached to a massive door bell high above on the castle wall and it is beckoning me. I can't resist and give it a good tug. The bell rings out loud and clear – alerting the entire village below that the castle has a visitor. Troy and I wait at the massive wooden gate in case someone opens it, while the others quickly walk away. Sadly, no one was home or perhaps they were just tired of people ringing their bell. Back in town we find an excellent outdoor shop, where David buys himself a decent tent. Lucas takes one of the bikes and his compass and sets off to visit yet another castle, the one at Grein, a couple of kilometres upstream from us. It is a good chance for him to get some quality practise in on the bike and provides another betting opportunity for the rest of the team. Will he return before dark (he has no lights)? Will the bike be stolen (he has no lock)? Will he get lost (he has a compass but no map)? Will he get to the castle before it closes (we did not think he'd get there before 5pm)? And will he call us for a lift home (he has no mobile phone on him)? Needless to say, he returns home just before dusk around 7.30pm with his mission successfully completed.

The naked people on the bike path are somewhat of a surprise. First we come across a naked old man walking along the path and we just presume he is a senile escapee from a nearby retirement home. But then we run into his mates. It seems that they are from some kind of nudist colony on the outskirts of Vienna, which the bike path crosses. We try hard to stay on our bikes and not show too much interest in the bare flesh surrounding us. Heather is the least fazed and, if anything, seems slightly saddened that there are no good-looking young males in the group.

A little shaken but not stirred by the experience, we power on to Vienna. Not much is going to worry me now: I am supercharged on antibiotics and my health is good again, the weather has cleared up, we are ahead of schedule and all feeling good. As we enter Vienna, it is hard to contain our enthusiasm. The city is like a goal for us, a halfway mark, a destination we want to get to. We are becoming very fit now and feel ready to go the whole distance. All the aches and pains seem to have gone and we are able to maintain a pace of at least 20km/hr.

But it is Troy who is looking forward to Vienna most. Bored with driving all the time, he is now looking forward to the arrival of Cindy, now confirmed, on Sunday 26 August – three days' time. Cindy, who is a young 48 year old, also happens to be the mother of one of Troy's schoolmates. Troy hasn't had much contact with Cindy since he was a pimply teenager, but thinks he will recognise her anyway. He can't imagine what it will be like riding and driving with his school friend's mum as a teammate. Maybe she'll have some good gossip about Troy's youth – we'll soon find out. But one thing of which I am certain is that Cindy will do a great job as part of our team. She is a hardy woman – fitter then me – and has great enthusiasm and common sense.

Cycling along the Danube is truly a holiday here. All the way to Vienna is safe and easy! Lots of pensioners and young families ride the bike-paths.

Cindy's imminent arrival is not the only news we have about long lost friends: our missing suitcases have turned up safely in Australia. British Airways sent them back to our homes in Tasmania and Canberra and it is now simply too late to try to get our gear sent over to us in Vienna for the last half of the trip. Frankly, I wouldn't trust the airlines to get it to us anyway. We have been reminded of the loss of our luggage everyday on the road as we constantly have to make do with inferior replacements or nothing at all. Without my PDA's GPS navigator, which I had so carefully prepared with European maps, we have struggled to find each other, especially in big cities; the replacement camping gear and clothes we bought in a rush have been found wanting; and the lost computer equipment means we are fast running out of space to store film footage and back-up files and that we have wasted hours hunting down stores to try to find replacements.

Because we got a little ahead of our schedule on the good flat paths, we will now have two days of sightseeing in Vienna before Cindy flies in from London on Sunday. Staying in a big city does have its advantages – we have more choice of places to stay and usually end up booking some good deals on great hotels, some with gyms and spas included in the price. Also these kinds of hotels nearly always accept my American Express card, to which I have transferred money and which I can now use again. Lucas drives ahead with Troy to book us into the Renaissance hotel in the central area of Ullmannstrasse and then Lucas takes off to collect a replacement cable for his hard drive – he phoned ahead to order it – from a Vienna store. Troy hops on the spare bike and rides back to meet us (which is not an easy feat) and guide us back to the hotel through crazy city traffic.

By the time we get to the hotel, it's getting dangerously close to 5pm, and today is a Friday, which means that if I don't get moving and find a Western Union branch quick smart, I won't be able to collect the money that has been wired to me until Monday – the day we are planning to leave Vienna. At this moment Lucas returns with his cable and tells me he noticed a Western Union sign on his way. I decide to discard the map marking a far off Western Union office given to me by reception and put my money on Lucas remembering how to get to the one he saw. The others relax in a café, placing bets as to whether we would make it or not. Amazingly Lucas walks me right to the place and just on 5pm they hand over my money.

Vienna is a beautiful, truly classic, city. And I really wanted to immerse myself in its culture and history – so what better way than to visit the spectacular State Opera House, which incidentally was the inspiration for that other great cultural force: the Muppet Show. Outside the opera building there are official State Opera House hawkers dressed in 18th century period costumes, and smoking. I tell them that I don't think Mozart would have smoked, but they insist that he did. The ticket prices are, as expected, very high. And, as the opera season is finished, the only performances are nice classical music concerts for the tourists, performed by a well-known philharmonic orchestra dressed in period costumes.

David is very keen to buy tickets and wants to hand over the cash right there and then on the street. Heather wants to just try to sneak in without paying or follow her guide-book's advice of buying part-used tickets from tourists who have paid for standing room tickets just to see the inside of the building and then leave after the first intermission. She is refusing to pay the outrageous price and goes as far as to say she would not go on principal, even if somebody else paid. While they argue, I scramble for my phone and call up Hildegard Grivell, an Austrian family friend whom I am expecting to visit us tomorrow. She used to live in Canberra but now runs a bed and breakfast with her family close to Salzburg. She is making the two-hour trip by train tomorrow to visit us so I ask her if she would like to see a concert in the opera house. She loves the idea.

That settled I immediately buy tickets for all of us for tomorrow night's performance of the Vienna Mozart Orchestra out of the entertainment kitty that Brent, as the Mad Bomber sponsor, had provided. The concert is to be performed in the 18th-century 'Musical Academies' style – a kind of 'best of' selection of single movements from Mozart's many symphonies and concertos, and overtures, arias and duets from his best-known operas.

The next pressing matter is to find somewhere to have dinner. As we stroll around looking for a restaurant, we pass lots of very good buskers, including a small group of young violinists who give us a new insight into classical music. Seriously good stuff, and fun to listen to and watch. No tramps with guitars here.

Wandering around randomly in a big new city looking for food is never a good idea when there are more than two people involved. It takes ages, and you never find something to please everyone. We eventually decide on a Russian restaurant and sit down at a quiet table on a terrace outside. It starts to rain, so we are forced to move on. Just then the waiter comes running out, and tries to sit us down again. Since it really is raining hard now and there is no room inside his Russian restaurant, he takes us to another place nearby that he says he owns. The restaurant is pretty new, but it's Friday night and it is empty.

To seal the deal, he offers to bring us the Russian dishes we wanted from the other restaurant. I want Borscht and so does Heather – she is curious to compare it with her family's recipe – and David wants the herring that he spotted on the Russian menu, so the waiter runs back in the rain to the other restaurant and duly returns with the dishes. The rest of the team, looking for simplicity, just order from the restaurant we are sitting in.

As if Vienna does not have enough wonderful sights to keep me occupied, I have the great idea that I should do the laundry – again. I hike half way around the city, dragging around a bundle of dirty clothes – Heather's Lucas' and mine – on the underground and then on several buses before finding a Laundromat. I swear I will never do it again. The drab Laundromat is a dismal place with a few sorry-looking people flipping lazily though seriously outdated magazines. Over the buzzing and whining of machines, I hear people speaking English, and soon discover a tired American family who are frantically washing all their clothes after spending the night getting eaten by bedbugs. It turns out that they have paid just about the same for their bedbug-hotel as we had for our five-star hotel – and theirs was obviously far less comfortable and probably rather cramped with all those bed bugs. I give them the address of the website that I often use to book accommodation (actually I bid on accommodation using the 'name your price' method on priceline.com where lock-in the price you are willing to pay for a certain city area, and a hotel finds you).

With the washing in the machine, I go in search of a new Nokia phone, which has built-in GPS navigation and I find a store that not only has the one I am looking for but it also accepts American Express. I return to the hotel in a good mood with fresh laundry and a new phone. My friend Hildegard is due to arrive at any minute and as I wait for her with a drink in the downstairs lobby, my new phone is hard at work in the room, downloading all the maps we require for the rest of our trip from the Nokia website.

Hildegard arrives exactly on time and we all gather in the bar, merrily chatting among ourselves and feeling very upper-class having pre-drinks before the Opera. As Heather puts it: 'As can happen when one is immersed in an environment for some time, we are all becoming quite refined and cultured here in Europe. Never mind that we sweat all day biking and the van smells like "boy"; put us in the glitz and glam of the city and we clean up good and go get opera tickets. Yep, that's where we're headed tonight to see the Wiener Mozart Konzerte at the Vienna Opera House.'

David is watching his clock. It's all very fine to have pre-drinks, but not if it means actually missing the performance. We catch the metro into the city centre and then stroll along leisurely looking for a restaurant near the opera house. David, still looking at his watch, impatiently herds us into the first one he sees. Fortunately the meals arrive promptly, something we are not used to, but as we are about to order dessert, David ushers us out the door – we do, he reminds us, have a show to catch. The Vienna Opera House - a cultural treat provided to us by The Mad Bomber!

David is always on the ball, making sure we get to places on time. I, on the other hand, see no point in setting an alarm clock as I always wake up before it goes off and get everywhere five minutes late no matter what I do. I always tell David that he needn't worry so much as things always seem to work out fine. To which he always replies that those things work out because he worries about them on my behalf and plans ahead. Perfect, I say, with still not a single grey hair on my skull! David really wishes he didn't worry so much, but somebody has to – and we all really appreciate his efforts. As long as David is around we are prepared for anything.

And so there we are in the Vienna opera house, right on time, in a crowd of tourists being guided along by people in period costumes. The atmosphere is fantastic and we all have huge smiles on our dials. Finding your way through the corridors and hallways, stairways, nooks and crannies of the old building is challenging, but with all the friendly ushers we promptly find our stalls high up above the orchestra. Photography is allowed during the performance, which is usually unheard of. As you can imagine there is a lot of camera flashing going on from the audience as the entire orchestra dressed in 18th-century costumes, not only perform the music but seem to act it out. The conductor is especially animated and even attempts a little audience participation at times. It is a really entertaining show and we all have a great time – and no one even thought of snoozing off. Troy treasures the CD that came with the entry price and will play it for many moons to come.

We come crashing back to the 21st century on the way home as we stumble across a battlefield inside the metro walkway tunnels. The emergency services are mopping up after a big fight. Young rough-looking men are looking bruised and bloodied; others are drunk and still keen to fight with anything and anyone. We quietly shuffle through the turmoil, walking past blood and gore as police try to disperse the rough crowd.

# CINDY'S CLOSE CALL

It is Sunday and David is worried. Cindy has just called to say she is on her way from the airport and David is concerned that she is going to be an excessive drinker. My fault really as David knows I met Cindy while running with the Hash House Harriers who have quite a reputation as drinkers. I took David on a few of the Hashers social running and drinking outings and I don't think he ever recovered from it. But when Cindy finally makes her entrance, looking the part, ready for action, animated and ready to hit the town, no one is disappointed. She is going to be a great asset to our depleted team and today, as she beams with energy and excitement, we know she is our saviour.

Cindy, Lucas and I head off to see the city sights, Heather stays back to catch up on her blog and David and Troy set off on a mission to buy a proper GPS for the support vehicle. It is hard to imagine how people ever travelled without them now, a bit like imaging living without email. A futurist recently predicted that getting lost is going to be a thing of the past and the next generation of kids will grow up not understanding how someone could not know where they are as every mobile phone, watch, car and even bicycle will have built-in navigation.

We all meet for dinner in town and spent two hours looking for the perfect restaurant, one where we can eat what appears to become our staple diet: spaghetti and schnitzel.

Cindy can barely remember our names as she mounts her allocated bike and follows us into the manic Monday morning traffic of Vienna. It's 9am and to our great surprise, we are greeted on the way out of the city by another nudist colony. It certainly brings the colour into Cindy's cheeks, riding trigger happy with her camera in one hand, she – as Heather notes in her blog – 'is quite happily taking not-so-inconspicuous photos of really leathery, wrinkled flab'. By the time we clear the section of the path populated by naked people, we realise we are not on the right track and, in fact, have to turn around and ride through the colony again. David and I cycle through calmly but steadfastly looking straight ahead of us, assuming that Heather and Cindy are on our tails. But when we stop at the place where we need to turn off, the girls are nowhere to be seen. I volunteer to ride back through the colony again to look for them. I can't see the girls at all and am trying hard not to catch sight of any drooping appendages as I scan the path for Cindy and Heather. Suddenly, just as I fear the nudists are tiring of me, the girls reappear miraculously – they had taken a wrong turn and had to retrace their tracks. For the final time, we ride through the colony, eyes facing front.

It is a hard first day for Cindy and after 80 long kilometres without a stop I wouldn't want to swap butts with her today! We haven't stopped because we haven't seen any coffee houses. When we finally spot one it is only three kilometres from the Slovakian border, where we are meeting Troy in the support vehicle. But coffee is coffee, so we stop for a break anyway – to Cindy's great relief.

# BRATISLAVA LOOKS GLOOMY IN THE DISTANCE

At the Slovakian border, I am fussing about trying to get a sales tax refund as I am, mistakenly, convinced that we are leaving the European Union. I had made sure that everybody kept receipts for all the equipment we had bought and assumed that we would now get a refund – like I did in Sydney when we left Australia. The bicycle border crossing is not the same as the highway crossing, it is slightly off to the side and very quiet. We are waived through very quickly. I notice a sign on a deserted building that says sales tax refunds, but nobody can tell me where the new building is so we cross into Slovakia without getting the refund. I think I am the only one who cares. We all assume that the insurance will pay for the replacement equipment, but I know my current cash situation and know that a few hundred dollars from the tax refund would come in handy.

We ride on through dead sunflower fields along huge bicycle tracks. In the distance, the capital, Bratislava looms. It is not exactly a pretty sight: a lot of grey apartment buildings merged into one big urban mess of concrete. We ride along the river and stop at a bridge that leads to the centre of the city. Troy has parked the support vehicle there, reluctant to take on the traffic of the city across the bridge, unless we really wanted to spend the night there. The traffic across the bridge and the city on the other side does not look appealing to us. We are distracted by the sight of dozens and dozens of exotic motor vehicles parked on the grass by the side of the river with lots of people milling about. Cars are revving up and some cruising around. Bizarrely all the cars are sporting Dutch number plates! I have never seen so many Porsches, Ferraris, Lamborghinis and the likes. It must be some kind of European road trip for Dutch millionaires. Suddenly I hear a roaring engine followed by screeching tyres.

A Dutch exotic car group is racing past Bratislava on their way through Europe just as we arrive.

I turn in time to see Cindy throwing her bicycle – and herself – out of the way of a speeding Porsche heading right for her on a footpath! It was a very close shave and could have easily ended with broken bones or a broken bike.Fortunately, though shaken, Cindy and the bike are both unscathed. This is not a good beginning to Bratislava.

With one of the cars now roaring off and flying past us every few minutes on their way to Vienna, we start to feel unsafe on the footpath and quickly make up our minds to cross the bridge and take our chances with the not so supercharged traffic of Bratislava's city centre. We cycle across and have a late lunch at a café, but we still have the chore of finding accommodation for the night ahead of us. David and I check out the big four-star Danube hotel in front of the cafe, while Lucas and Cindy head off to find the tourist office in the centre. We have no luck at all, while Lucas and Cindy come back armed with a tourist map covered in circles, which they tell us represent various accommodation options. Options are not always a good thing, especially when presented to a group of tired cyclists who all have different ideas about where they want to stay, what is a good location or how much they want to pay.

As Heather is the most exacting when it comes to accommodation costs David and I suggest that she should go to the tourist office to book something for all of us, and we would go with it. She resents the implication that she is difficult to please and refuses to go, so I say I'll do it. Lucas, Heather and Cindy follow on behind. I walk into the tourist office and make an executive decision to book us all into student digs, the Summer Youth Hostel Svoradov. The only campsite is 10km out of town – just too far for us. Although the hostel is very cheap, Heather still isn't happy and tells me that she is annoyed that I am always content with the first place that turns up or whatever accommodation the support vehicle finds and do not look hard enough for something cheaper.

The truth is that I'm just happy if someone makes a decision. Sometimes even deciding who is going to the tourist office to find out what accommodation is available is too difficult a choice for a group to make. Often no-one feels like taking the lead, no-one thinks it is necessary for all of us to go and most of us do not specifically care where we end up. So if anyone has special needs or wants, they can always volunteer for the job. It really is a blessing when the support vehicle team drives ahead and takes the initiative to find us somewhere to stay. There is nothing worse than being tired at the end of the day and trying to make group decisions: David likes hotels, Heather likes to camp, Troy gets a sore back, Lucas wants something scenic and Cindy is yet to have her say. But the support team always tries to keep all our wishes in mind and always looks for the least expensive, yet practical, option.

Camping with our inadequate equipment is not very comfortable and the campgrounds are often way out of town, but the hotel bills are getting out of hand too, and hostels have disadvantages such as not opening till late in the afternoon and poor security for all our expensive gear including film equipment, bikes, cameras, GPSs and laptops. It is not an easy decision to make, and the support vehicle often has the best chance of making an informed decision on accommodation. When faced with Bratislava Troy had looked at the map and thought we might like to push on and try something out of town, not to mention the traffic across that bridge looked horrific. Troy was still recovering from Vienna traffic this morning. He had bought a new GPS on his way out so that now the support vehicle had one. All this time he had relied on the large scale country maps and the vague bicycle routes that we had.

We move on to the student hostel not far away; it looks very uninviting from the outside. There's a rough-looking pub nearby with a few big motorbikes parked out front. I venture inside the hostel and speak to the old women in charge, but unfortunately we can't understand each other – in any language. I recognise a few Russian words but that is not helping. She gives me lots of paperwork for all of us to complete. I'm a little worried now as I can't imagine this working out – it's especially tricky with the bicycles. In the end we are given two room numbers and shown a lockable shed with other bicycles in it and they open up a big gate so we can park the support vehicle inside their courtyard. Cindy is an art appreciater, she hugs statues.

The building is enormous, reminiscent of an old hospital perhaps. It is pretty much empty, we see no one else, and the accommodation seems clean enough. Each room has three or four beds and a little wooden desk. There are shared bathrooms down the corridor with shonky showers. But apart from that, the team all agrees the hostel was a good call – plus it is virtually underneath the Bratislava Castle - a massive square building with four corner-towers perched on top of a rocky hill. We walk back into the city centre for dinner.

Bratislava is teeming with young people, full of life and busting with energy. There are cafes and restaurants, cobblestones and lovely old buildings everywhere. After seeing all the concrete high-rises on the horizon as we rode toward the city, this cosmopolitan downtown area is definitely not what we had expected. When we get to the main square, Troy and David get out the laptop they brought along and sit down on a bench. On our earlier trip into the centre, we had noticed some students were hooked up to Wi-Fi, so the boys take advantage of the internet connection to download maps for Troy's new GPS for the month ahead. There are a few other people using laptops in the square so we feel safe here but are still cautious.

Another surprising thing about Bratislava is the art. There are sculptures literally popping out of the pavement and other interesting art installations scattered around. We notice a hippy-looking bus parked in an adjoining square – it seems to be preparing for a public movie show and people are settling down in front of a large outdoor screen. This is only Monday, so Friday night here must be amazing. While we have dinner, fireworks start to explode over the river – unfortunately our view is blocked and we can only hear them – but that doesn't stop Cindy and Lucas from racing off with their cameras to catch the show. I try asking some people if there is something special going on, but everybody seems to agree that this is just another Monday in Bratislava. (It may have been the celebration for the Anniversary of the Slovak National Uprising!)

Cindy and Lucas get up early to walk up to the castle. At 8am we ride our bikes packed and ready to go into the old town to catch breakfast in one of the many nice cafes. What a surprise Bratislava turned out to be. We got off to a bad start here, but the city won us all over and we all wish we could spend another night here – but if it's Tuesday, we should be in Hungary, so our short sojourn into Slovakia must end.

# HUNGRY, HUNGRY, HUNGARY

'We are hungry all the time because we keep saying 'Hungary'! The food here, from what we have experienced, is amazing. I know, we're always talking about the food, but seriously, it's so good.' – Heather's blog, August 30

An insatiable appetite is a typical symptom of Cystic Fibrosis. This can be expensive, but it will rarely cause me to put on any weight – I have weighed between 69 and 71 kilograms for more than 10 years. Cystic Fibrosis must be the only medical condition that requires snacks between meals and deep-fried food on doctor's orders. I don't have to worry about cholesterol or fat as people with CF can't digest fat. That keeps us skinny, but the downside is that we miss out on fat-soluble vitamins and minerals in a regular diet. To help us digest fat, we have to take pancreatic enzymes throughout every meal, swallowing a capsule after every couple of bites. If I don't take enough capsules in a meal, for instance if I underestimate the fat content in the food, I will get complaints from whoever tries to enter the bathroom after me – unless the room has a powerful exhaust fan! The bad smell is caused by the undigested fats. At age 42, I am well accustomed to my medication – but this does not mean that I smell any less offensive from what I hear from the others sharing rooms with me. Maybe this is why my sense of smell is so lousy – damaged by exposure to my farts. Actually, my impaired sense of smell is more likely to be caused by thickening of my mucous membranes.

It is often the case that young people with Cystic Fibrosis have stomach trouble, and older people with CF have lung trouble. But now that people with CF are living longer, new complications are arising such as CF-induced diabetes. My endocrinologist in Tasmania believes I am on the verge of needing to take insulin, so I have to keep an eye on my blood sugar levels (BSL). Unfortunately, my BSL measuring device was in my lost luggage and so I do my best to eat regularly, eat low GI and healthy foods and avoid drinking gallons of juice at breakfast and putting sugar in coffee. I estimate my BSL to be too high most of the time (7-15 mmol/l). Nothing much I can do here, not even measure it. At least we are aware of it.

Lunch and dinner are often blurred on the road because we like to get to our destination before lunch, and if we don't make it in time, we will often just ride on through lunch, snacking instead on chocolates, fruit and sports bars and lots of Heather's fabulous healthy mix. Heather is doing a great job in finding low G.I. snacks – such as nuts, dried fruit and whatever cereals she can find in local shops – and mixing them up in big bags for us to nibble on during the ride. Hence she is now unofficially responsible for making the 'mix'. When my breakfast energy runs out, I heavily rely on it. I had expected to be able to buy muesli bars along the way, but the European bars are full of sugar, soft and gooey, and certainly not the energy food that I need. In Austria I stocked up on a few energy sports bars, which I use in 'emergencies' – I swear they give me an extra hour of bounce when every other option is exhausted.

It is nice to ride into Hungary. I have good memories from my previous trip to Hungary a very long time ago – 23 years ago in fact. The roads are now getting smaller and narrower, the towns are all quaint and cobblestoned and we are spending more time riding through nice fields and forests. We are now getting off the beaten tourist track and our hearts are beating hard in anticipation of the unknown! One thing that doesn't seem to change is the rain and clouds following us everywhere we go. Although we are drenched almost every day, it fails to dampen our spirits.

The riding is becoming a bit more challenging as the route takes us away from the river for many kilometres at a time, taking us up and down many hills. We have to cover greater distances – at least 10km more than I had calculated for each day. We have no real trouble cycling the extra distances, but we do have to make sure we are on the bicycles and away by 9am each day. We are pretty fit now but each hill is still painfully slow – they never seem to get any easier. Being fit just means we can climb more hills without falling over from exhaustion and we don't get as sore.

Our first stop in Hungary is Gyor, a regional capital and the most important city in the north-east of Hungary. Considering that it has been conquered and occupied by just about everyone, including the Celts, Romans, Slavs, Mongols and Turks, it is remarkable that many of the buildings are in the Italian renaissance style. The reason for this is that in the early 17th Century the commanders in charge did not want to succumb to the Ottoman Empire but were also unable to defend Gyor so they burned the place down. Gyor was later rebuilt by leading Italian architects who not only built an entire castle there, but also put up a big wall around the city.

It is a very pretty city and has a fantastic market-like feel about it with lots of shops spreading their wares on the streets. We are waiting for a message from the support vehicle here and while we are waiting we are approached by a friendly lady who is trying to get us into her hotel. It is tempting as we are all keen to explore this interesting city, but we receive a text message from Heather and Lucas in the support vehicle, saying that they have found a campsite for us and that we should come to the stadium site marked on our maps, and then follow the signs to the campsite. The Győri ETO Stadion is due for completion in 2008, but the spot is marked on our guide-book map.

Reluctantly we leave the town behind, knowing that camping out of town means we will not come here for the rest of the afternoon. We ride five kilometres out to the stadium, then note with horror that the sign for the campsite points down a road that looks awfully busy. We brave the traffic on the road for another five kilometres and we are now getting a bit upset that not only is the campsite so far out of town, but that we are choking on exhaust fumes trying to find it. We finally reach a campsite, but we can't see our support vehicle anywhere.

We make a distressed phone call and ask them where they are. It seems there are two campsites, and they are at the one right next to the stadium, which we had obviously missed. We have to ride back again – another five kilometres on the busy road. This is not cool. We have ridden over 100km already today and are not pleased to cycle along this rotten road again, we find a little side-road back. We finally get back to the stadium and ride around it until we come to another camping sign pointing at a well hidden campsite only a few hundred metres from the stadium. I am so annoyed; I get off my bike and sit down at the cafeteria, and order a cold beer before I can face anybody. Again beer is the easiest thing to buy anywhere, from petrol stations to campsites! It has been a very long day for us on the bikes. I am also cheered to find all our tents already set up, that Lucas and Heather have done the shopping, there are chips and snacks, and there is a meal in progress. I'm happy again, and the warm and fuzzy feeling is slowly returning.

We decided to use latitude and longitude co-ordinates from now on to communicate positions. I hope this resolve will help, but my fancy new Nokia phone with built in GPS is already the laughing stock of the group – though it could be down to user

error. Not only does the phone have enormous trouble locating our position, only managing if I am standing under a clear sky without even so much as a tree within 25 metres, it also takes as much as10 minutes to get a fix – by that time we have found our way with the map. Darn technology is very complicated! What do you expect when you buy a brand new gizmo. I wished I had my tried and trusted Mio PDA with its GPS which was in my lost luggage and now safely back in Tasmania.

Considering the very hefty price we paid for the camping, I am disappointed with the rudimentary facilities. The communal bathrooms have showers that are no more than pipes with water pouring out of them and the laundry sinks are blocked and have no hot water. By the time you add up all the additional expenses of camping, sometimes you are better off in a hotel. I have no idea why camping is so expensive. As it turns out the only other campers we see are two young men and a woman from Germany. They have some bicycle problems and our hero Troy comes to the rescue. He has a real thirst for fixing things and to date on this trip his skills have been seriously under-utilised. He beams with confidence as he attacks their first little problem, something to do with a pannier. He then moves on to the next problem, and then the next and then the next, until he is presented with a major mechanical problem. But it is now getting dark and Troy's legs are cramping as he squats over the bike with the rest of us crowded around with torches.

Troy had ridden over a 100kms today too. It is a very tricky situation with a very cheap built bicycle and he is missing the tools that we lost with our luggage. He ends up searching out the owners of a work vehicle parked outside the adjoining hotel and borrows a bigger wrench. An hour later, well and truly dark by now, he finishes the job. Troy, a mechanic back home, is quite pleased to get his hands dirty again. Even the oil underneath his fingernails had completely gone after a month on the road – the only time he had previously ever had vaguely clean hands in all the time I've known him was at his wedding. Washed up again and sitting around chatting, our fellow, happy, campers reveal that the two young men are in fact mechanical engineering students. Troy doubts very much they will graduate.

The next day we stop at a particularly pleasant little town, Tata, on the shores of Öreg-tó, 'The Old Lake', cradled in the valley between the Gerecse and Vertes Mountains. By chance, we run into Troy who is just on his way back to the support vehicle after visiting the local tourist office. He tells us the town is chock-a-bloc full and virtually no chance of accommodation for the night, but the office had given them one glimmer of hope which Cindy, his co-pilot for the day, had gone to check out. Whenever Cindy is not cycling, she likes to go for a long run, so – despite the rain – she offered to kill two birds with one stone. We discover Troy had parked the car right outside a restaurant-bar called the Phoenix. Seeing this as a sign – and the fact that it is still raining and we are starving – we decide to settle into the bar, have a late lunch and wait for Cindy to get back.

The bar has a covered terrace where smoking is not allowed but no one else apart from us would think it is a good idea to sit out in the rain anyway. We see smokers sitting inside; we like it outside and put another layer of clothing on instead.

Cindy returns from her run with good news: she has checked out the hotel and, not only does it have availability, but it looks really nice too. We have to book through the tourist office for some reason. Troy races off to reserve rooms for us, while we leisurely finish our late lunch. With bloated bellies, we head off to our charming hotel on the lake shore. We are split into two adjoining rooms and they tell us we can store the bikes in the dining room overnight. The hotel, Volán Panzió, seems strangely empty in a town that was meant to be strangely full. The hotel, whose own restaurant is closed for some reason, recommends a quaint lakeside eatery nearby for our dinner. After such a late lunch at the Phoenix we are not really hungry, but decide to go for a walk to check it out anyway. The building is exquisite and we find that the menu is the same. The prices are so reasonable that we just have to take advantage. It feels really luxurious eating in such lavish dining room with all its art, plush carpets, crisp white tablecloths and nice furniture.

Lucas is missing out, preferring to shoot some footage of the sunset over the lake and left the hotel before we did. Not only does he not know where we are, he doesn't know that the hotel staff locks up the hotel at 8pm and that we have the key to the outside door with us. When he tries to return to the hotel in the dark, he also discovers that he can't remember where it is – and spends ages walking up and down the streets searching for it in the rain. When he does find the hotel – to be fair, its lights have been turned off – he also discovers that the door is locked and we are nowhere to be seen. He knocks on the door of the neighbouring hotel, whose friendly staff calls the owners of our hotel to let poor Lucas – cold, hungry and wet – back into the hotel. Just a few minutes later we roll up – almost literally after all the food we've had – and hear of Lucas' ordeal. I take the responsibility (read pleasure) to take Lucas back to the nice restaurant for his dinner – and even manage to get through some more cocktails and a fancy dessert.

Tata turns out not to be an exception in Hungary. Along the way we find other good-quality hotels at not unreasonable prices, friendly towns and truly fantastic food – though we still have trouble buying regular water. As Heather points out in her blog, sparkling water is a problem on the road: 'The bubbles tend to become somewhat explosive in our water bottles and plastic bladders after a few kilometres of bumpy travel. If you're not paying attention, the water sprays into your mouth from the pressure build-up, causing a few choking fits here and there.'

# CHOCOLATE MILK AND HONEY TRAPS

I am genuinely surprised that Hungary has changed so much since my last visit. This would perhaps seem a little less ridiculous had 23 years not passed in the meantime. I was expecting a more rural experience. When I was last here, before the fall of the iron curtain, life in Eastern Europe was very different. I remember catching a bus with Brent and Martin back in the 1980s to the Aggtelek caves in northern Hungary and it felt like the Middle ages. There were no fancy restaurants and cafes to be found then (on our budget especially), and if we ever did find a cafe it was always rustic and old fashioned, and often had people playing Gypsy violins. We would sit down and the locals would just stare at us.

One time, in search of a place to eat in rural Hungary, we ended up in a stone cottage pub, with heavy iron bars on the windows and even the single entrance had a big iron gate across it. We walked in and tried to get a drink, but were refused service, probably for being foreigners. We left in frustration and as I closed the heavy iron gate behind us, being a bit cheeky, I put my padlock on it. It wasn't locked, but immediately people starting swarming towards the one exit and shaking the grate thinking they were locked inside. We ran for the bus stop and just as the bus showed up a group of angry patrons came running towards us. We managed a hasty escape. Eastern Europe at that time was probably not the best place for practical jokes – especially considering the 'police' presence then. We were supposed to register with the police every time we changed accommodation, but we rarely bothered. Today tourism is big business in Hungary, and economic growth means that the places I knew are now transformed.

Take Esztergom, our next stop, for example. In my mind, a small village nestled on the bank of the Danube; in reality, a town of around 30,000, which even boasts the

European Suzuki Factory. And my dodgy memory gets us into even more trouble when we leave for the capital, Budapest.

But now, just as we are standing in the town centre, busy with tourists and shoppers, and wondering which way to go, Lucas appears with a local woman who is offering us accommodation for the night. She leads us up a steep road, muddy with roadworks to her hotel. She tells us only half of us can stay there, with the others having to stay in a unit a little further along up the steep muddy road. Heather and I go with her to have a look at that unit and figure that all of us could stay there if some of us slept on the floor on camping mattresses. The lady agrees and offers us a fair price, breakfast included, and even finds us real spring mattresses to put on the floor of the apartment. The car is stowed into a tight garage and the bikes in another. Mud is everywhere.

That settled we join the tourists and walk up to the Basilica, a beautiful church on top of a hill surrounded by gardens and statues which has earned Esztergom the name the 'Vatican of Hungary' – the Basilica is also the seat of the Catholic Church in Hungary. Just like the other tourists we try out a photo booth, which not only takes your photo, but also emails it to a friend. We have a few excited goes at it, posing in front of this odd machine but none of the emails were ever to arrive. At least the food doesn't let us down, and after a great meal, we fight our way back up through the mud to our apartment where we all bed down together – except for adventurous Heather who finds some fresh air by sleeping on the veranda.

'I'm sure you all want to know how we're all getting along! Well, as you can imagine, it's hard for people to bite their tongues or conceal character flaws 24-hours a day. Add to that being over-tired from a night or two of cacophony-snoring that even deciding where to have dinner can bring on an argument or two. However, we still like to spend our rest days together doing the sightseeing thing and we even had a big slumber party when all six of us crammed into a room to save a few forints,' - Heather's blog September 2.

I am excited to see chocolate milk on offer for breakfast. I never forgot the really good chocolate milk which was sold in plastic bags last time I was here. Back in the 1980s, staying in student dorms, we lived off the stuff. Sadly the milk at our breakfast buffet, which we share with a bus-load of school children, is pretty awful, but we still fill up on cheese, bread and weak milky coffee. I tell the team that we have a nice quiet bike-path along the Danube to look forward to as we leave Esztergom for Budapest. But time can make a liar out of anyone and we have to cycle on a road. To make matters worse we have trouble navigating the route with maps in the GPS that do not correspond to reality. I have also given Troy the wrong directions to the hotel that I booked over the internet, but fortunately he's already lost faith in my poor memories of the place and when he clearly sees the grand hotel on the wrong side of the Danube he has no trouble ignoring my clear directions and sets off to find his own way across the river to the hotel. Leaving Vienna and the rest of Western Europe behind we now feel like we are really starting on our adventure as we cycle through rural Hungary.

Budapest is another important landmark for us: by the time we reach it we will have earned another bottle of champagne, having ridden more than 2,000km and reached our halfway point. But first we have to get there and the increasingly manically busy road makes the going tough – though a steady tail-wind helps us to power along. We cycle through Visegrád, where the Danube splits in two – creating a 10km-long island – before it reunites on the outskirts of Budapest. We jump on a ferry at Szentgyör Gypuszta to cross the river to the village of Kisoroszi on the central island, which is known as Szentendre Island. It is a haven of peace and quiet, dotted with little villages, fields and crops.

We are reluctant to leave, when we reach the end in less than 30 minutes, knowing that one short ferry ride away we will be smack bang in the middle of all that chaotic traffic again in the small satellite city of Szentendre. We can't find any cycle path, the map doesn't seem to correspond with what we see, signs don't make sense and the locals can't understand us. Then I spot a small bicycle shop. When all else fails: go shopping. I buy five sets of brake pads to replace the seriously worn out sets on our bikes. The man in the shop replaces the pads on my bike to ensure they are compatible, we do a deal and he points us in the right direction towards Budapest.

Stopping only for a quick burger on the way, we continue along the Danube toward central Budapest. Hydrofoils, full of people going places, race up and down the river. We have seen tourist boats and lots of cargo vessels on the river before, but now the river is an integral part of city life and the public transport backbone of Budapest. We ride past old buildings; some nicely renovated, with people sitting out on their terraces having lunch or preparing dinner; others terribly run down. We follow the river and see more immaculately manicured lawns and well-tended gardens, and the odd overgrown jungle.

The traffic increases to manic levels now as we ride into the city centre. We too have spotted the hotel, the Marriott, on the other side of the river. It is under renovations, which is probably why I got such a good internet rate for us, but it is a beautiful hotel none the less, and in a very central location right on the river with lots of stars for our comfort. Troy, having ignored my mad directions which included castles, is already there. He has already put the car in the hotel parking lot and reserved a spot for our bikes.

Keeping with our custom of eating the stereotype national dish, we have a good Hungarian goulash and some local ale for dinner at a restaurant in Vörösmarty Tér, a town square just a stone's throw from our hotel.

I am very keen to take the team to the amazing Gellért Hotel baths, which I visited 23 years ago as a skinny 19-year-old. The thermal baths, part of an old Art Nouveau hotel complex built in 1912-1918 for the very rich, are surrounded by mosaic-covered terraces and marble balconies and their facilities even include an artificial wave pool. The Ottoman rulers also built baths on the same site in the 16th century to take advantage of the same natural hot springs, whose mineral content is claimed to have healing effects. So the next morning, on a well deserved rest day, we take a leisurely stroll over to the baths for a day of pampering. Lucas, who modestly prefers not to show his body to every man and his dog decides to stay dry and visit the Fisherman's Bastion, a beautifully restored castle that was first built in the 1900s. Unfortunately the Gellert's hotel wave pool is out of action and, being a Saturday, the other services are limited: that means no mud baths or massages. At this point, Heather decides she won't go in either and goes for a walk around the city instead.

I just want to get wet – and see the glorious inside baths again. Cindy is keen to check out the male Hungarian physique and David and Troy want to see what all the fuss is about, so we pay our deposits and complicated charges, take our multiple receipts and tokens, collect towels and find our way through the warren of rooms and hallways – up and down stairs, across miles of tiled floors, past hundreds of semi-naked people and attendants – to get to the baths. It feels very Roman in here. We spend a few hours bathing in the natural spring-fed pools, subjecting ourselves to the extreme cold and heat of the various outdoor and indoor marble baths. It's fantastic, but I am developing an annoying stomach ache. At first I think it is the goulash from last night, but I realise that it may also be related to my Cystic Fibrosis.

Back in Australia, I used to suffer a lot from stomach aches and I attributed it to stress for years. But actually, it is a common complaint for people with CF. Three years ago, Annie Munnings, an ambulance officer who was in training with my wife, introduced me to kefir, a fermented milk drink originally from the Caucasus region. She gave me a little cloth bag containing kefir grains, which are basically a culture of friendly bacteria, and told me to leave it in milk for a few days to create a yoghurt-like drink. I have not, until now, had any stomach aches since. Considering I have not had any kefir for over six weeks now on the road, I should not be too surprised to finally get a stomach ache again.

So it seems like a small miracle that just as my ache is becoming a problem, I notice by chance a small shop in the hotel lobby area that sells a readymade kefir drink. I drink a container full immediately, while we wait for Cindy to reappear from the women's changing area.

Half an hour later, while walking through the less touristy and less flashy Buda part of Budapest, I raid the first grocery shop I see, buying all the goodies that I remembered from 23 years ago – the chocolate milk in plastic bags and the great Hungarian chocolate bars – plus a variety of kefir products ranging from drinks to yoghurts. My stomach ache almost disappears overnight. I wish it were so easy to buy kefir products in Australia – there you have to create and keep alive your own kefir culture. Back in Tasmania my wife Katherine is busy keeping my kefir culture alive by making mini batches – but she won't drink it! As you can imagine, leaving milk at room temperature for a few days makes it look pretty gross.

Back at our hotel, we notice some fire hoses in the car park near to where the bikes are stored and decide it's time they had a wash. The hotel staff say we can use the hoses as long as we don't spray all the cars, which is easy enough as there are not many cars parked here and there is ample place for us to wash the bikes. We set up an assembly line. Heather and I take all the accessories off the bikes to prepare them for cleaning; David takes charge of the hose; Cindy the brush; and Troy replaces all the worn brake pads on the sparkling finished product. Lucas stays dry by filming the whole process, while the rest of us get a soaking, but it is a good bonding experience all round.

On our last day in Budapest, one of us who shall remain anonymous gets caught in a honey-trap. We are on our way back to the hotel and he decides to walk off his dinner a little. He hasn't had the best day – earlier he was ripped off at the money exchange for about AU$50 – but he was still willing to help when a couple of strangers tell him they're lost. The two young women ask directions and then suggest that he goes for a drink with them. '

'After a couple of cognacs and special coffees in a trendy bar, the women suddenly declare, "Oh! We only have 1000 forints (about $4).

He looks at the bill and is rather alarmed as the amount is over 40,000 forints ($160). While the women tell him it is "customary for the man to pay in our country", he thinks about how he is going to get out of this: he knows it is a scam, but how can he get away. He tries: "I haven't got enough money – I'll need to go to my hotel and get more." To which the bar staff reply: "We'll come with you." They walk the short distance back to our hotel, and he is relieved when the henchmen say they'll wait outside. He runs into the lobby and tells the receptionist he is being scammed. She tells him not to worry and to continue on to his room - this happens all the time and she'll handle it. In the end, he didn't have to pay a cent.' - Heather's blog, Monday 3 September 2007.

This is the first time one of us has been scammed, though I think a few times we have paid excessive prices because people see us coming on our nice new Batavus bikes, with matching jerseys, and a new model support vehicle with sponsor signs on it, and mistake us for a wealthy team. No matter how hard we explain about Cystic Fibrosis and how we are raising awareness, it doesn't seem to ever lower the price. The other side of the coin is that we also attract a lot of favourable attention, sometimes from those who also have a connection with Cystic Fibrosis People are always very impressed and supportive of what we are doing and always very surprised that I have CF and yet am managing this ride.

# SINKING FEELING

Thank god it's Sunday – leaving Budapest is a blessing for my lungs. The city pollution makes me cough an awful lot on the way out. Riding and coughing is always a little difficult. It often means that I cough so hard that I also start to bring up my breakfast as well. It can get messy with coffee and juice squirting out of my mouth – I do hit my shoes, my bike or my shirt sometimes, but I am so used to it that I can generally keep clear. Sounds gruesome and it is not very pleasant for people cycling near me, but it's all part of living with CF. At least the traffic is lighter today than the weekday rush we encountered on our way in to the city. Passing Keleti Pu, the railway station where my Trans Siberian journey started 20+ years ago, David quickly navigates us safely away from the busy thoroughfares and on to nice quiet country roads, some a little rougher than others, but still a welcome change. Southern Hungary saw us on some seriously small farmers roads, often not knowing if the little track would stop in a field or a farm-house instead of the next town!

It is overcast and drizzly and we ride along muddy lanes, past fields filled with huge stacks of round hay bales, farm-workers on tractors and pigs foraging on the side of the road. Old farmers, busy with their chores, give us strange looks as we sail by on roads that seem to lead to no-where. At times, we seem so far off the beaten track that David breaks out in sweat – wondering if he has sent us up a dead end. We are relying on his guesswork now as the maps are inconsistent and do not show all the roads and even our hi-tech GPS gadgets are having trouble.

We need to cross the Danube again when we get to Ujmohács, about 10km from the Croatian border. We have already spent nearly all our Hungarian Forints ahead of entering a new country with different currency – this time, the Croatian Kuna. So we are at the ferry terminal, going through our pockets to get enough money together for the fare. We scrape together enough – with a little left over – and Lucas, who is navigating in the support vehicle today, volunteers to head back up the hill to the ferry office to buy the tickets for all of us. But just as he is out of sight, the ferry turns up. As there is only a crossing every hour, we are worried we might miss it. The cars that just arrived on the ferry drive off the ramp and the waiting cars on our side start to drive on. Still no sign of Lucas and we panic. Sure that Lucas will come running along with the tickets any second, Heather, Cindy and I make a dash for the ferry, expecting David to follow. He didn't. He sensibly stayed with Troy and the support vehicle and waited for Lucas, who ran into difficulties trying to explain that he was paying for five bikes, one car and seven people. Five minutes later and Heather, Cindy and I make it safely to Mohács on the other side of the river, having not been asked to show our tickets once. We feel quite smug until we realise that, not only do we now have to wait an hour until the others catch the next ferry, we are also separated from the last Forints we had. We don't have a single forint to spend between us and

stand defeated, counting pigs in a truck to pass the time, while David prepares for the next half of the day by drinking a nice relaxing beer on the other side, bought with our last Forints.

Probably just as well I missed out on a relaxing beer – I am still on antibiotics. I figured it was good for me to stay on them for a while longer as we had three big cities – Vienna, Budapest and, soon, Belgrade – to ride through in a period of just a few weeks and big cities are the places where I am most prone to lung infections. According to the medical profession, this kind of preventive use by people with CF is not 'abusing antibiotics'. Most doctors recommend that we either stay on antibiotics permanently, just switching from one to another when we develop resistance. Sometimes it is possible to take them one month on, one month off, but often your lungs will just infect as soon as you come off the antibiotics. It is also recommended that we have a bi-annual 'tune up', for which we are given intense therapy and serious intravenous antibiotics to regain as much lung capacity as possible. The truth is that I would prefer to be off them all together if I could manage it, but that seems impossible at the moment as the infection keeps coming back so quickly. Luckily, at least, the antibiotics that I use are a very standard broad-spectrum variety easily obtained and I am able to stock up on supplies almost anywhere in the civilised world.

Actually, apart from my CF-related problems, we are all very fit now and are covering more than 100km a day with relative ease. There are no particular aches or pains or feeling sick and, today we even manage to break the magic 20 km per hour daily average – despite the hills, some of which were quite serious. So our new record is 21.5km per hour – it feels great as breaking this barrier has been on my wish list for some time now. Although we have often ridden many long stretches at a time at over 20 km per hour our final daily average on the trip computer would always be in the 15-18 range. We have even been granted a few sunny days lately, maybe that also helped speed us up. The Cinderella of our team is still Troy, who despite adding to our number, rarely gets to go to the ball and is still driving almost every day. It is what he signed up for – official driver/mechanic, and he wears the badge with pride. Cindy, Lucas and Heather take turns to keep him company in the support vehicle, while David and I are always on the bikes.

Buoyed by my record breaking success, I decide to try my luck for a third time to get my sales tax back at the Croatian border at Udvar. The crossing itself is a little primitive so I am surprised that there is an office that can deal with my claim. They take my receipt and my passport and ask for the shop's paperwork. Shop's paperwork? Apparently you need to have a special form filled in by the shop where you made the purchase. I don't have any such forms – not one of the shops told me this although they knew I wanted to claim the sales tax back. Still clutching a fistful of receipts, I go back to the team, with my fantasy of getting some cash back shattered. When it comes to bureaucracy I often fail.

# WAR AND PEACE

These people have been to hell and back. You can see it in the ruins of apartment buildings blown to bits, but still standing; in the little villages where every house is pock-marked by huge bullet holes; in the new tiles that replace old roofs blasted by the bombs, and in ancient churches with modern glass windows. The damage suffered by Croatia's civilian population seems immense. It is overwhelming to see it as we ride south through the country, which was at war with Serbia from 1991 to 1995 after declaring independence from the former Yugoslavia. It seems terrible to stop to take pictures, I almost can't help myself, but keep it to a minimum. I hope that the locals who see me taking photos aren't reminded just how awful the war damage looks – I wonder if they might now be used to it or perhaps even desensitised by it, having to get on with their daily lives among this devastation. I'm sure that they'll never forget and I'm not sure if any of us should. We should all learn from it and remember the reality and consequences of war. I take a moment to take it all in and then turn to look for David who keeps on going steadily. He seems miles away now. I pack away my camera and try to keep my mind on the ride.

We find that while the people in Croatia are extremely friendly, the bicycle paths are not. The roads go up and down and, occasionally, through villages with steep roads paved with cobblestones that really rattle our bones. While it is not bad therapy for me – the vibrations really loosen up the phlegm inside my lungs – it is a little hard on the bikes. The cheap Dutch panniers that David and I bought –

designed for a casual ride to the shops or maybe to school – are hardly designed for this kind of treatment. While we are impressed at how waterproof they turned out to be, the attachments holding them on to the bikes are pretty flimsy and every bump we ride over makes them fly up like wings. They look pretty comical, but they are still doing the job – and at €25 each they are still a bargain.

We usually have the lights on while riding in the rain so that we can be more easily seen by cars. The headlight on my bike keeps flying off its bracket too. The lights are not the best quality and are certainly not waterproof – when wet they either go off or become impossible to switch off. On a few occasions, Troy has had to unscrew the lights that fail to turn off and dry them overnight for us. We need the lights to improve visibility in the rain, so when mine pops off I have to go back, find it and screw it back on. This is becoming more frustrating than the rain itself: not only do I lose all my hard-earned momentum by stopping, but it puts me even further behind the others – and I am already lagging behind most of the time now.

Today, we have already been on the bikes for 110km and now we are riding around and around a city block in Osijek, trying to find our hotel, Hotel Drava, in Osijek. Osijek is home to roughly 100,000 people, was settled by the Croats in the Middle ages, sacked and conquered by the Turks in the 16th century, then returned to Western rule by the Hapsburgs in the 17th century – most evident in the abundant Baroque architecture (random Wikipedia Trivia!). As lovely as the city is, we are exhausted by the time we discover the hotel, hidden down a driveway in the centre of a city block. Although worn out from the ride, we are never too exhausted to eat. Soon we are walking down to the beautiful old part of the town, Donji Grad, where a few bullet-ridden walls again remind us of the city's more recent past. A restaurant down in a dungeon just on the main square seems just the place to try a traditional Croatian pizza with kulen sausage meat and paprika sauce accompanied with local Baranja wine. As we are leaving a chatty waitress, who seems pleased to see some tourists this late in the season, asks us if the food was OK – as sometimes it is not that good she confesses with a smile.

The Danube now becomes the border between Croatia and Serbia and we pass through the war-ravaged town of Vukovar. The damage here is serious, and we are in awe of what we witness. In 1991, a battle raged here for 87 days as 2,000 self-organised defenders held off the Yugoslav People's Army supported by Serbian paramilitary forces. Such devastation had not been seen in Europe since the Second World War. In the end, the army overran the shattered city; around 2,000 defenders and civilians were killed, around 800 went missing and 22,000 fled into exile as the city was ethnically cleansed of Croats. When the Serbians entered the city, several hundred people took refuge in a hospital. The Serbian army removed around 300 men to a farm a few kilometres out of town, where they were either beaten to death or executed and buried in a mass grave.

The shelled ruin of a large water tower, that looks like it is barely standing, has been preserved as a stark reminder of the devastation suffered by the city. I think of how lucky our generation of Australians is to not have lived through a war at home. My own parents and grandparents, being Dutch Jews, suffered in the Second World War and many of them did not survive.

In 1942, two years after the Germans invaded Holland my mother's parents decided to make a run for it and used the underground resistance network to get the family out of Holland on foot. On their arrival in the un-occupied Eastern part of France, they reported as refugees to the French authorities and were imprisoned as illegal immigrants. The North and West of France was already occupied by the Germans, but it wasn't long after their arrival that the rest of France surrendered to the Nazis and my grandfather was taken away to the camps – sent to Maidanek in Poland and never to return. To save her children from the same fate, my grandmother swore that she was not Jewish, even though she was. The authorities measured her up for an ethnicity test – she passed, so my mother and her brother were allowed to go to a Red Cross children's camp, where they were safe. Many adventures later my grandmother brought her children back to Holland after the war.

There was more to the story of course, but the important thing is that my mother survived the war! My father and his parents also survived after being hidden during the Nazi occupation in different places by a number of good people in Holland in Anne Frank-style. The majority of our relatives who did what they were told by the Nazis mostly perished. I feel fortunate that I have never had to go through something as horrific as a war. I must say that I am proud to be the result of a seemingly endless line of direct forefathers/mothers who all survived long enough to become a parent, despite the wars, genocides, epidemics and other disasters that came their way through the hundreds of generations (this should in theory apply to all who read this...) and hence consider myself a small miracle despite not being able to father children myself.

Today, with the freedom to ride a bicycle across a united Europe, I only need to worry about fighting my health (and the mucous monsters!) and getting up the next hill. (Reference to 'Walter and the Mucous Monsters' written by wife Katherine!).

And there are plenty of hills to keep us occupied as we ride on down to Ilok, Croatia's easternmost town, climbing inclines of up to 12 per cent – according to the road signs – on cobblestones or brick paved roads. Troy has not only found us a place to stay for the night, the stately-looking Dunav hotel on the riverfront, but we also end up on Croatian television to boot. A TV crew doing some sort of travel show wants to interview us about why we are in Croatia and how we like it. We say that, apart from the persistent rain, we are having a good time, meeting lots of friendly people and eating lots of nice food – then we get in a quick plug in about our ride and why we are doing it. I hope we spread a little bit of CF awareness to Croatia through their show.

The hotel has wireless internet for its receptionist and we discover that the signal just reaches to the top of the lobby stairs. We don't think the management realises that anyone can hook up and enjoy their internet connection, but there is a comfy lounge chair at the top of the stairs which seems set up for just this purpose. It may not be the most comfortable spot to sit to chat on Skype to your friends and family, but needs must be met. We take turns, but I draw the short straw and end up sharing my Wi-Fi space with the high fidelity groans and moans of a randy couple in a nearby room that seem to be breaking longevity records. Meanwhile, during a walk around the hotel's garden, Lucas and Heather bump into a fellow cyclist, Ivan, who is also on his way to Istanbul, having set out from Germany. By coincidence, we had already passed Ivan earlier during the day. Although a German, Ivan, proudly sports a cap that has Perth written on it, to remind him of another ride he did – around Australia. He is a seasoned cyclist all right; carrying all his gear, and camping out or staying in hostels and pensions most of the time. He bids them farewell and heads off to his cheap B&B for the night, and we return to our three-star hotel. Heather is visibly very jealous.

# ALPHABET SOUP

Day 41: When we got up this morning we had 2,523km on the clock and were in Croatia; now, about 40km and a good two hours later, we are in a different country again and riding towards Novi Sad, the second biggest city in Serbia. New town, new country and a new language – and even a new alphabet. The Cyrillic alphabet is hard to decipher but we quickly learn one word: – Efe – which gets us a beer.

To get to Novi Sad, which is on the other side of the Danube, we have to cross an enormous bridge. From here, the city doesn't look very appealing – a big grey mass of buildings in a haze of smog. We are now not so keen on cities anyway. Not only is it stressful to navigate the busy city traffic while choking on the smog, but it nearly always proves tricky to find parking for the support vehicle and a place to stay. So it seems much more appealing to us all to bypass Novi-Sad and just continue along our way in the rain until we find a place to stay further down the road. Troy drives ahead, but the first hotel he finds is an hour further east in a town called Sremski Karlovci.

He sends us coordinates but our GPS doesn't seem to think it is such a good idea to go there and sends us on a wild goose chase up a busy road past Novi Sad and into the hills. The altitude and the exhaust fumes of the fast moving traffic are proving a challenge, but when the GPS points 250 metres over a steep ditch towards a forested hill off the road we lose faith in its wisdom altogether. So we just call Troy for some old-fashioned verbal directions. Seems we have to turn around and ride back down the same road we just climbed up. We fly down with a furious pace, keeping up with the traffic, and are at the appointed hotel, Hotel Boem, in a couple of minutes.

By this time, it is well after lunch time and we are all a little exhausted and very hungry. It takes ages for us to check in and the reception staff make us all register separately with our passports before handing over the room keys. I dump my luggage in my room, have a quick shower, I race downstairs to the hotel bar where I really expect to be able to eat something. But the empty bar only has alcohol and they don't even sell potato chips or peanuts to stave off my hunger. I order a beer to console myself and wait for the others. Lucas, Heather and Troy are the first to turn up and I drag them to the one other establishment in sight, another pub across the road, in search of food.

In my broken German, I discover that they don't serve food either. We rub our bellies and motion hunger to get across our pressing need. The barman, also struggling in German, tells me that there is a soccer club that has a restaurant not far away. He tries to give me the directions and we struggle to understand each other in German. After about five minutes, Troy suggests that the barman might speak English. And the barman, who does speak English, immediately understands and gives us easy directions to a club 10 minutes walk away. David and Cindy manage to find us and join us there shortly after.

'At the restaurant, we settle into the booth and open the menu. It's written in Cyrillic script – great, friggin' characters and symbols.

Luckily, the owner speaks a little English and when we say things like "salad", "chicken" and "pig", she nods yes and goes to the kitchen. She brings us a big basket of three different kinds of homemade breads to satiate us while we wait. Our meals arrive, some of which are terrific mounds of pork, sausage and indecipherable flesh.

The mixed grill for two people, which Troy and David order results in them both getting a meal for two. But we are all very hungry and put away plenty of the food and several local refreshments. The owner comes over several times to chat and eventually brings us a business card. On hearing our story, she claps her hands and asks us if we would like a drink.

Lucky for us, David once had a Serbian girlfriend. That was about 38 years ago, but apparently, she left enough of an impression for him to remember Slivovitz, which in Serbian translates to How to melt your oesophagus. Apparently it is plum brandy.

After two rounds, we made a reasonable call to leave. Little did we know that an innocent card game of Slaves and Masters would unleash the Slivovitz again. Back at our hotel, trying to sober up, as it was only 5:30pm, we decided to play cards downstairs in the foyer. The hotel owner motioned for us to use the dining room, which was empty and dark. She turned on the lights and cleared the cutlery away only too happily, then clapped her hands and said in halting English, "Yes, okay! So, in Serbia? Slivovitz!!" to which we groaned yet somehow found ourselves accepting, of course.

The last I saw of the rest of the COFE team, they were ordering a round of beer after someone claimed it would be 'refreshing'. - Heather's blog, 6 September (2711 km - 156 hours of peddling since Paris).

The next morning we make a mental note never to accept drinkable gifts from strangers again. Slivovitz hangovers really hurt. Not only are we pleased for the first time not to see a bright blue sky, our bloodshot eyes appreciating the subdue greyness of the heavy cloud cover, but even the colour of our shirts is proving too bright to handle. There's not even any coffee at the hotel to help ease our pain so, hung-over and suffering caffeine cold turkey, we hit the road for Belgrade. The combination of these two diabolical conditions is unbearable and when my bicycle light falls off for the thousandth time I explode in a fit of temper.

The map does not show the speeding trucks and diesel fumes or the rain!

'Walter stops, picks the light up and throws it as hard as he can on to the road. It doesn't smash into tiny little particles, which is not satisfying at all, so he tries again and again, yelling at the same time. But the seemingly indestructible light just flips over a few times on the tarmac so Walter gives up, abandoning it. But when Lucas goes over and picks it up, it is still working – frustrating Walter even more.' – Heather's blog.

The plastic bracket that held the light on the bike had broken off completely this time – ensuring it will not ever back to haunt me again! About five minutes later Heather's light bracket also snaps and David's does the same soon after. The lights are expiring one by one!

Just outside Belgrade, we stop for an emergency caffeine stop at a river-front cafe and wait for a call from Troy, who has gone ahead in to the city to try to find somewhere for us to stay tonight. Here we bump again into Ivan, the German cyclist also heading to Istanbul. This time, David and I get to know him a little better as he shares the story of his travels with us. He has been riding bikes all over the world, including around Australia. While Ivan looks fit, it's hard to believe that a man of his age does so much cycling – he does look like he should perhaps be riding around a lake, not the world.

The mobile phone rings, it is Troy, and the news is not good. Not only has it been a nightmare for him to try to navigate Belgrade's city centre with our poor maps, but even when he manages to get to the right area to look at a hotel, he can never find a place to park. To top it all off, he has been booked for speeding. The fine is more than Troy has on him, so the policeman just takes the €40 Troy has, telling him that it will suffice after all. The policeman promptly pockets the cash without issuing a receipt. Troy feels he has been scammed, but maybe this is just how things work around here.

So, understandably disgruntled, Troy tells us that we should ride into the city and try to find a hotel ourselves. We do just that, say goodbye again to Ivan. The traffic is incredibly busy and the going is tough. Discovering that my phone receives Wi-Fi in front of a shop, I make a humble attempt to book something via my favourite websites, but standing on a busy Belgrade side street with dubious internet and no proper keyboard or screen, I soon lose patience and give up. The hotels we try along the way are too expensive. David is ready to pay up as the situation is starting to look miserable – Troy had already spent hours looking, so what are we going to achieve? We decide to persevere at least till we find the tourist office. It is below the main street of Belgrade in a shopping tunnel of sorts and we have to carry the bikes down the steps to get there – only to find that the office is closed for an unofficial coffee break. We wait patiently outside until it finally reopens. It is worth the wait and we are soon dispatched in the direction of the only affordable hotel in the area.

Previously I have booked hotels in the big cities online, getting great internet discounts for luxurious international hotels. But I can't help but wonder if we could have found a more modest local hotel at an even better price by just searching around once we get there. Also these big hotels are a sure way to miss out on the local culture completely. So, this time I wanted to test the situation out to see if we could get a decent local hotel and didn't book online first.

As it turns out, the hotel, hotel Splendid, is quite good for its two stars – definitely comfortable enough, although extremely smoky. It is centrally located, the drinks downstairs are cheap, a sparse breakfast is included and, unlike the big hotels, there is no mini-bar temptation and no expensive distractions such as massages to tempt us. The city itself also does not disappoint. It is a truly bubbling town full of life and we have the most exquisite meal of the trip so far and some nice wines at the fine looking Opera restaurant with white starched tablecloths and fancy looking menus. The bill at the end is so modest it deserves a standing ovation (as well as a good tip). It was the finest dining we had so far.

# FATAL ATTRACTIONS

Saturday September 8, day 43 and a rest day in Belgrade. Well, I say rest, but in reality we all have chores to do: washing clothes, buying maps, and finding parts for the bikes. But Lucas' task for the day is really making him sweat: he has to call his girlfriend, Alix, in Australia to mark their 18-month anniversary date! Clearly besotted, Lucas will do anything to please his girlfriend – bend over backwards and leave no stone unturned to give her what she wants. If he has promised to call at a particular time (in Australia) and that turns out not to be very feasible time where we are to able to call, he will still find a way to keep the promise. I tell him to relax – I'm sure she'll understand if he can't call sometimes, after all he is travelling and is kept very busy filming and cycling, and we don't often have easy or affordable access to phones.

On a few occasions Lucas has kept us up well past midnight fussing over phones to call his girlfriend, so I give him a hard time about being 'too nice' but no amount of lecturing is going to stop him from trying to please her. David is worried that I am riding Lucas too hard. He is young and in love, I guess, but I was too soft when I was young and I wish that someone had told me to toughen up then. Anyway, without another option, at precisely the time he had promised, Lucas phones his girlfriend – using the hotel phone. He just thought he would tell her that he couldn't really call her at that time, but it still ended up as a five or ten minute call and cost him dearly.

It is quite a chore to keep in touch with our friends, partners and family on the road. I continue to buy local SIM cards whenever I can, diverting my Skype calls to it. Heather's sister, celebrating her own birthday, rang the USA Skype number just after I had found a Serbian chip at the Post Office across from our Splendid hotel. Heather was just scrubbing up in the shower, and I was willing to rush the phone right into the shower, but was intercepted by Cindy who asked the sister to call back in 15 minutes.

David is not deterred by the high global roaming rate on his mobile and calls his wife, Tiina, for a few minutes every second morning or so, before breakfast. Troy and his girlfriend Kim have a purely text-onic relationship on the road, and Cindy also uses text messages to keep up to date with her friends and family. Because of the time difference, the best time to call Australia is early in the morning when we either rush to get on the bike or wish to sleep in – or very late at night when we are well and truly crashed out and exhausted in our beds.

Lucas, Cindy and I visit the Belgrade fort, Kalemegdan, the next afternoon while David and Troy watch some TV, catch up on sleep and have some serious down-time. Like many ancient European cities, Belgrade was originally confined by a wall and this fortress is the old city centre. The first settlement here was founded in 3BC and, despite the walls, was later conquered by the Romans and Byzantines. Wandering around the ruins and the gardens in this huge park today is quite pleasant. There are even tanks and other old restored military equipment on display from twentieth century battles and little museums in the towers of the old wall. The views are wonderful with the greater city of Belgrade sprawling out in all directions, far into the dusky pink haze of pollution.

That night we decide to eat McDonalds for dinner, but after the amazing meal we had last night, our appetites fade as soon as we walk in. While Troy still manages a hamburger, the rest of us continue looking. David and Cindy decide to just have coffee and cake and I spot a restaurant that is also called Opera and Heather and I can't resist. It turns out the restaurant is owned by the same family as the other Opera, and has the same menu. While Heather digs into a salad, I order the chilli spaghetti that caught my eye the night before.

I love chillies and would go so far as to say it is becoming a fetish. David is also hooked and we are particularly enamoured by the hot chillies that we have found in Eastern Europe.

The first task in our quest for chillies in each new country is to find out how you say chilli in the local language. With the promise of nice fresh chillies with our dinners we go to great lengths to overcome the language barriers, but often fail, ending up with chilli powder or chilli sauce. Occasionally we see the chillies growing in fields and pass through villages with strings full of chillies and peppers hanging out to dry. The first time we saw them was when we were cycling through Mohacs in Hungary. We bought a nice-looking wreath full of chillies from an old lady at a roadside stall. From that point on I knew I would not be without a chilli fix and always tried to keep a couple in my pocket for emergencies. Unfortunately, often when we sat down for dinner I'd realise that the chillies were still in my cycling shorts back at the hotel or locked up in the support vehicle.

We are leaving Belgrade in heavy traffic on a Sunday in persistent rain with trucks passing by within inches of our lives, their fumes spewing over us. I am crawling along as the road steadily goes uphill, pulling away from the Danube. The road is narrow, the edges are rough and tricky, and I am lagging behind already. Then my mother calls. I answer while riding and reassure her that everything is going well as I huff and puff, cough and spit throughout the entire conversation. Luckily, she is used to it and is happy to hear that the ride is going well.

Eventually, what goes up must come down and at last we are heading downhill. I am really picking up speed now, the traffic now doesn't bother me as I am travelling at a comparable speed and I'm no longer being blown away by drafts from trucks.

After flying down one big winding hill, David and I stop to wait for the girls just before entering the satellite suburb of Kaludjerica. We usually try to regroup before entering any new urban area, where we have more chance of losing each other. We wait and we wait and then we start to worry. Where are Heather and Cindy? We fear that one of them might have fallen off – or worse – and start heading back up the hill to search for them. We are relieved to catch sight of them coming down slowly just as we start off – relieved because they look fine, but mainly because we don't have to make it up that hill again. Cindy had a flat tyre and without the means to repair it on the go, she had to take it easy on the way down with a seriously deflated tire. It's the first flat we have had in the whole trip so far – more than 2,000km, so that's not bad going at all. David quickly replaces the tube in the tyre with a spare he had and we all continued on together.

It seems there is a wedding taking place in every town we ride through at the moment, and Smederevo, where we stop for lunch, is no exception – in fact, as a sizeable town of about 80,000, it seems to be hosting several weddings at the same time. There are nice, shiny, decorated vehicles with fancily dressed happy people in them, waving and tooting their horns.

The town square is full of happy people too and the terraces are full of tables and chairs and people sitting in the little sun that appears to be coming through the clouds. We also take a seat but are disappointed to find that these establishments don't sell food – and it is lunchtime. After checking half a dozen of the cafes on the square, we find one with some old rolls in the back. I buy the entire supply while Heather wastes no time in sniffing out a nearby supermarket and returning with snacks and juices.

We eat our makeshift lunch and gulp down yoghurt drinks when two cute little Gypsy girls approach us and start hassling us for money. Just as they are about to become unbearably annoying an old man tells them off severely. It does not completely deter them and we start to feel a little insecure. We worry that the girls might pinch something from the bikes and run off with it or perhaps are merely a distraction to allow someone else to steal from us. Although we have not been robbed once on this trip, we have been ripped off a couple of times now. Life on the road is making us paranoid.

When we mount the bikes we notice Cindy's tire is flat again, so Troy swaps the whole wheel. He'll look at it later. We head out along a small rough road, peppered with pigs and chickens and the occasional dead dog. We are slightly relieved we haven't seen any live ones today – especially Heather, whose mere presence is an invitation to the chase. I don't know what it is, but dogs love her. To be honest, we are all a bit afraid of dogs and are petrified of contracting rabies. Australia has never had rabies so it's very scary to us – especially to Troy, whose doctor gave him a stern warning about the danger of the disease.

So far we have safely escaped many dog chases. None are too serious for us, though packs of dogs can be quite scary. Often the first thing you know about it is the sound of them growling at your heels and as it would often be more dangerous to take your eyes off the pothole-pocked road ahead, you just imagine the dogs as being huge and vicious and speed up as much as you can to escape them. I may have been chased by poodles for all I know, certainly the dogs I've seen chasing Heather – apart from looking scruffy and keen for the kill – don't seem to be trained guard dogs. The further east and the more rural the landscape, the more often we get chased by dogs. Despite that prospect, we like these little back roads as they are more fun to ride on - dodging pot holes, mud, muck and other gooey stuff generally produced by animals.

# JUST A LITTLE SCARY

It all seemed so nice. Pozarevac; Nice city, a nice hotel, Hotel Dunav. But sometimes all is not as it seems. While the hotel looks big and modern from the outside, for example, once inside it's pretty rundown and drab. I head out to change some money. On my way I see a lively restaurant and bar area with lots of young people milling about right next door to our hotel and start mentally mapping our night out. But by the time I get back to the hotel with the cash, the others have hatched a plan of their own. Seems they had asked the reception for a dining suggestion – a little place not far away, just a left right left right left or something simple like that – and seemed sold on the idea. So we all head off together, dutifully turning left then right until we realise, about 15 minutes later that this is not going to be such a simple journey after all. We are lost. We search the streets for the restaurant with no luck.

Small gangs of young people that we pass start to hassle us, whistling at Cindy and Heather, and sniggering behind our backs as we walk past. We are starting to feel uneasy and find more suspicious-looking young people around the corners as we walk the fairly empty streets at dusk. Cindy decides to hold on to us to pretend that she is with one of us for safety. Not that I think that would make much difference – unless it is David she is holding on to, at least then she may have some fighting chance. But the numbers are definitely against us, and it seems not out of the question that some of these youths might just carry knives. Adding to our paranoia is the fact that we have run into a stack of undertaker shops which are advertising coffins. On every second post we see notices of deceased people – a common practice in the East where people post obituaries on telegraph poles, houses and gates, but we are noticing an awful lot of them here. We decide to try to find our way back to the hotel along a main road.

Suddenly we spot a restaurant. I race in first. It is not the restaurant we are looking for, but it seems to be the only one around these deserted streets. And it is a fancy one at that: inside are civilised people with children having dinner. The beers that soon land in front of us taste better than ever. We have had enough surprises tonight and don't stray from our familiar schnitzel, and cucumber and tomato dishes and French fries. Lucas, however, does try something a little different: his meat dish comes wrapped in a pig's lung. And he loves it.

The next morning we ride on in the rain. More mud and dirt and fewer trucks. We seem to have left the big smoke of Belgrade well behind us. It isn't until we are settled into our sobe – Serbian guesthouse – on the outskirts of Veliko Gradište that night that Troy finally has time to work out why Cindy's tyre is still flat after David threw a new tube in it on the road – he discovers a small piece of metal embedded in the tyre wall which we had not seen in the mud when we changed it. It is not the only piece of cleverness of which Troy should be proud – we all love the sobe he's found for us, it seems small and personal and not too touristy. The Srebrno Jezero Sobe, which means Silver Lake Guesthouse (Srebrno Jezero is also the name of the area), is run by an elderly couple, the Stojiminirovics, who are very interested in our trip. Chatting in a simple variation of German that I just understand, they ask us all about our adventures and then start to shower us with gifts – mostly boiled lollies and tea.

David and I are too tired for the hospitality and walk around the river-front looking for a good spot for breakfast in the morning. The pension does not offer breakfast and, although we have a little kitchen at our disposal, we don't have any breakfast supplies. Heather took the car out in the afternoon to see if she could find a shop, and reports that there are none. How a town with 6,000-odd people does not have an obvious shop is beyond me. Not to worry, as David and I soon find the perfect restaurant for breakfast and decide that, indeed, it would be perfect for dinner too, not surprising it is called the Srebrno Jezero Hotel. We head back to fetch the others, but find our hostess Ljiljana has them fully engaged.

'Our very affectionate hostess blessed us. Even though we could hardly understand her, we figured out she was telling us to put the little laminated angle she had in her hand in our car so as to avoid car crashes, then she kissed us a lot and stroked our cheeks and hair. It was a little like being nurtured again by our mothers. She was so sweet she even started crying when we left, waving while we rode away following her husband as he escorted us out of town. She gave us gifts, including a giant gourd, which she told us was over 200 yrs old. We are meant to give it to one of our sponsors. We think that is what she means. The odds that it doesn't get completely demolished in our over-stuffed vehicle are somewhat slim, but we'll certainly try to keep it intact so we can send it to you, Brent!' - Heather's blog September 12.

Her husband is particularly interested in our route and as he pores over our maps, he tries hard to convince us to stick to the highways: new modern roads that are very smooth and very fast, and a much better alternative to the little scenic roads along the river which we show him we are planning to cycle on. It takes David and me a long time to convince him that, for us, the highway is smelly, noisy and dangerous, and we don't mind the extra distance involved taking the back roads. That settled, he kindly walks us to his mate's restaurant nearby where we politely sit down and consume dinner and copious amounts of refreshments even though we really would rather try the restaurant we saw earlier on our walk.

The next morning we wake up to the fussing of Ljiljana, trying to give us tea and dry biscuits for breakfast. It is still raining outside and we really would rather get going and maybe even try the restaurant we found yesterday, but we do the social thing and have tea with our friendly host, and obligingly take a picture. The couple are so friendly, they even apologise for having to charge us when it's time to leave. They tell us that next year they will be in their own home in Belgrade and we can come to visit for free, but now they have a boss who wants money. They charge us a fortune, more than she quoted the previous day, but arguing in Serbian is out of the question and we are running late. David pays.

As we are getting on our bikes, Mr Stojiminirovic gets out his car and starts warming it up. Turns out he is intending to drive his car slowly in front of us to guide us into the centre of Veliko Gradište, 3km further to the main road. We do not want to insult our kind hosts by stopping for breakfast straight away at the restaurant we saw yesterday so we ride on to the next village about 20km further along the river. By this time we are really starving and desperately in need of coffee. The tea and biscuits were nowhere close enough to meeting our dietary requirements of the first mile. We ride and ride but don't see any cafes, then finally at about 11am as we ride into the tiny village of Golubac which has lots of cute little red tiled houses we spot a shop, possibly the only shop in the village, and buy all sorts of biscuits and chocolates – which is all it has to offer – and stuffing ourselves with totally inappropriate riding food.

Sure enough, five minutes further down the road just when we thought we had seen all of Golubac we see a little roadside cafe that probably could have cooked us breakfast. We get our first Turkish-style coffee. Heaven in a cup, we need more of this, bring it on! I order seconds. I then discover the toilet: a squat variety in a little wooden outhouse. It is seriously soiled. Luckily, no one else needs to go. I know Heather has just made use of bushes along the way. We don't bother to order a breakfast.

Food is becoming our obsession. The supplies in our support vehicle are seriously depleted and our failure to find a supermarket is testing our foraging skills – all these strange foods and no obvious places to find them. Sadly we are lost without a supermarket. It's not even that we have that much time to seek out supplies as we are continuously on the move to cover our mileage goal each day and even the support vehicle team is flat out with their daily task of finding us a place to stay. Whenever they come across anything resembling food they buy up big. The other problem is that we don't have any cooking facilities – my camping stove was in my lost luggage – so we are rather limited in what we can buy.

Planning the ride, back in Australia, it all seemed so easy: the support vehicle would drive ahead, arrange a nice picnic lunch for us, then continue on to the planned destination where they would then find us a nice safe place to camp along the river, where we would cook a meal and enjoy a nice peaceful sleep on our comfy camp mattresses on virginal green grass in waterproof roomy tents. The next morning, after a nutritionally sound breakfast of porridge, coffee and some fresh fruit, we'd be on our rosy way. Well, they were dreams.

You know you have not stopped at the right place when you are told the lunch options are either beer or Slivovitch. The rain hasn't let up since we left the cafe and the hit from the sugary snacks has worn off completely, so cold, wet and hungry, we try a pub that Troy has found for us in a town called Dobra for some lunch. Alas, we discover they only seem to serve beer or Slivovitch. We were hoping for something a little more solid so we decide instead to fashion a picnic out of some supplies that Troy has found in a little nearby shop. We take cover from the persistent rain underneath a roof built over a well next to the pub. There is a little table near the well, so we sit on a rock wall next to it and lay out a snack of bread, cheese, salami and bananas.

A local man walks up to the well, nods hello to us and proceeds to fill some bottles with well water. Heather is inspired and races off to the support vehicle to fetch an empty 10-litre water container which she fills from the well. I am a little anxious that it will make us sick, but it turns out to be fine after all – none of us are poisoned. The people around here certainly seem as tough as nails – we watch in surprise as an old lady carrying a load of vegetables heads for the creek flowing along the road, then walks into the freezing water. The water may only be knee-deep, but it must be freezing – especially on such a cold, miserable day and in the rain.

We push on in the rain after our picnic, feeling better again. The road is wet and passing vehicles splash mud on us. In the low light of the overcast sky we feel very vulnerable as trucks skim past us. I'm sure they can't see us with our flimsy little flashing LED lights. A few hours later, about 3pm, we take refuge from the crazy lorry drivers in a roadside restaurant that is serving up riblja čorba, a traditional Serbian soup made from carp and catfish.

# TUNNELS AND CASTLES

When we stop along the road for a rest the next day, David points at some huge mountains up ahead and suggest that they are in Romania, where we are headed. Don't be crazy, I reassure him, Romania is flat and the cycling will be easy, most likely downhill with tailwind. But there is no way my promises are going to wash with the others now as I have been wrong so many times before. Sure enough, the mountains, on the Romanian side of the Danube, are the Carpathians: home to most of Europe's bears and wolves, and also Dracula's castle (on the border of Moldavia and Transylvania). The mountains regularly peak over 2,500m and we are heading straight for them. They look challenging, and I get this gut feeling we might not finish the ride in the next six months if that is what we have to face.

We continue on with trepidation. The road starts going up and up and down and down, and up again. We are heading into the World Heritage listed Djerdap National Park of Serbia, where the Danube carves a passage of over 100km through the lower Carpathian Mountains to its north and the Balkan Mountains to its south. The hills get steep and we are climbing lots. The riverbanks turn into high cliffs. We see lots of road signs that indicate steep roads with inclines of initially six, eight, and later on even twelve per cent, but then we come across one that warns us of a 20 per cent incline – which we doubt is correct. As if the hills are not enough to deal with, we are now also going through a lot of tunnels that range from about 50m to 400m in length. Those tunnels longer than 200 metres are pitch black in the middle and as the sides of the road in the tunnel has harsh curbs we are really worried about accidentally running into them and falling off. The lights on our bikes are useless – the flashing LED style that are just meant to help other people see you – and we crawl along blindly in search of daylight at the other end.

The four major gorges formed by the river are known as the Iron Gate. At the last of the gorges is the Iron Gate I dam, which has one of the biggest hydro-electric plants in Europe. It is also past the point where we plan to cross over into Romania tomorrow. As we ride past an abandoned quarry of sorts, I suddenly spot a castle in the distance. It looks as though the road up ahead leads right to it. This is great luck. Though I expected to see some pretty amazing sights along our route – it would almost be impossible not to in 4,000km –we had not planned to go out of our way to visit tourist attractions, so the castle, which turns out to be the Golubac Fortress, was an unexpected bonus.

The medieval fortress has 10 square towers which are connected by walls a couple of metres thick - they must have come in handy throughout the tumultuous history of the fortress, which was the object of many battles. It changed hands repeatedly, passing between Turks, Hungarians, Serbs and Austrians until 1867, when it was turned over to the Prince of Serbia.

Troy and Lucas who are just ahead of us in the car, have already climbed some of the castle's standing steps and ladders, discovering the vastness of the ruins. We also stop to admire the spectacular scenery. We take a lot of photos, but have to ride on. Troy climbs to the top of one of the walls and looking down on the huge structure now wishes he had paid some more attention in his history lessons at school.

We head through the big arches of the castle. These arches, like the tunnels, are barely high enough for the trucks that race through them every 10 minutes or so. One almost gets stuck as we watch it go through. We hope we won't meet one of these trucks in any of the long dark tunnels that might lie ahead of us. We decide to stick together for the next long tunnels, believing there is safety in numbers, but after a few scary moments we enlist the support vehicle as a shield. There is no safe way to negotiate these tunnels unless you have a proper light – as it is David, being extremely well prepared, is the only one who carries a flashlight with him on the bike.

As you can imagine the views are stunning all along, with mountains, cliffs, and rain clouds of course, and did I mention plenty of uphill?

We are, also unbeknownst to us, cycling through the northern reaches of the Balkan Mountains. The Balkan Mountains are primarily a Bulgarian range that stretches from here pretty much all the way to the Black Sea and Turkey, our final destination.

As for health, David thinks I look a little gray when reaching the tops of hills when I push it hard, but other than that I am fine. I stop the oral antibiotics. The only medication I am on now, apart from the dozens of pancreatic enzyme tablets, is vitamins, salt water and Pulmozyme in the nebuliser and Fluimicil (mucolytic). Not bad! And feeling very fit and healthy, and missing my wife awfully.

The last town we come to in Serbia is Donji Milanovac. We find Troy standing at the turn-off to a hotel he found for us. He apologises for finding us a hotel on top of a hill, but it was the only one he could find. We ride up the steep little road and find this huge massive hotel, perched on top, overlooking the Danube Who would've expected that off the beaten track. I guess we are not off the beaten track. I must admit the road we ride on is fantastic, apart from the scary tunnels! The reason the hotel is so massive, it turns out, is because Donji Milanovac is the town nearest to the Lepenski Vir archaeological diggings where archaeologists found human settlements dating back to 7000BC. The hotel is named after Lepenski Vir. Of course the Djerdap National Park with its Danube Gorges is incredibly scenic too and draws a large number of visitors in summer. The hotel is humongous. There is a complete convention centre inside the hotel, a massive dining room for 500 people, and over 100 rooms. There are crowds milling around in the hotel lobby. The whole complex feels very Russian, Russian as in large, smoky, and bleak perhaps. The gloomy rain does not help the atmosphere.

As is our usual habit we explode our luggage in the rooms and fully test the showers. We rummage around and get our stuff sorted, and eventually all but one of us is ready to go for a relaxing drink before dinner. Lucas is still busy doing backups of chips filmed full of scenic footage of the day and rushes around trying to get ready to come with us. As we walk down the stairs he remembers something and disappears and says he will catch up with us in the bar or wherever we end up. He disappears in the corridors of the hotel.

We find the bar and settle in. The prices are reasonable and we sample the local ales. Heather goes for an umbrella drink, and Cindy decides on a Black Russian. We are living it up, and enjoying the vista outside overlooking the Danube. The rain still pours down outside, but we are dry and warm inside, and cannot wait to go for dinner. We are ravenous. Lucas does not show up, and we imagine he is absorbed in technology or filming something interesting, like the rocks or earth, an ant colony or a snail. Sometimes we wonder what exactly he thinks should be in the documentary. We trust him and leave it up to him.

In the mean time Lucas was in fact only a minute behind us. He walked down the stairs, came to the hallway, looked all around the big hotel but could not see us. He assumed we walked out of the hotel, down the path, to the village and found a place there. He walks down the muddy steps, through the rain. He looks in the first restaurant, the second cafe, the third establishment. Annoyed he walks back up the steep stairs through the little forest that separates the hotel from the rest of the town. Back inside the hotel he finds us. Turns out there were more than one bar here, and where we sat he may not have seen us from the entrance. Lucas looks wet and cold. We sit him down and let him order a blue umbrella drink from the menu. Although the beer is cheap, mixed drinks are not. But the few spirits that the girls, oh, and Lucas, drink barely shows up in our still modest bar bill. These are the joys of travelling in countries where the Australian dollar is stronger. At home there is no way we could just stay in hotels and drink and eat like we do here. We enjoy the lifestyle when we get the opportunity and feel we are rewarding ourselves for the distance covered. We rarely come across luxuries like this. Who could sit in their room and read a book and watch the cable channels!

We are united, and we are hungry like a horse. We move to the hotel restaurant for dinner and once there are ignored for about 15 minutes. There is only one other table, with a large extended family having dinner. The waiters are completely ignoring us as they occasionally walk up and down to serve the family. We are used to slow service by now, but being ignored like this is becoming painful. We need beverages, a jug of water at least. Lucas is the first to run out of patience, and he walks upstairs to the lobby where he asks if we could get served in the restaurant. The rest of us hear the phone ring in the restaurant. After 8 rings the waiter comes out and briefly speaks to somebody on the phone, glances up at us, and walks back into the kitchen. We give it another 5 minutes, and decide to leave. Not bothered by the rain at all we negotiate the steep slippery steps through the forest to the township situated a few hundred metres below our hotel. We find a perfect restaurant, the first one with a proper menu and have a good meal with friendly service to boot. It is nice getting some fresh air, and the rain does not bother us in the least. We are used to worse!

When riding our bicycles beer is obviously not an option, and we are fortunately able to buy our water in large five or ten later containers in most shops for not too much money. We always have one or two of them in the van to fill up our water bottles. Now which one is the one we filled up with well water again? Oh yes, the one we scratched the label off.

We joke about putting beer bottles on the bicycles, but that just looks so wrong! David once experimented with a Jim Bean bottle on his bicycle, which we all thought looked very cool, but totally inappropriate for the documentary that Lucas is filming!

My bicycle computer is keeping track of the various interesting statistics, such as how far we travel each day, how long it takes us, and what our average speed is. I still have a fascination with our average speed for the day, something I have always had. The aim for me is to maintain a 20 kilometres per hour average for the day, but that is still almost non attainable. Going up these hills, and of course flying down them at breakneck speeds, our speeds vary from four kilometres per hour to the high fifties! At the end of each day my average is normally roundabout 17 to 18 km/hr as per usual. In the past few weeks we occasionally had days where the daily average exceeded the 20 kilometre per hour mark, but they were unusual - and usually explained by a persistent tailwind! To put this in perspective, the average well equipped cyclist commuting to and from work on good roads could easily average thirty or more kilometres per hour.

The National Park we are now cycling through, the Djerdap National Park, ends at a large hydroelectricity plant, but just before we get to the plant we will cross a long bridge into Romania. We are all a little anxious about Romania as we are warned about Gypsies and criminals. After all, most of the credit card phishing attempts and scanners originate from Romania. On the other side of the Danube we see Romania and soon we will be crossing over! Before we even get to the border Romania comes up with its first surprise. From high up on the bank on the Serbian side of the river we can see this huge carved out face on the cliffs. I notice David and Cindy stopped along the road ahead, and I presume they stopped to let me catch up. But no, they are staring at the other side of the river looking at the monument of King Decebal. King Decebal, one of the greatest military strategists to have ever existed, a Dacian king who was eventually defeated by the Romans. His face is carved out of the rock only recently completed in 2004. .

Serbian modern art fades in comparison to the Dacian King across the river!

Standing precariously alongside the rock wall guard of the road, with the odd truck roaring past, we stand there mesmerised taking in the view and taking photos

Further along, where the cliff was less severe we find a pull-off for cars. It has a sign that we cannot read, a bin full of overflowing garbage and litter all around. The view of the Dacian King is poor from this vantage point, but at least it is a safe spot to stop. To make their claim to art the Serbians had put a big globe statue here. An odd piece of abstract art. It is obviously used as a toilet as you can see the icing (wet toilet paper that has dried over time) and the other obvious evidence. Us boys make good use of the facility and do our bit to make the grass green behind the globe.

"Day 47- Just short of 3000km - The last few days have been a welcome relief of gorgeous scenery and fresh air. We have had 4 or 5 days straight of heavy traffic and nasty exhaust fumes – we are all coughing the distance now!

We are back with our beloved Danou (or Danube as we know it) and the views as we ride up mountains, are of cliff faces straight down into the river and lush, almost tropical foliage. We are in more hilly areas now. We are still having mostly wet, windy days, but the days are definitely warmer.

Today we crossed into Romania and are now in a border city called Severin. So far on our trip, we have experienced no trouble whatsoever at the borders. Today we were even given VIP status and ushered past several waiting cars – must have been the sponsor stickers!

It looked like it was going to be a long wait as the line-up was long and slow-moving. Although we could easily get through with our bikes, we usually like to travel through these crossings with the car and all together. Of course, on the one day when we are able to jump the line, Wally goes missing. One minute he was there, all excited about his energy drink, the next he's not and has left us with his bike. We are literally right at the window of the customs agent, stalling and feeling bad about all the cars behind us, when he casually pops out of nowhere. He had decided to go to Romania to use the toilet....classic Wally, no?

We plan to stay on the Romanian side of the Danube for now. Eventually we will cross into Bulgaria!

We have been advised, both by our instincts and the" Let's Go Europe" book, that camping is not a good idea, so we have been hotel-ing it every night for about 2 weeks. Although camping would be nice and cheaper, there isn't much in the way of decent patches of grass in most places, as industry or huge piles of litter occupy all spaces. We have also noticed in these Eastern Bloc countries that it is sometimes next to impossible to find a restaurant. We have been known to wander around trying not to look like tourists with cameras and wallets, desperately inquiring, "Restaurant???" to anyone who looks in-the-know. When we do find a hotel that has a half-decent restaurant, we are pretty excited.

The food is no longer quite as spectacular as it was in France and Germany, but it is still okay. We do suffer a bit with breakfast when we are usually offered up white bread and tea (not even coffee seems to be popular and jam and butter are extra), and usually find ourselves gorging on sweet energy bars and bananas when we can find a store." – Heather, September 12.

Before officially crossing into Romania I stop at the duty free shop on the border, and spent my last Serbian penny. I invest in a bottle of Slivovitz and a bottle of Serbian chocolate liqueur with a matching bottle of Serbian vodka. The first item is really to give away on arrival in Istanbul to worthy supporters, or to be shared with them, and the latter two are intended for us to make "Black Serbians", a variation

of a "Black Russian", which Cindy had recently invented. We expect that in the coming nights we might have a need for a stiff drink, when hiding from Gypsies in bushes on dark nights".

Turnu Severin, the first town in Romania that we come to seems just like any other bustling little town. We find a hotel, the Continental Portile De Fier Hotel, just before the town-centre which seems pleasant enough, a tad more expensive than we had hoped for, but we feel safe with our bicycles and it looks clean and secure.

As I get off my bike David starts to speak to a tourist in a rental car, a German lady travelling with her husband. She saw the mention of Cystic Fibrosis on the vehicle and was enquiring about what exactly we were doing. Her daughter has CF it turns out. David calls me over, and I speak to the woman. She can hardly believe I have CF, that I am 42 and am cycling around! Totally inspired she leaves with her husband on her way back towards the direction we just came from. I feel all warm and fuzzy again, knowing I am inspiring people. That is what this ride is all about! All along we try to explain what we are doing to people we meet, but after Austria it has been next to impossible to get people to understand. I take a mental note again to ensure that next time I go on a trip like this we must carry an information leaflet in the language of the countries we are passing through. How can you raise awareness when people just think you are on some organised tour of sorts, something a lot of people must think.

I wave at the German couple's car, and hope we inspire more people along the way.

The hotel has a restaurant with a non smoking section, totally unheard of in Serbia. Everything is clean here, unlike in Serbia. Don't get me wrong about Serbia, but the difference between Serbia and Romania is noticeable here. An added advantage is that we can read the menus! Not that the food choice changed much, but the slight variation is very welcome.

Heather and Cindy decide to go into town and look for an Internet Café and a shop to buy supplies. They take the car, and disappear. An hour later we decide it is time for dinner and without our women-folk we make our way to the appealing restaurant downstairs. There are only a few people in the restaurant, and they are smoking, but at least there is an official side of the dining area that is designated smoke free, according to the many signs posted on the walls. The abundance of non-smoking signs had given me the false belief the whole dining room was non-smoking, but I am not that lucky. The smoke obviously does not read the signs and wafts all through the restaurant. The no-smoking area makes no difference at all except that there is no ashtray on the table. There is a TV with its volume turned up loud, but nobody is watching except for staff. It, and the smoke, get to me, and I have to go and ask if at least the TV can be turned down, which was promptly done. I am not brave enough to challenge the young dudes about their smoking. We order from the English menu, feeling very elated to actually have some vague idea what we are ordering.

Knowing that Cindy and Heather in an Internet Café could take a long time (says I, the geek who never gets enough of the Internet), I decide to send an SMS to Cindy's phone. Cindy does not reply. David gets a little worried, this is our first night in Romania and we are separated from the women. We have no idea about the security in town or how safe it is for them on their own. David also texts them, this time specifically asking for a reply. We sent them a few more messages, including offering to pay a handsome tongue in cheek ransom for Cindy in case she got kidnapped, and a slightly smaller budget for the return of Heather in case she was kidnapped too. We love teasing Heather like that. We get no replies to our messages, and start to get worried about them. They could have had an accident in the vehicle, they could have been robbed, anything was possible.

We finish our dinner, and want to pay. This is when we discover that no credit card is accepted in the restaurant, we cannot put it on the room's account as the restaurant is apparently not part of the hotel, although you could have fooled me. The hotel itself, despite the credit card stickers on the front door, does not accept credit cards either it appears. Credit cards here need a PIN, which we do not have for our Australian cards. And something we were not used to. In fact it made us suspicious. Australia is a little behind.

While we are trying to sort out this mess we ask Lucas to stand in front of the girls' hotel room and listen for a mobile phone. When we ring Cindy's phone Lucas can hear the ringing in their room. This explains why we are not getting answers from them. Heather does not have a phone. It is only a marginal relief to have an explanation for no answers to our messages. A few hours have now passed. Where are they?

We are sent into town by the restaurant staff to get cash from an ATM. David and I hop on our bikes and cycle into town to look for one. We find one very quickly and return with cash just as Cindy and Heather rock up in the car. I greet them like a father greets their naughty children who are coming home five minutes after dark. More relief then anger. How could they know how worried we were. They are surprised we got worried, and think we are overreacting, but we are all pleased to have them back in one piece, and decide that this is the right time to trial our Black Serbian concoctions, less than 12 hours after purchasing the ingredients. We pay our restaurant bill in hard cold unmarked random notes, fresh from the ATM.

Our credit cards from now on are pretty useless, despite the whole gamete of them being advertised on many doors. Turns out that all credit cards here have security chips built in, and ours do not. Credit cards here also have PINs, not all ours do. Although the machines that read the cards also have a facility for the good old magnetic strip card we could not get the operators to use them, especially with the prevailing language barrier, and not without rudely leaning over the counter! The same with the PIN, for which there was a question on the credit card machine straight after swiping it. This message is usually in a foreign language, plus the operator presses the buttons, and they always choose to do the transaction with a PIN instead of a signature. We do not discover this till very late in our trip, when it is really too late. Fortunately I had brought Euros from the Western Union agent in Vienna, and exchanging money is not too difficult in most places. Unfortunately money does have a habit of running out very quickly, especially cash!

Having survived that first night we now feel better about Romania. We have a good breakfast, for a change, and mount our steeds nice and early, about 9am. No different from other mornings really but we define early mornings by the amount of urgency there is in leaving, which is directly related to what David had discovered on the map. The cycle route book is in German, and I now try to at least translate the relevant bits before leaving each day. I look for the hints, tips and cautions. With my German language skills it is often difficult to say for certain if the warnings apply to one or the other option, and often get it wrong. For instance if it says, in German, that the roads are very sketchy and hard to follow, full of potholes and broken bottles if you do decide to continue along the river, I would always have doubt about my translation, wondering whether the warning applies to following the river or not. My German improved immensely during this trip! Unfortunately I have to learn through mistakes.

This morning there is a mighty gale blowing in the direction of our destination which is directly east of us. We belt down the road at 35 kilometres per hour for about 15 kilometres before we come to the turn-off at Hinova. Our guidebook tells us the intended Velo6 bike route along the Danube follows the big bends in the river, but we can see that the main road cuts the corners, which really is not bad at - with minimal traffic and a nice tailwind to boot. We are not sure where the main road goes to, but it heads of in the right direction. Determined to follow the Danube we now head West (!), following this big bend in the river. The crosswinds are incredibly tough and the road surface deteriorates quickly. We wind along a little road and come to a sign that says we are entering Tasmania. Hello, Tasmania? I live in Tasmania. I thought I was hallucinating. Nope, I was not hallucinating, just misreading the sign. It said Tismana. Still, I felt a little at home! The road now turns to dirt and eventually becomes loose and deep gravel.

The wind is now very strong, and it certainly appears to be blowing right against us. In actual fact the river does wind so severely that we do face the wind. We battle on, and on and climb over many hills as well. We pass small rural farming villages, Batoti, Vrancea, Gogosu, and start running into animal drawn wooden carriages with car or tractor tyres for wheels. I try hard to be inconspicuous when taking a photo of an elderly Gypsy couple riding towards me on a cart, pulled by a cow! They slow down and ask me if I want to take a photo. I pull out the camera again, and duly take a photo. This couple does not appear particularly friendly, and they start making gestures which I understand to mean they now want money. I am not prepared for this, and offer them a handful of local muesli bars which they reluctantly accept, but I can understand that what the man is trying to say is that he has a family to feed and needs money. I pretend not to understand them as pulling out my wallet to find some local currency from amongst the hundreds of Euros seemed so wrong at the time. I quickly get on my way, leaving the old couple terribly dissatisfied, but from now on I will carry a small amount of money in an accessible place.

This was my first attempt to take a photo of Gypsies, and also my last. I get very little opportunity as we are always on the run in these rural areas, fearing to stop out of safety concern when there are groups of people around. Also being the last in our group the last thing I want to do is stop and let the others disappear even further ahead of me.

We ride on, and the going is tough. With the soft gravel roads we are riding on now I am starting to doubt we will make the 140kms to Calafat where the guide book tells us is the next chance of finding somewhere to stay. If the winds are going to be this tough and the road surface this bad we may have a struggle on our hands!

The road surface changes from soft gravel to hard and rocky as we enter a forest. We bounce along at a slow pace. Lucas is getting behind, it is the hardest day he has had on the bike. The terrain makes it hard for all of us, but especially for Lucas who to date has ridden less than any of us as he was still learning to ride! I think he was still putting too much weight on his bicycle seat, or maybe it was plain metal fatigue, but suddenly his seat broke off! He yells at me, I yell at Heather, Heather yells at David. We all stop. What are we going to do now; we have a long distance to go today, at least another 100 kilometres. David calls up Troy and swaps seat posts and puts the broken seat on his bike. David now rides standing up. Very exhausting process for him, but he does it without hesitation. We are lucky to be in mobile phone range, most unexpected I tell you! We feel far away from civilisation here, and in Australia I can assure you there would certainly not be a cell phone tower anywhere within range! Troy was almost in Calafat, looking for accommodation. Finding us on this little road in a forest between Crivina and Vrancea seems highly implausible, but at least we have the same map books now. Troy and Cindy arrive in a cloud of dust on the dirt-road half an hour after we called them. I am impressed. Troy swaps the seat post with the one from the spare bike on the back of the support vehicle. We fill up our water supplies and quickly mount the bikes again. We are moving slow today despite our fast pace this morning.

The villages we start to cycle through do not have shops, or at least not shops that we recognise as shops. Certainly there are no cafes and restaurants, nor can we find a regular corner store to buy anything. The villages and towns that we cycle through have crowds of old men sitting together looking at the dusty road and talking to each other, and crowds of elderly women doing much the same but in different places along the main road through the little towns. The houses in the street, the churches, it all seems very old and poverty struck here. There is no wealth here, there are no fancy cars, just rickety carts pulled along by horses, donkeys, bullocks and cows, some of these look seriously decrepit. No idea where the young people are or what they are doing, we assume they might be working in the field. We do see people dotted about the countryside appearing to do some work, but the ones we see working are elderly too. Are the young people in the big cities? Are they in Bucharest the capital or other big cities? If they are it is obvious they are not sending much money home!

Some carriages we see are pretty much past their used-by-date. Often these are the ones with young people on it. They cheer us on and wave. I am embarrassed to show my wealth and do not take a photo. Lucas is filming already, we have a record. At one point we see an old carriage with a worn tire falling of its wheel pulled along by an old horse with young people smoking on it, and the horse is dragging the carriage along. I feel sorry for the horse. These are painful sights to see, and when the young people ask us for money we wave back and continue. I wish we could help them, but we are struggling too, in our own way. Are these young men the unemployed who return to their villages with no skills to speak of? We are all too scared to stop in fear of getting robbed, since we have been repeatedly warned about that.

There are several drinking establishments in each town, but none serve food. In Tiganasi I venture into one of them, and ask directions to food. We know better than to expect this drinking establishment to just serve us a steak sandwich or point us towards a supermarket. We are really far from civilisation here, and a drinking hole is exactly that, a hole to drink in. Well, maybe not a hole, a small bare dusty pub with old people drinking beer. As I ask directions I notice Lucas standing behind me filming, and then Heather comes in trying to help too. We are told to continue to the next village, Gogosu, where there is a market. When we walk out of this particular place we find David fighting off the locals, who are hassling him and standing around him and the four bikes. The young people are excitedly shouting and gesturing at David! They seem friendly, but we smell volatility in the air! We fear that it is possible in these situations a so inclined person could steal a bike and get away with it. We have to be more careful and sacrifice some filming!

We cycle through the tiny settlement of Gogosu without seeing anything resembling a market.

"We knew we were in for a long ride when our guide book basically said, Good luck finding accommodation in the next 140km. We had started our ride an hour early and were hoping for the best when we leaned into some of the strongest cross winds we've encountered thus far.

After a good 20km, done at about 12km/hr, we left the shoreline winds behind only to jump onto rocky, deep gravel for another 10km. Here was where we had a casualty with Lucas' bike seat - it just broke off. This was the kind of riding that vibrates your feet off your pedals, so it was no surprise that something would rattle off.

We put in an SOS to our support driver and continued on with David having swapped seats and now riding on the spinning gravel standing up. Soon after as we were riding through a small village and starting up a long, steep hill, a nice old woman stopped us as we rode by and handed out bunches of grapes, a very welcome treat!

As we were concerned about accommodation that night, our support vehicle left us after we grabbed another bike seat from them to check out the situation in the next town - 85km away. We were now 60 odd kilometres into the day with no food or water resupply - a slight oversight on our part. Several villages later, in a place called Gruia we came across something that looked like a cafe. We were able to communicate that we needed food and water and they provided us with bread, salami and pickles and a giant bottle of pop and water. It seemed that upon closer inspection, it was really just a small mom-and-pop store, but we were welcomed to eat what they had in their fridge!

Resupplied and caffeinated, we flew through the next 70 km with hardly any effort as we now had the blustery winds behind us, acting as a push. At times we were clocking 40km/hr on the flats. We made it into Calafat that night shortly after 6pm after starting at 8am, and over 9 hours of ride time! But that wasn't the end of our long days." – Heather's blog September 15.

Riding through Romania is tricky at best, and although it is always difficult to find accommodation we invariably find a larger town with one hotel. I am almost convinced there must be more hotels in these places, but with our language skills, or lack thereof, we may be misunderstood. Personally I think that we look so organised and professional in people's eyes that people assume the hotel in their town is simply not good enough for us and advise us to cycle another 30 km to a larger town where there is a bigger, perhaps more appropriate hotel. It is just hard to imagine that hotels are that scarce! The guidebook we have for this area along the Danube also tells us there is little or no accommodation, so the author of the guide book must have had the same experience.

In the guidebook we sometimes see tent icons, camping signs, drawn on the map. We get very excited when we see them, happy at the prospect of camping; something we have not done since leaving Hungary. When we come to these marked sports, or when Troy or Cindy, whoever is driving, goes to check them out they are either not there or they are totally abandoned. With all the poor hard working people and farmers in the fields all around us at all times we do not feel safe just setting up the tents. We are already attracting a lot of attention by just standing still. There are people everywhere, even along the roads there are groups of people harvesting chestnuts and walnuts from the mature trees lining the road. Going for a pee break is not easy either, but I don't think anybody objected to me watering a tree every 10 kilometres or so.

I do really have to pee a lot. Every half an hour I have to go again. My Camelbak is tied to the front of my bicycle and every time I think about water I take a sip. Camelbaks are a great invention. My Camelbak (a name brand) comes in the form of a little backpack with a water-bag inside, and a tube with a mouthpiece that you suck water from. It means you no longer need to drink warm water from a plastic bike-bottle covered in dust and grime! Very convenient for regular sips. It is still rare for me to drink even three litres of water in one day, not counting the drinks before and after riding such as with breakfast when I drink multiple glasses of water, juice and coffee. Three litres of water is probably not even enough given all the exercise we do. Maybe the peeing is an age thing, maybe it's the onset of diabetes; my blood sugar levels are not as low as they should be. In fact, the endocrinologist warned me last year that insulin injections were inevitable for me in the very near future. I had an appointment with her prior to me leaving on this trip, but I received a letter in the mail to advice that the appointment had to be moved, which made it impossible for me to see her. I have been monitoring my blood sugar levels on a daily basis for months and months and do know roughly where I stand (When I arrived back in Tasmania I was prescribed daily insulin injections, so my sweet diet on the road was far from ideal). My blood sugar reader was in my lost luggage.

We eventually complete the big loop of the river and return back to civilisation, if you can call it that. We are welcomed by Troy in the town of Calafat, 140 odd kilometres from where we started in the morning. Cindy had gone for a run… This had been a long day, and we are glad to be in a good looking modern hotel. Looking out of the hotel window it does look very rustic (read 'poor'), and we wonder how many people stay in these fancy hotels in these seemingly remote locations. I ask two men in the dining room what they are doing here, and discover they are charting the Danube, travelling down the river with a boat full of scientific instruments taking readings for a survey.

This particular hotel has an incredibly slow service in the dining room because of a wedding feast they are preparing for. Wedding? Yes, everywhere we go there are weddings it seems. But we are used to slow service; it is not unusual for us to wait an hour for our meals, or even 20 minutes for just the order to be taken even though very few people might be in the restaurant. We have very little else to do, except sit down with a beer and the alternative is to sit in the hotel rooms watching the cable channels – which surprisingly they still have in most hotels. Here, like we have seen in other hotels, the cable comes complete with a free porn channel that none of us are able to watch no matter how bored we are! So sitting in a restaurant, talking to each other debriefing the adventures of the day is always a good alternative. You would not want to be in a hurry. We are tested to the limits here. It is now 8pm and we still have no sign of dinner, we are totally starved by now. Even the beer service is lacking, we had one beer… Funnily enough we always manage to get a beer within 15 minutes of sitting down anywhere, but even getting that replenished anywhere east of Vienna was sometimes a challenge.

You might get the impression that food and drinking are now dominating this trip, and you might be right. In the mornings the most important thing to get done properly is eating as much as possible to get enough energy for the ride ahead. Come lunchtime we are starving again from all the exercise and keenly looking for lunch. The support vehicle's main task in the morning is to look for groceries and supplies and think about our lunch stop; can they feed us or do we need a café. Organising food has become increasingly more difficult as we cycled down-river from Hungary. The afternoon's objective for the support vehicle is to find a suitable place for us to stay the night, which is the hardest task of all. Troy and David need to guess how far we can ride, and decide to look further or closer along our projected path, and not stray too far away from our route, and avoid up hills of course.

Every night we need to find a restaurant where we can eat, or a place where we can cook. Home cooking is almost impossible for us, as the car does not have a refrigerator and only one Esky (Ice-box) which we cannot always keep cool. We could technically carry all our cooking stuff up to the hotel rooms and try and eat on the beds; unlikely! Finding a suitable restaurant, or any restaurant for that matter, is never straightforward and presents a mission in itself. If you count the time you start looking for a restaurant till you are back in the hotel a sizeable chunk of our afternoon/evening is gone. Tired from the day's ride there is very little else you can do. Doing touristy things is often out of the question, unless it is a rest day. But even rest days are often used for housekeeping chores, search for camping shops that might sell tent poles suitable for our tents, other needed gear, or search for an Internet Café to update the blog, post pictures on the net or check Email. We did find some spare tent poles in Vienna that we have been able to use sections from to fix our broken poles – requiring intricate repairs from Troy. Correct tent-pole lengths are crucial, and this is difficult to maintain as you cannot just cut a bit off. We are not getting many opportunities to camp, but we feel the tents need to be in order in case we need them one day.

It is very fortunate that most of us like food, looking for food, eating food, sleeping, shopping and cycling, as museums and culture is mostly out of the question on this trip. There are numerous historic and cultural points of interest along the way that we just cannot stop at. When Lucas wants to film a certain section or stop at a significant view, Troy still feels there is too little time to stuff around even in the support vehicle and will only stop briefly for Lucas - if at all. It is hard to imagine that even with a navigator on board he needs the whole day to basically organise our accommodation (and lunch if possible) and has no time to muck about.

Troy is not stupid and he is not lazy at all, but it really is a tough task to drive the support vehicle even though he can cover the daily distance in a couple of hours of driving if he knew exactly where to go! It is not straight forward at all, and we do not know where we are going to be at night. It should also be mentioned that the maps we have, including the guide book, are very unclear (and in German) and not always correspond with the roads. Cindy and Lucas are also not experienced navigators, although they are picking up the skills fast. David still does all the day to day route planning with the German book and the GPS. He plans the days, briefs and confers with Troy as to where to go, where to meet us etc, and takes the blame for every wrong turn and unnecessary hill! David takes the job very seriously, unlike me who would just stumble on turn by turn as they happen. When Troy finds a suitable hotel he texts us the GPS coordinates so that we can find him with (relative) ease on our bicycles using David's GPS.

Heather's job is primarily to keep track of what happens (too much to write about all of it really!) and after her day's cycling venture out into the new (scary) cities looking for internet cafes where she has to put up with youths listening to bad music which they turn up when they see her coming. Heather often uses the laptop to prepare the blogs to minimise time in the cafes, and carries photos (which she takes as well) and content on a USB stick. Heather does regular shopping too, when she ventures into the towns, aided by Cindy or Lucas.

Lucas is constantly on the go trying to film each and every moment. He often tries to ride with us and charges ahead to shoot us coming up hills, or hangs back to shoot scenery and then race to catch up again. He films anything from open coal mines to castles, but always trying to catch us impromptu interacting with locals. Not bad for someone who had trouble even mounting his bike in Paris!

Lucky he is young and has endless reserves of power. When we get to a hotel room Lucas has to immediately recharge batteries and empty the memory cards on which he records the high definition video footage from our stealthy camcorders. When he is not cycling he is navigating with the driver.

Cindy helps by rotating with the driver and navigator and sometimes gives our aching bodies a massage at the end of the day. The massages do not end up in 'happy endings' and our wives/partners can be reassured. In fact there is absolutely nothing romantic about riding these distances with the resulting aches and pains focusing our attention to food, shower and sleep (where does the beer come into it?). Cindy helps out all-round, with everything from navigation to cleaning eskies and shopping, sharing Heather's bedroom, and keeping us all entertained.

Me? I feel I do very little except ride. The team says all I need to do is survive to Istanbul. I try doing my bit where I can, help David translate the German language trip book that we were given by my friends Hans and Marjan - without it we would have had enormous difficulties. The book was only published months before our departure and we are very pleased to have it.

Romania along the Danube proves not to be a tourist trail.

# OILS AIN'T OILS

Heather: "The next day, the guide book showed no signs of accommodation for 145km as well. Lacking the adrenaline rush of the day before, we started out again an hour earlier than usual. Luckily, we had no wind that day and gorgeous blue skies again. The first 100km was uneventful and we did them all before lunch at 1pm. After a hearty feed of meat, cheese and bread, we set off to tick off the remaining 44kms to Corabia. About 10km down the road, we saw an unusual sight - our support vehicle was pulled over with the hood up. Troy let us in on the catastrophe - petrol in a diesel engine...Turns out WE were now the support team

When he and Lucas had pulled into a gas station specifying diesel, the attendant pointed them to the pump that said diesel. Troy double checked the pump, and with no reason to think otherwise, the attendant filled the tank - all 80 litres. Two kilometres later Troy stopped for a photo, and the car would not start again.

As luck would have it, we were within about 100 metres of another gas station. There was some discussion whether or not to push the car all the way back to the original station, but why? Try to get back our money or get the job done now and get out of here? We chose the latter and after a lengthy discussion with the attendant involving a lot of hand gesturing and drawing on a note pad, we were finally able to get him to understand that we needed to siphon the gas out and replace it with diesel. Easy, right?

Somehow we managed to be there for over three hours as several back and forth trips were made to find the right size and length of hose to stick in the tank. Then when the right hose was found, it still didn't work - anti-siphoning device? The only thing to do then was to methodically turn the key on and off to prime the fuel after the hose was removed. This leaked the fuel out at an agonizing pace while we all stood around and watched and tried to shoot film for the documentary. The gas attendant seemed to be quite upset at seeing the camera and asked for us to stop.

A few minutes later, he came up to me and said, "problem" and asked for the notepad. On it he wrote the word Mafioti. Like the classic dumb blonde in a bad B-rate movie, I said the word out loud with a questioning face. The attendant shushed me loudly and looked over his shoulder in all directions. He pointed to the guy helping us - by now, there was quite a crowd - and said "problem" again. Apparently, we were being aided by the mob. We now became concerned about the rather large crowd beginning to surround us.

But as you can see, we are all alive to update you on our progress. Aside from donating a few litres of oil and prolonging our longest day yet (144km), we had success. All the fuel was hosed out and the new diesel replaced. The crowd was very willing to help and incredibly friendly - we were even invited for beers, but even that didn't tempt us as much as visions of our hotel and food did.

Our last 35 km was an impromptu race just to test our merit and we made it in a little over an hour and just in time for a gorgeous sunset from the views of our hotel, situated on the Danube River. – Heather's blog, September 15

I think that we were extremely lucky because of the following points:

• The support team found us a hotel before lunch so we already had that sorted out. Normally this is arranged after lunch. Imagine if we still had to look for a hotel after the whole affair...

• Troy had taken over driving after lunch as his knees were getting very sore. If Cindy and Lucas had the diesel/petrol incident happen to them we would have surely attributed blame to them! But with the support crew mechanic doing this it added credibility to the fact the pump was incorrectly marked,

• Troy filled up the tank straight after lunch and stopped to take a silly picture of some old trucks behind a fence. This meant he was in a safe position, he did not run the bad fuel into the engine - just was not able to start the engine again.

• As it happened straight after lunch we cycled into them within minutes of getting stranded – safety in numbers.

• Another fuel station right behind the car was very fortunate; imagine pushing the vehicle a kilometre or more!

• The petrol station owner who helped us took David in his car to get some other hoses and whispered to him that his fuel wasn't the best and we shouldn't fill up our tank with it! We took 1/3 of a tank after siphoning the petrol out and went to another petrol station to fill up the car completely.

• We had the brutal wind on our tail and averaged 30+ to the hotel - which was 35km away, arriving just before dusk. Imagine riding our bikes after dusk without proper riding lights! Death defying. Cars drive well in excess of 100 kilometres per hour. The most common car here seems to be what looks like a Renault 12, only it is not a Renault 12, it is a Dacia. Dacia is a Romanian car maker that worked in close cooperation with Renault since the 1960s, and it appears they still built the old Renault 12 under license. I hope not to meet one by accident.

The trip average for that day was 22.7km/hr. Not bad for 144 kilometres!

# BUMPED BY A WEDDING

Heather: "Needless to say, we were resting the next day. The sights we were seeing lately were very entertaining as we rode through village after village. It seemed like we had stepped back decades into an era where the horse drawn cart was predominant and people still spent all their time in the fields. We saw the oldest, most withered faces and women bent 90 degrees at the waist still walking down the street. Children yelled and stood on the streets with their hands out so we could high-five them as we rode by. Everywhere, we got waves and Bravos! We were really feeling that what we were doing was more and more of a novelty the farther east we went - it is true travel now!" – Heather's blog, September 15.

We have come to Turnu Magurele, a place with a castle on a nearby hill and a nice hotel to stay in. The hotel is nice enough and staying here for an extra night seems a very good idea. After settling in we make our way to the dining room. The service in the restaurant is so incredibly slow that we realise we probably need 24 hours just to get breakfast tomorrow. After checking with reception the next morning they tell us we can stay for the second night if we move rooms; apparently a wedding had specifically pre-booked the rooms we are in now. We pack up our gear and move promptly. No big deal.

After breakfast Troy and David settle in front of the TV of their new room, ready for a day of relaxation and refreshments. Lucas, Heather and I go in search of an Internet Café and (amazingly) we find one not far away. Turnu Magurele is only a small town with a shrinking population currently under 30 000 happy and clean inhabitants. It has a nice feel to it with the cobbled and bricked roads with people that acknowledge us with friendly gestures.

I had just completed my duties on the Internet and went to look for a Romanian SIM chip for my phone when it rang (with my Australian chip still in it). It was David with the bad news that we had to evacuate the hotel; apparently the wedding needed the rooms we had just moved into as well, and they needed it by 5am tomorrow morning. There is no other hotel in town that we know off or that the hotel could recommend to us. David tells me they are in the dining room attempting to order lunch. If I can get cash that would be good as the hotel does not accept any credit cards. Lucas had already gone walkabout from the Internet Cafe, and David reports him present at the hotel. I do not want to rush Heather with her blog, so I leave quietly and find an ATM to get some money of my MasterCard. Miraculously I walk past a phone shop and am able to buy a Romanian SIM chip without any complicated paperwork or questions. Back to the café to pick up Heather and quickly access my Skype account to divert the USA number to my new Romanian mobile phone. Before heading back to the hotel we buy chocolates at the Internet café which is about the healthiest foods they had, just in case we are too late to have lunch in the hotel; It is foreseeable that we return to the hotel and find the bikes ready to go just waiting for us latecomers to quickly pack and grab our luggage.

Back at the hotel we are dumbfounded to find the others still sitting around an empty looking table in the restaurant impatiently waiting for their lunch - which had been ordered over an hour ago. Before we eventually mount our bikes at about 3pm. almost every one of us individually had asked the staff where in the next town we could find a hotel.

We are lucky that the next town, Piatra, is only about thirty kilometres down the road, and not 140kms! The hotel we are all advised to go to we are told is bigger, better and cheaper than this hotel. This hotel certainly is not cheap, but what do you expect when it is the only one in town and it has cable TV (with porn!). We are pleased to find the suggested hotel with no problems, and well before dusk.

We have cycled two 140+ km days in a row now, a rest day with a mere 30 kilometre relocation ride was still a rest day for us. The last big day, with our petrol incident, was on a pretty straight forward road and we pumped the miles steadily. Up the hills I run out of puff while Heather and Cindy, Troy, David or Lucas, anyone who rides, powers ahead of me and patiently waits on top for me to watch me arrive in coughing fits. Fortunately the hills do not appear to be too long on these long stretches, but one 22% incline road sign had me worried. I occasionally stop and cough (and lose some of my breakfast...) and catch my breath, then get back onto the bike in a tree climbing gear. Sometimes when we cruise at over 20 km/hr my eyes sting with the very salty sweat dripping down my eye brows!

Living with CF makes my sweat very salty, and getting sweat into my eyes is like diving into the Dead Sea for those who have ever done that. The Dead Sea is 8 times saltier than regular sea water; you can float in it high enough so that you can read a newspaper without getting it wet. You should not submerge your head in that kind of salty water. But that is the kind of sweat that I have pouring into my eyes it seems.

No-one along the way knows about cystic fibrosis and we still cannot explain what we are doing... We are seen as some corporate group of flash tourists with MONEY. No concessions or discounts, and not really raising much awareness really. The onus is on Lucas' documentary 'Coughing the Distance' to do that for us!

We had ridden some good distances lately due to there being nowhere in between to stay, and we had to have a rest day or else we would get too far ahead of our schedule. There is no way we can arrive in Istanbul too early, I want to plan something which involves us arriving exactly on time; noon on the first Saturday of October. It is the time and date I had originally planned to finish on.

And so we casually ride into Zimnicea shortly after lunchtime. We have ridden a quick 50 kilometres since Turnu Magurele and we find ourselves going through a town of about 20 000 happy Romanians. Zimnicea is where Russian troops were stationed when they defended Bulgaria, on the other side of the river, from the Ottoman Empire's army 150 years ago. In 1977 this town was almost totally flattened by an earthquake as well, and what wasn't flattened was flattened by the Russian bulldozers. The Russians wanted to rebuild it from the ground up.

We drove past some old ruins and fortifications, most of which were only marked on our cycle map as historic sites, but little was left of them. We decide to stay, and Troy had already located us a hotel. An interesting hotel it is, it seems to be either half demolished or under re-construction. The large dining room is getting decorated for a wedding. The rooms are cheap, we stay! Due to renovations in the hotel there is only cold water, and lots of mosquitoes are coming through the windows.

The wedding guests start pouring in and we are treated to party noise for the rest of the night. After dinner in a nearby restaurant we decide to play cards in Heather and Cindy's room but in the end Troy and I want to see what is going on downstairs with all the music. We loiter out the front, trying hard to get invited for a beer, but fail miserably. No one wants to talk to us and invite us into the festive dining room with the after dinner dancing.

One of the waiters walks out of the dining room into the lobby area, where we are standing, and we take the opportunity to ask him if we can get a beer. After ten minutes of waiting for the beer we decide to investigate and go down the dark corridor the waiter had disappeared in. It is dark and dinghy, mouldy and decrepit. It smells of food. We come to a few intersecting corridors but follow our nose.

Eventually we end up in a kitchen-like dungeon, but not before we see this caldron of death; a large pot (the kind you expect cannibals to cook humans in) full of dishes suspended on a gas flame, bubbling away in a loading dock area. It is like a big bowl of soup with dishes in it. Putrid. This place is messy! We find staff, and pretend to be looking for a beer. In reality we are fascinated with the dungeon like labyrinth of corridors and almost forgot about the beer. We are handed a bottle each and are told we should not be here. With the original mission accomplished we walk out into the more conventional looking public part of the hotel.

Later on in the evening Troy brings Lucas there with the camera, but they get stopped before getting to the cauldron of death. In the morning I take note to see if our beers found their way onto the bill, they surely did! Basic breakfast in the girl's room and off we go to Giurgiu, the next main town, about 75 kilometres on our way.

"Unfortunately, because there were 6 of us playing cards in the small room that night, we had the windows wide open and noticed too late that the room was slowly starting to swarm with mosquitoes. As it was Cindy and mine's room, we suffered the consequences - too hot to sleep under any covers, we tried various unsuccessful techniques, like lying fully clothed on top of bed sheets, or lying completely naked under thin sheets.

After about 2 hours of trying to get to sleep, we both got up in a maniacal frenzy, ran to Troy and David's room to get the key to the van, ran down to the van to get the mozzie spray and then I proceeded to spray everything in the room with the toxic shite. That only lasted until the coughing started from all the fumes.

Did I mention there was a wedding going on downstairs that was playing really loud techno music until 6am? Yep. Apparently, Romania has the largest concentration of married people (in the world/Europe?). We have definitely noticed this in the form of decorated cars and most restaurants where we might have to wrestle our server away from blowing up balloons to order." – Heather's blog, September 18

Along the dusty road leading through a tiny town I see a man along the road sitting on a chair, as all older people seem to do, but he has oxygen tubing on! I stop and explain what we are doing. We both cough and understand each other. Heather films us and I take a photo of him. He tells me he has been on Oxygen for 12 years or so and offers us drinks. We have no time to spare. I try to give him money which he totally refuses. His family stands by watching with horror as he knocks back the money so I hide it under his tubing in the window sill.

Cycling near the rural town Malu as we are approaching Giurgiu I see a large grass fire in the distance. Smoke is blowing towards where we are heading. It means that soon we might ride in barely noticeable smoke and even at that concentration that is enough to affect my lungs. Although I might not realise it as I ride through, I will cough significantly more that night and the next morning.

I pull out the video camera I am carrying for the afternoon and record the plume of drifting smoke. I continue filming the hills as I get onto the bike. Within 10 seconds a small flock of sheep cross in front of me with an old shepherd. I feel lucky to film him. I next notice two little dogs helping him. As I am filming the dogs spot me and start chasing me up the hill! I randomly aim the camera behind me to film the chasing beasts. I am convinced they are in it for the chase as they probably could manage to run a little harder and give me a bite or two! Instead they hang with me, and keep a safe distance as I slow down up the hill. Maybe they are getting tired too. They give up just as David shows up, coming to look for me already! With a big coughing fit of excitement and adrenaline I make it to the crest of the hill where Heather and Troy are waiting for me. We have been plagued by daily dog chases and it is tricky business getting this on tape as the camera-man is also scared to fall of f and chance being eaten alive by the mongrels! Hopefully this footage works out for Lucas. Now let's knock on wood for 5 minutes!

We continue our ride on the dusty roads and are approaching the very dusty township of Giurgiu. We ride in through harvested corn fields and we see industry on the Bulgarian side of the river, there is even a bridge here to the other side. We decide to stay in Romania because if we are to cross now we will need to get back into Romanian territory again when the South Bank of the Danube becomes Romania again in a few more days of riding. The Danube here is reasonably active, we see barges going up and down, and wonder what is all on board. The river is blue, wide and open here, a slow and steady current heads East. We are now counting the days to the end of the Danube. In a couple of days we will reach Calarasi and there we leave the Danube and bee-line to the Black Sea leaving the Danube to flow into its sizable Delta area North of where we want to be. We like the Danube, it has become our friend. It travels with us, and has been with us for about 40 days by now.

Troy awaits us as we finally ride into the dusty outskirts of Giurgui. Troy gives us directions to the hotel he had found and booked with Lucas. We enter the town and go past a busy market place where we all take a mental note to return to for food. We ride further and further through the town, leaving behind the lively market following Troy's directions, and hopes fade of seeing the market again. We come to the hotel, well, the place he found. Despite Troy's understanding it is locked up. It doesn't even look like a hotel, how did he find this one?

There is a cafe restaurant next door and we gladly park our butts and sit down on the plastic chairs under the roof of the terrace. We have a late lunch, a big one. Food is good here, we like the service, and we can communicate almost effectively with the waiter too. Eventually the man who belongs to the accommodation next door shows up with a key for us, and leads us inside his place. We were starting to get worried he was never going to show up!

We head up the steep stairs of his establishment. It is a bit of a bed and breakfast without breakfast. We are assigned two rooms, and a third room has some Romanian young men staying in it. It is rickety here, and old fashioned. It is the home of this gentleman who has most of his furniture moved into his kitchen, where he has an improvised desk. The bikes are squashed between the steep stair railings and the windows. The bathroom area for all of us to share is clumsily designed and gives little privacy. We like the fact we are finally in a modest place! Student accommodation!

Heather and I go walk about looking for an internet cafe in the area. The streets are ripped up and under construction, it is dusty and there are holes and obstacles along the temporary footpaths. After receiving directions here and there we find something that looks like a kids' entertainment cafe. It is a little room adjoining a bar. The bar is smoky and full of drinking men, and the computer room next to it is jam packed with noisy kids playing computer games. This is the internet cafe we are told to go to. I cannot stand the noise and go out to the covered area between the bar and the computer room, a little patio. I ask the waitress directions for a toilet but she smiles and gets me a beer instead. In the end I pretend to unzip my pants and she gets the message. I am shown the one toilet in the place. Surprisingly clean considering 30 people and maybe 20 kids are all using it - or at least I make that assumption. The waitress has a beer waiting for me as I walk out the toilet. It is a very cheap beer, and it brings home the fact that we get charged tourist prices in the hotels we have been in. Not that beer ever was expensive anywhere. Beer beer beer, there is always beer. I buy relatively expensive lemonade for Heather and bring it to her. I also want to fix up the young teenager who seems to be in charge for using the computer. No idea how much I owe him. The young man, a head taller than the other kids tries to think up a good figure for me to pay, and all the kids excitedly stand around suggesting other prices. With a look of daring anticipation he scribbles down 5 Romanian Leu (about US$2) and I act outraged for about one second. His face immediately changes expression from happy to scared. The other kids all wait with abated breath. I smile, pull out some money and pay them 10 Leu, and tell them that is for Heather as well. They all laugh and cheer and celebrate at their victory.

Many decibels later Heather appears out of the den and we walk a different way home. We find a supermarket, and man, this really is a supermarket! We buy as much as we think we can possibly consume in the next few days, keeping in mind that we are unlikely to find places to really spread out and cook, and remembering that we may not be able to keep things cool.

I am dying to go for a leak again; I pee every 10 minutes it seems. Inconvenient for sure. A sign of high blood sugar levels too I realise. I worry and wonder what my sugar levels are doing. I certainly slow down during the day and get tired lately. There is no toilet anywhere near the supermarket I am led to believe by staff. As a matter of urgency I find a quiet spot behind the building and risk it. No one catches me, but that is a matter of luck really. Heather and I lug our proudly obtained possessions back to the hotel.

"Right now, day 52, Wally and I are in an internet cafe in a town that we have all forgotten the name of...again. What we are finding in most internet cafes in Romania is a plethora of kids playing computer games, all blaring their own music as each tries to out-blare the other. The decibel levels and mix of rap and what sounds like Latin/east Indian (I don't know!) pop and computer beeps and squeals are enough to make me want to pull out my own hair and then start on the person beside me.

One boy stands reading over my shoulder - can he understand? Who knows... anyway, I'll try to concentrate enough to write now.

At last check we were 5 days ahead of schedule and so to combat this, we are planning a few days on the beaches of the Black Sea, lapping it up and for some of us, contemplating our next move for when the trip is done". – Heather's blog, September 18.

The next morning we hop on the bikes all happy to have spent one night in budget accommodation and fully resupplied with nutritious snacks and a fresh blend of Heather mix distributed in plastic bags.

Wednesday 19 September. We are approaching Calarasi, the town where we leave the Danube. We are riding along a narrow busy road, full of trucks and smoking vehicles into the very industrialised city of Calarasi, surrounded by abandoned Russian style factories. We have a possible rest day scheduled here, as it is going to be a long ride to the Black Sea which we have to do in one hit as there is nowhere obvious for us to overnight in between. We try not to overdo the riding, avoiding injuries is very important with Cystic Fibrosis. If I cannot do aerobic exercises or cough for a few weeks due to an injury that could really have dire consequences on my lungs. Imagine having bruised ribs from a fall or a pulled tendon. If we find a place where we can comfortably stay an extra night now that we are ahead of schedule and wince we have been riding longer than planned distances, we will!

We arrive at the longitude/latitude that Troy had sent us, and find hotel Calarasi, a large modern looking high rise hotel. We really would not mind crossing the Danube and riding another 30 or so kilometres, just to shave some distance of the 140 kilometre day ahead of us - the distance to Constanta on the Black Sea! Troy and Cindy go and investigate the other side of the river, and head for the ferry to look for an alternative place for us all to stay further on our route. Lucas, David, Heather and I sit down in the hotel's restaurant and have some greasy spaghetti for lunch. There is a sign for a pizza restaurant across the road, something we have not had for a long time, but it is closed.

There are a number of people eating and drinking coffee in the hotel's restaurant. I can't say it is an inspiring location, lots of concrete and unfinished surrounds. The hotel is going through a major renovation by the looks of it. After lunch I walk around the hotel wall to the reception area. There does not appear to be a way through the restaurant to get there. Strange place. The first thing I notice as I walk through the front entrance is the Amex sign on the front door, then I see the extend of the renovations going on in the lobby. Excited about being able to pay with the Amex card I tell the ladies behind the desk I am happy to see the Amex sign.

'Oh, no, sorry, we no accept American Express'. That really annoys me. They sport the American Express stickers on the door, it is a really large hotel, and they will not accept it? The excuse is the renovations going on. The entire lobby really is covered in plastic and dust, and work men are running around. Should they not have the manual swipe machine? The room prices are advertised on the wall, but when I try to book the rooms I get told those rooms are not available. In fact every affordable combination of rooms is not available; we would have to get the expensive newly renovated double rooms. To me this is just a scheme to get more money out of us, or to scare us off from staying there for some reason. They even readily recommend another hotel to me. Apart from the diners in the restaurant who appear to be locals, no other guests are in sight.

I need some fresh air, I am agitated now. There is a Cosmote office right next to the hotel, the Romanian telephone company whose prepaid SIM chip I currently have in my mobile phone. I am often unable to send messages to the other crew, and also often unable to receive them despite having full coverage. I will come back and speak to these people later, I make a mental note. As I double check the SIM chip in my phone, to see if it really is Cosmote, I notice there is a wireless Internet available here, and it comes from the Cosmote building. Perfect. Internet! Quickly I collect my email on the phone and walk back to the restaurant.

We are expecting Troy to come back any time, so while we go looking for the newly suggested hotel we leave Lucas and Heather to wait for them. David and I go and scout out the alternative hotel. Naturally it is not easy to find, despite the simple directions of straight ahead and then left… Fortunately David spots something that looks a little like a hotel, but does not have the word hotel (or anything else for that matter) written on it. He opens the door that leads to a small lobby inside to ask for directions and discovers it is indeed a hotel. He immediately checks the rooms and makes a booking for us. I go back to find Lucas and the others and take them to the great find. The rooms are fantastic and we unanimously decide to have a rest day here. It is even affordable.

My first mission is to go back to the Cosmote office to send some emails using the free wireless Internet! I am able to sort out the SMS problem too. The problem was them and their network, and not my phone. It is a known network issue they are currently experiencing.

On our second day in Calarasi, our rest day, Cindy gives David, Troy and myself a trendy haircut; either a number 2 or a number 4 on the shears! This is the last time we see Cindy's professional hair dressing kit and caboodle... We carry the laptops to the Cosmote office and do some quick blog updates and do some emailing. It is not exactly an internet cafe, Lucas, Heather and I sit there on concrete outside the office. Fortunately there are not many people milling about, and we are left alone. Lucas and Cindy take the support car and go for a drive to film some Gypsy communities in the neighbourhood. They come back with photos of very poor people working and living on the land.

Lucas continues his exploration and goes walkabout in town now. He finds young Romanian students who show him around. These new friends also want to have dinner with us, but when Lucas tells us we are all a little reluctant; we are tired and just want to eat and have an early night in preparation for tomorrow's big ride to the Black Sea. Another issue was whether we could trust these people! We may sound a little over anxious about security, but we do have an awful lot of gizmos and feel that we cannot afford to lose any of it or deal with such situation. We are running low on cash and already have one insurance claim to make when we get home.

Lucas and I wait for the Romanian friends and the rest of our team heads for pizza in the restaurant we had seen yesterday. Heather decides last minute to join Lucas and me and we stride off with our new Romanian friend, the only one who ended up coming. It is interesting to hear his stories, the Romanian history as he saw it, about the Romanian car called the Dacia (the Renault 12 'imitations'), and about 'the Gypsies'. Romanians call Gypsies the natives and do not seem to respect them very much he tells us. Apparently some are very wealthy, but we only hear and see the poor ones. Our friend is going to take us to an especially nice restaurant, and let us taste extra nice Romanian Food. We walk for about an hour, looping around the park next to the Danube before going to this fancy restaurant near the Calarasi zoo. It is a little out of the way, but it is renowned we are told. Would you believe who sits there when we walk in? David, Cindy and Troy had just ordered dinner! This just shows you the number of restaurants available to us is very limited.

We occupy a table with white tablecloth next to them. There are no big tables set up, and besides, David, Troy and Cindy are almost done with their meal. Our friend orders us dinner and wine, but has none himself! He sits there as he watches us eat our usual Romanian schnitzel, and we try to have casual conversation. He is a local student. He is busy with his mobile phone and eventually gets a girl to join us as well. They both know about my Cystic Fibrosis, or at least that I have lung problems, but still insist on going out for a cigarette on several occasions. We have dessert and coffee, walk the girl home, and our new friend takes us home to the hotel again. It was a fun night talking to local people, something we rarely get a chance to do. Our friend sees the Gypsy wedding preparations going on at out hotel, and explains how these are the wealthy kind and they will start the wedding at midnight and celebrate till dawn. Wealthy Gypsies, wow. How stereotyped are the Gypsies in my narrow-minded world that I only think of them as poor people living in camps living of crime! I feel ashamed to even refer to them as Gypsies as I know it is a derogatory term, and to portray them as threats to our safety. My attitude is akin to how the Jewish think about the Arabs, how the Americans used to think of the African Americans and how Hitler thought of the Jews (and the Gypsies!). Being Jewish I don't like people stereotyping me, or even assuming I must be wealthy and have amazing political and business contacts (if that were the case I would have a real publisher and a movie deal in Hollywood by now instead of a larger mortgage)! Anyway, back to the Gypsie wedding.

The hotel was indeed fully geared up for the wedding by now, in time for our last night. There were black robed men running around, which to me looked like priests. I had spotted them through town as well. Apparently they were the wealthier Gypsies, but with their beards and fancy robes and black suits they looked like orthodox religious people. Dare I say I almost thought they looked like Hasidic Jews – who incidentally also originated in Eastern Europe (Belarus and Ukraine). The black double-breasted rekelechs and buttonless coats and black hats almost unmistakably looked Hasidic. There is a lot of ignorance in this world, but I have to believe our young Romanian friend who told me these are 'rich' Gypsies. Could it be these people were in fact Satmarer Hasidic Jews who actually originated in Romania (albeit in a completely opposite corner of this country)? The Satmarer Hasidic Jews were displaced during WWII when Hitler invaded Europe and tried to eliminate all Jews and Gypsies. Most of the Satmarer Jews now apparently live in New York, London and Jerusalem. (According to http://en.wikipedia.org/wiki/Satu_Mare)

We had already experienced several weddings on our journey and are prepared for a little bit of noise. Turns out it is not too noisy, and we all have a reasonably good night's sleep. It was tempting, especially for Lucas with his camera, to restrain himself and not go and check out the wedding.

The music coming from downstairs from midnight till the wee hours of the morning was most unusual, with a fast and constant hypnotising rhythm.

After a good breakfast we head for the ferry and cross the Danube for the last time. It is very wide at this point, and the ferry takes its time getting to our side, and then took a fair time to get us to the other side. A delay we are not keen to have considering it is a 140 kilometre ride with possibly hills in between. Pleased to find good coffee at the ferry's café and entertained by a man trying to sell us a flick knife we impatiently pass the time before boarding the ferry. When we finally board it is with the impatient cacophony of car and truck horns and rings of my bicycle bell. We squeeze on with not an inch to spare. Some cars have to wait for more than an hour for the next trip. As the ferry approaches the other side of the Danube we get to see our first close-up glimpse of Bulgaria. The Danube is the border between Romania and Bulgaria for close to a thousand kilometres, but at this point the Danube diverts away from the Bulgarian border. We are crossing to the first Romanian part on the Southern bank of the Danube. What we now see of Bulgaria is not pretty. It looks like a Lenin-esque residential area, dilapidated concrete apartments where poor people appear to be living.

# TOWARDS BULGARIA, THE BLACK SEA AND MAD DOGS

It is the Bulgarian town of Silistra. Most unusual is the sight of a big passenger jet abandoned in the middle of it! Right now we do not feel comfortable with the prospect of having to go into Bulgaria if it is as bad as the poverty stricken chaotic mess indicated. For now we are pleased to remain in Romania a little longer!

The presumably illegally parked airplane that we see sitting on the Bulgarian shore looks forlorn and derelict. It is a Russian Tupolev Tu-134, also known as the Crusty. It is very similar to a DC-9, and normally carries about 84 passengers. First built in 1967 many are still in use today, mostly in Eastern European countries. No idea how this one got here, and although it does look impressive complete with the escape slide, it is not a good advertisement for Balkan, the Bulgarian Airline!

The first few kilometres on the Southern bank is alongside the Bulgarian-Romanian border; a large barbed wire fence with the occasional uniformed and armed patrol. We are cycling on Romanian cobble-stones, and glad we do not have to cross the barbed wire barrier into Bulgaria yet.

"Crossing from the Danube to the Black Sea was really our longest, toughest day of the trip so far. Just a hair off 150km, this time with wind, hills, rabid dogs and even a nasty little kid who ran after us and tried to grab stuff off our bikes! We were only an hour or two into the day - very slow going as most of us were up all night involuntarily listening to the music from yet another wedding. We were riding through a small village along a cobble stone road, when I heard a kerfuffle and then David yelling. I turned to look and saw a young boy, about 12 or so, running alongside him grabbing at the bag on his back pannier rack."- Heather's blog, September 22.

The kid dislodges David's plastic-bag wrapped helmet from his bicycle and David had to re-secure it. I stop my bike behind David and hold the little brat off. He is standing there balling his fist and inviting me to fight him. What do you do? I try to look intimidating, and try not to cough. I manage to keep him away for the ten long seconds that David needs. We jump back on our bikes and race up the cobble stoned road and up the hill, trying to out-run him. My greatest fear is that he is so brave because his older brothers or some other thugs could be hiding somewhere close by waiting to join in and surely get away with some of our gear. He is a quick little brat and runs fast to keep up with us. I struggle gaining any kind of speed going up this hill. He laughs and falls behind a bit, still gesturing at us aggressively. He makes one more attempt, and tries to sprint after us in vain now. But a dog appears out of nowhere and starts barking. The kid spurs it on and so now we have a dog and a kid chasing us. As I ride frantically up the hill I am also trying to find rocks to throw at the dog (or the kid!) but again, we are just pedalling as fast as we can and stopping for rocks is out of the question. Finally an old lady along the road, probably his grandmother, stops him from harassing us any further. It all happened so fast that no one knew how to react.

Surely cycling along the Black Sea coast, after we reach Constanta, is going to be flat and with tailwinds!

Phew, it is a long ride, although no major mountain ranges the terrain is undulating to say the least. The road surface is poor and the distance to be covered to get to Constanta is long. There is nowhere along the road for us to stay, and after the kid incident near Ostrov we now do not feel like stopping in any of the towns we pass through – not that there are any obvious places to stay! To cover 140 kilometres is a big ask for us, and we still might be surprised by a range of mountains prior to getting to the Black Sea. We had an hour delay waiting for the ferry, we have to keep pace. The countryside is relatively dull. We see some ancient ruins of Roman walls, but we cannot stop. We try to pass the time playing cards on the bicycle, just to say we could. Shuffling the cards alone is difficult on the bike. Then there is the holding on to the cards and sorting them in your hand. In the end we can't even play Go-Fish and after 3 minutes we give up. Whose idea was this anyway? Heather? We wave back at the locals who occasionally wave at us as we pass the many villages along the way; Lipnita, Baneasa, Ion Corvin,.. The villages are generally less than maybe an hour cycling apart. We have no serious winds to deal with, which is fortunate. I am getting a little chilly and wish I'd worn my tracksuit pants. When we see the car parked in the grass just outside of a little town called Adamclisi I quickly rummage through the back to get to my bag, naturally on the bottom of the heap, and grab some warmer gear. We all swallow some lunch that Cindy and Troy prepared for us and get on our way. Now I am positively hot. I stop again. This time I am stowing away the warm tracky dacks and fleece that I had only retrieved from the car minutes ago.

Without carrying lights for riding at night we are anxious to get to Constanta at the Black Sea before dusk. Prior to leaving I had booked a nice hotel in Constanta over the Internet. I got an excellent price for the Best Western Savoy Hotel. The Internet website showed a map and a picture of the hotel. The location is perfect, as it is exactly at the end of the road that we are on, and the hotel is newly renovated.

We are making progress, we pass Cobadin, it is now only 40 kilometres to go. We cannot see any mountain ranges ahead, we might be lucky. We get to Basarabi and merge onto a much busier road now. The road we are cycling on is the main highway from Bucharest to Constanta. We have crossed Europe from West to East! We are approaching the Black Sea and have reason to celebrate again.

Constanta is a prime holiday destination, and the highway we are riding along is busy. It is approaching peak hour and the road is a blur of trucks and cars enveloped in a smelly cloud of emission fumes. The wind seems to be helping us a bit and we are screaming along the highway's edge, heavy traffic narrowly screaming past. It is becoming industrialised now, we are going into a much bigger city than I had imagined. In fact Constanta is the second largest city in Romania with almost half a million residents.

Boats are a common sight in Constanta! Are they just abandoned?

As we approach the city of Constanta we run into a huge welcoming sign; a boat! It is a welcomed photo opportunity where I can legitimately get off my (tired) bike (two tires in fact!). The boat, prominently named Constanta appears to be one of many in Constanta, and we are to spot a few more dotted around the city. We never found out exactly why this was done, but may have something to do with Constanta being the biggest port on the Black Sea (and the fourth biggest in Europe).

Troy in the support vehicle runs into trouble looking for the booked Best Western Savoy Hotel, but eventually finds it on the map, in a location about 10 kilometres further North up the road. He calls us on the mobile, and catches up with us before entering the town limits. He is very agitated and tells us that the traffic is frantic and dangerous, and that the hotel is located in Mamaia, Constanta, at one of the outer beaches. It is not where shown on the map. Troy has not been there yet, but he was shown where it was by friendly people who helped him find the wrong address. Troy gives us instructions on how to get there; follow the main road into Constanta and then follow the signs to Mamaia, away from Istanbul!

Cindy is looking pale sitting next to Troy. Any passenger in a car driving around this traffic is bound to be pale unless they actually have a death wish. Later on Troy calls us back to revise the instructions as his GPS has led him to a dead end road, and he wants to catch up with us again to give us more detailed directions. In the meantime we have hit the big traffic too, and start following the signs to Mamaia. Our tired legs take us past numerous hotels, all looking very inviting, and Lucas is cursing me for booking us a hotel so far away! Well, it was conveniently located and right where we were to enter town… according to the Internet. It is Friday afternoon, or should I say early evening by now. The light is starting to fail us. You can tell this is a touristy place by the entertainment parks we ride along, including a large water park complete with big slides, but it looks very closed. In fact the pools are drained. We wonder why.

The traffic is truly scary, difficult to follow, weird intersections, and dangerous drivers. The fumes are terrible, and I go into video game mode! Video game mode is where everything suddenly seems surreal, you weave in and out of traffic, attempting to avoid the suicidal drivers as if you are in a video game where some vehicles are out to get you, and losing one or two lives before ending the game is a distinct possibility, but you only have one life left of course. Adrenaline completely takes over and I forget all about the sore muscles, the long day behind us, and the real danger that we might be in. Having been brought up on a bicycle from before I could even walk I am very comfortable playing this game and oblivious to the danger. I have a lot of fun in these situations. This could not be said for Lucas who has very little bicycle experience, and Heather who right now is swearing at the traffic and the dogs.

"It is sad that some little punk got us all in a tizzy, but we are rather paranoid about our stuff and what we have heard about Gypsies and thieves, so the best option was to keep moving. Nothing was stolen in the end. I guess after 3500 km plus, we can expect a few mishaps. Our only regret was not having caught it on film!

But Lucas did get a bit of doco material when I had a nervous breakdown, spat the dummy and threw a wobbly at a few dogs at the end of the day. Since we entered into Croatia, I seem to have 'something' that dogs sense and like to chase. On more than a few occasions, I have been seen in the distance, frantically pedalling my ass off while hounds chase me down and leave everyone else alone. So far, I have managed to outrun them, but my nerves are wearing down. Cindy tells me the best tactic is to stand firm ground and snarl back at them. I was reluctant to use this advice as I thought standing my ground would give a canine the perfect opportunity to latch onto a limb and drag me off.

Our last 20km to the Black Sea was in agitating traffic. We were getting honked at, mowed down by fumes and gusts from giant trucks and riding along a shoulder about 2ft wide. Personally, I'd had enough. We had just started off after stopping to figure out directions to our hotel; a truck flew past, a car honked and two dogs came out of nowhere, snapping and snarling and chasing. I screamed a really bad swearword at the top of my lungs and they stopped in their tracks - I even heard a whimper, but I think that was from David in front of me....

Anyway, it was like heaven to see our hotel, all lit up from the evening's sunset and right on the beach! - Heather's blog, September 22.

When we finally get to the hotel it looks nothing like the picture we had seen on the Internet, and it most certainly has not recently been renovated. Not that we are concerned, but we are slightly annoyed that we had to ride an extra 10+ kilometres out of the way to get there. They do have our booking; we are at the right address. A rest day is planned here and we can relax for now.

It is about 8pm when we finally get to the dining room for dinner and discover that nothing on the menu is available. There are other guests, but the excuse is that it is the end of the season and the hotel is closing down for winter. I size the situation up by my beer. The situation must be desperate; the beer choice is limited to one very expensive choice of local beer. After ordering food the waiter still comes back several times to ask us to change our order as they only have one or two of the dishes and not enough for all of us.

When during our meal we start hearing a tumultuous sound coming from the outside and start smelling insecticide inside we quickly abandon the dining room and retire for the night – we have crossed Europe West to East!

Today, we are all well-rested and are feeling the need to celebrate. Walter and Troy scoped out a Kentucky Fried Chicken on the way in, and are off to get the makings for our romantic beachside dinner: KFC and Champagne, baby - nothing but the best for the COFE Team!"  - Heather's blog, September 22.

A well deserved day of rest is now ahead of us. After a leisurely breakfast Lucas leaves the hotel to go on a Lucas Side-trip. Troy and I go for a drive to pick up fried chicken and champagne. Kentucky Fried Chicken signs had been spotted all along the way through Constanta.. As we are accustomed to, nothing to do with food is easy, we should know that by now. After one hour of driving around looking for the shopping mall in which the alleged store is supposed to be we stop and start asking people. Eventually we get a taxi to drive in front of us and point it out.

Driving through Constanta we notice there are road signs that not only have many of our next destinations on them, but also Istanbul! We try hard not to get too excited about it; it is still a fair way to go, hundreds of miles in fact. But it sure seems closer now, and we are coming to the end of our adventure. The signs are received with mixed feelings. We do not want it to be over yet! We still have Bulgaria and Turkey to go.

In any case, we find the KFC, get our chicken, pay with cash, and next on the agenda is Champagne. Given the availability of beer everywhere I cannot imagine this to be difficult. It is. Just like us trying to celebrate our first thousand kilometres with Champagne, this too is proving a challenge. We find a large variety shop, as big as you would find anywhere in the West. It has everything you can possibly imagine inside it. Surely I will find Champagne here. I locate the liquor department and find lots of wine and beer and lots of Spumante, but no Champagne. None of the wines are chilled either, and after asking around I find a bottle of expensive and warm Champagne. I buy it as the chicken is getting cold quickly, and the others are wondering where we are and getting hungry. At the checkout I discover this store is for members only, and have to plead my case with other people in the queue. Fortunately somebody speaks English, understands my predicament and lets me use their membership card to pay. As big as the store is, credit cards are not accepted. Imagine taking the huge sums of money to the bank each day, or imagine the cost of the Armor Guard truck to pick up the takings each day. Why don't people catch on that electronic payments are good? In Australia it is also common to take money out when buying groceries. The standard question when paying with a card is whether you want cash out. This reduces the money in the till and reduces the money that needs to be taken to the bank each day. We now have chicken and Champagne, we safely made it across the continent to the Black Sea and we will drink to it in style!

Lucas had left us this morning to catch a bus to Tulcea to visit the actual Danube delta, 5700 km$^2$ of the second largest and best preserved of Europe's river deltas. Lucas had trusted us to be in charge of one camera in case we did something noteworthy. By the time Troy and I return from the chicken mission I, like the chicken, am truly cooked and no longer enthusiastic about anything. We make our way to the beach to celebrate us reaching the Black Sea. We leave the camera that Lucas left for us in the hotel room because we notice it does not have a memory chip in it – which apparently was lying next to it (we did not look).

At the beach we are enthusiastically greeted by a pack of dogs that follow us like sheep. Cindy had already met these dogs on her morning run and was chased, barked at, and intimidated by them. This time they are timid and friendly, as they know we have nice food. I must say they are extremely well behaved dogs right now, keeping their distance, and patiently waiting for us to feed them. Occasionally a motorbike, runner or cyclist comes down the beach, and the dogs immediately run after them, only to return to their position next to us. The sun is shining, the sky is blue, we could not have wished for a better day. Even though I come from Tasmania it was too cool for me to consider going in the water. This is not the case for the others, and after we feed the dogs and clean up after ourselves, the brave people go for a dip in the Black Sea and I go for a nap and drink lots of water on David's recommendation. I am still recovering from the shopping expedition; what a sissy! (I now know that my blood sugar levels were very high as I typically drink LOTS of juice when faced with buffet style breakfasts. That morning we had a buffet style breakfast…)

When the troops come back from their dip I vacate the room and go walkabout. Although it is a pleasant afternoon there are not many people around. The season had just about past and apparently this town is going to be vacated for the next nine months! Still feeling crappy I walk around the block and find a pizza joint which appears to be closed. David had scouted out a pizza restaurant earlier and liked it; hence I decided to investigate this one closer. On approach I notice a pack of dogs hanging around but assume they are just like all the other dogs everywhere else that are in begging mode when around food. Because this place is closed there is no food, and the dogs are in defend mode. I just about get attacked as I approach. I am in no mood to be harassed by a bunch of silly dogs and growl back. The leader of the pack does not appreciate being intimidated by me and seriously growls at me, baring teeth. I really feel like killing it on the spot, but figure I would end up the loser in this situation. It gets my adrenalin going and I am now truly ready for a beer on a quiet terrace on my own. I find a local hangout within a stone's throw of the dogs. I sit down, turn on my mp3 player and listen to my favourite podcast with a local beer.

It is nice having my mp3 podcasts with me. I can update them every few weeks from the internet after I have listened to them all. I listen to NPR programs from the USA, including Car-talk, and JJJ Hack and JJJ's Dr Karl Kruszelnicki from Australia, as well as Dutch radio programs. Podcasts are a wonderful invention, you can listen to your favourite programs from anywhere in the world at any time.

I am only just calming down when a family shows up and sits down and starts smoking, something that everybody in this continent does, or so it seems. Now, more than ever, it really annoys me. I relocate upwind from them. From this new spot I see a young good-looking couple arrive on fully packed bicycles. Only then do I discover that the small space between where I sit and our hotel is in fact a campground. Despite the sign, it looks highly unlikely a safe or appropriate place to set up a tent, but a man appears to organise a spot for them. They are the only ones there and after they finish checking in I approach them and hear their story. They are Polish and had cycled from Bucharest, camping most of the way. Heather would have been very jealous again.

Cheered up I return to the hotel where the others are ready to go for dinner. Lucas has just arrived back from the delta. Unfortunately we had not placed bets yet, but were certain he would not have made the delta which is hundreds of kilometres north of us. Considering he had casually left around 10am to look for a bus we expected his chances to be slim! Good thing we did not place bets on him yet, he made it there and back as per his plan. Even managed to charter a little Delta boat for a tour there! Boats are the preferred way to see the maze of natural waterways, which make for the perfect breeding ground for countless species of birds. The Danube Delta has the highest concentration of bird colonies in all of Europe. Why do we ever doubt Lucas? Perhaps because he is the youngest? Maybe we should follow him on his outings.

Altogether we make our way to the pizza restaurant that David had located earlier, situated in the opposite direction that I had ventured in earlier. The waitress recognises David and Cindy and immediately serves us a complimentary shot of

Tsuica, the local equivalent of the Serbian Slivovitz. The drink makes up for the food and lacking service that we are to receive!

On our way back from the restaurant we pass yet another wedding, going on, and Lucas feels compelled to film, being the dedicated person he is! We all laugh, and think it is funny how Lucas is always filming, knowing that the documentary could possibly be made into a 37 part series, one dedicated to weddings between Paris and Istanbul! Lucas has enough footage to make a 3-hour feature movie out of all his side trips alone! Out of all of us he takes most advantage of the tourist attractions along the way, perhaps because he is the youngest, has more energy than any of us, and the new culture perhaps makes more of an impression on him then on us cynics.

We are well attuned to riding it seems, we are not feeling the strain from the last 150+ kilometres ride. All it took was one rest day and we are keen to get out of Constanta. Keen as mustard (Australian expression) we leave on a nice Sunday morning through a relatively quiet Constanta, following the signs that actually read Istanbul and are heading down the Black Sea coast. We spot another huge boat with the name Constanta on it as we ride out of town.

The wind is less favourable, but it is not raining for a change. I cough up half my breakfast on the road through Constanta, and Cindy is following me with the helmet cam mounted on her helmet. Traffic fumes, yuck. We soon leave Constanta behind and are cycling on a pretty busy road with long straight stretches. We fight the wind which is increasingly less favourable every time the road swings into a more Southerly direction. Today we ride mostly South Easterly, but soon we are heading South. Let's hope the winds change direction after tomorrow. It is slowing me down.

Just before lunch time we come to the first petrol station in Mangalia, and the road is getting really quite busy now. We have not heard from Troy yet, so we sit down at a road side cafe adjoining a petrol station and drink a cool drink from the civilised and very western looking facility. There are clean toilets inside, and the counter is very busy.

When I come out of the toilet a queue has appeared at the counter. I still need to pay for my drink. The others are sitting outside relaxing. The holdup is one customer who is being difficult about his car and requires the attention of all the shop assistants. I try to motion to the staff that I am just sitting outside, but I don't think they see me. I walk outside and sit down with the others at the outdoor table and eat my nuts and drink the drink I just stole. A few minutes later a lady walks out and tells me the rush-hour has passed. I go in and pay for my snacks in retrospect. Troy and Lucas text us the location of a place to stay, and we leave this place that reminded me awfully much of western civilisation that could have easily been in the UK, USA or Australia if it wasn't for the language.

Not far down the road we meet Troy outside a flash looking roadside motel. Everything is clean and shiny, the staff seems professional, and obviously the petrol station was not an exception. This is not the Romania we saw in the past week or two! We get shown to our respective rooms. One magnificent room for the women and one equally magnificent suite for us three men. Considering the most modest price we are charged to stay here, this is unbelievable! Is this still Romania? Is this a farewell gesture from Romania? Tomorrow we cross into Bulgaria. Is this how Bulgaria will be as well? Let's hope so. This is impressive! We have wireless internet, TV, clean bathrooms, this is better than I would find in the average Australian motel!

We go and check out the food scene, and right there, next door to the hotel, is a little cafe with a good menu and a point and shoot buffet bar. You point at it and they scoop it up for you. The food is wonderful. We have potatoes, meat, vegies and other goodies. It is so nice being able to see what you order. This beats translating menus and dealing with language barriers. After lunch we settle in our newly found luxury, update the blog, email our friends, and watch TV. I think we can get used to this!

Lucas decides to shoot some nice scenery on a nearby beach. Of all things one could find on a beach he finds probably the most unlikely item; a bottle full of messages! He duly picks up the bottle and takes it with him. Anyone would have opened it there and then, smashed it if necessary. There could be young maiden on a desert island in need of a rescue. The bottle is full of little bits of paper with crayon writing on it, and does not exactly conform to the proverbial letter in a bottle coming from a stranded shipwrecked person in distress. He returns to the hotel and shows us his treasure. We can recognise some German words, but the messages are all neatly rolled up.

My theory is that it is a German or Austrian school project where they had tossed the bottle into the Danube, many miles upstream. The bottle would have had to float 2000 kilometres to the Black Sea and there it would have washed up on the beach. David swears he will swallow a Bulgarian Penny if that is in fact the case. His modest theory is that it was a local school that had ambitiously thrown the bottle into the sea at the same, or perhaps a nearby beach. The waves have washed it back within a day or so. If that is the case we decide to take the bottle to Australia and place it on the popular Bondi beach in Sydney. There we plan to alert the paparazzi and the rest of the media circus and make a big hooh-hah about a bottle from Bulgaria washing up on Australian shores.

A date is set for the ceremonial opening of the bottle; our last night together. That night is not really all that far away now.

Lucas also spotted a nice place for us to look for dinner. We have faith in our young expedition member who finds treasures, and gamely follow him fearlessly. Winding our way down to the Black Sea shore we come to a scenic path along the water. It is quiet here, and we feel relaxed. We soon come to a cafe that is partially built on the water and decide to go in. The music sounds good, and loud. In fact the music where we choose to sit is almost too loud, but it is worth the vista; overlooking the Black Sea on a semi-outside terrace right above the water. We happily put up with the loud music, and beer is served instantly. Food takes a little longer, but is good when it comes. On my way to the toilet I find two old Dutch ladies in the restaurant. I say Gidday. They are on a therapeutic holiday at one of the nearby health resorts where they get spa treatments and massages. I tell them we are doing something healthy too, and brag about us being featured in the Dutch Press.

We leave shortly after sunset, walking back to the hotel in a different way, and somehow end up going through a dark car park surrounded by gloomy looking apartment buildings. Lucas tells us how he was already advised to avoid this area as it was unsafe. Un-phased we walk on. We almost all hold hands, pee our pants and pray we are not robbed and attacked on our last day in Romania. There is no one about. The place is deserted. There are large garbage hoppers scattered around. We bravely walk on, and reach a civilised area again. I dive into a shop and buy goodies for on the road tomorrow. Who knows what we can buy in Bulgaria, I'd better stock up on snacks and kefir drinks. We safely get to the hotel and crash out for the night.

Breakfast is consumed in the cafe next door where we eat breakfast with everything we want on display. Complete with coffee, bacon and eggs, even chicken drum sticks, the works. And all so very reasonably priced we cannot get over it. Reluctantly we get on the bikes and leave town. With a bit of luck this is how Bulgaria will be tonight. I have visions of crashed airline jets and Lenin-esque buildings in my mind! The breakfast feels good in my belly and I am ready for whatever Bulgaria has to bring. Bring it on!

Monday 24 September. We begin our day cycling right through the centre of Mangalia, which turns out to be a bustling city full of hawkers and money changers. Money changers even approach us in front of money exchange shops, looking very sleazy. David is whipping us on, and urging us not to slow down as he senses a security risk. The fact that Heather and I have to pee is a complication too; it involves leaving Lucas and David to fend for the bicycles while we use the facilities of yet another KFC. KFC must be popular in these necks of the woods.

Actually leaving Mangalia is also tricky it turns out, and we are forced to ride over a very busy bridge. Heather and I try very hard to use the pedestrian walkway which is separated from the road. Unfortunately it is so narrow that our bikes do not fit between the railings and the lamp posts that are on the path. We are forced to go on the road with the heavy traffic. Off to our right we can see the Romanian naval fleet, of which I secretly take photos. Secret is not normally a word in my dictionary, and being discreet for me is very difficult; I stop, pull out my camera, and take my time taking the picture. I am sure I can see very worried naval officers peering back at me through binoculars.

Our route is hard to find now, the maps are sketchy and seem to be outdated. My phone navigation is useless - it takes 20 minutes to know where it is to begin with (Now I know it is a network assisted GPS, and without using the telephone network it has trouble functioning correctly, if at all. These are problems you get when buying new toys in a hurry and need to use them immediately. As data charges can sometimes be very expensive, when the phone asks me if it can use data when you switch to navigation my standard answer was 'no'. qed.). The Garmin GPS's we now carry only has basic maps for these distant regions. Even Google Maps is void of roads here. We are driving on very busy dangerous roads. Dead cats and dogs strewn bloated and disfigured on the side, others trying to attack you as you ride past. We have seen waiters in restaurants with air-pistols, carried in holsters, shooting at unperturbed cats. Trucks and buses fly past, and traffic is generally horrible.

# BULGARIA PROPER AND WHAT A TREAT

We are fearful of what might await us in Bulgaria. We have no decent maps or books for this area and the GPS as well as Google Earth show frightfully little detail!

We are ready to cross into Bulgaria. We had plenty of time to psych up to it, it is coming up in the next hour... we push on. The wind starts to blow against us now, but slowly we make it to the border. Troy is riding a bicycle today, and we meet Heather and Cindy at the border in the support vehicle.

The last time we saw Bulgaria was when we took the ferry across the Danube and saw the crashed plane in the run down suburbs, and cycled past barbed wire on the Romanian side where we were chased by the kid. We are apprehensive about Bulgaria, but we bravely approach the border. The border crossing itself is small and seems friendly enough. The crossing proceeds smoothly, passports collected by a not too friendly officer who disappears into his little roadside shed. Heather and Cindy get through the Bulgarian customs in the support vehicle singing loudly to a rock radio channel. The customs officers return all relaxed and friendly and give us our stamped passports. Elated we continue, and now we are in Bulgaria. The road goes on and on, and in a great mood we cycle hard towards our next destination. We also discover that the traffic has slowed down, the road sides are cleaner, and our overall impression of Bulgaria is improving by the minute.

Apparently there is an 80 kilometre bicycle path in planning to connect Mangalia with Balchik, a Black Sea resort that we will have to pass through. For now there is no sign of it and we have to follow the regular roads. Just like Velo 6, the trans Europe bicycle route along the Danube, this cycle path is also due for completion in 2010. I am well ahead of my time. Or as David puts it – 'typical Wally fashion'.

Heather and Cindy, today in control of the support vehicle, are determined to find us a campground adjoining the Baljik Bay, the part of the Balchik Sea, which in turn is part of the Black Sea, along which we are cycling.
    David and Troy showed Heather and Cindy which little roads we are trying to cycle on, and roughly where we hope to find accommodation. They are well equipped with maps and GPS in the support vehicle. According to plan we find a way off the main road and head back towards the coast. The main road had been going inland lately. The wind is awful along the main road too, and I am not doing very well today and am lagging behind a bit. I am very pleased to veer off the main road when we finally get the chance and not be cycling straight into the wind anymore. I prefer the coastal hills and side-winds instead.

Soon we start seeing the Black Sea again and find unexpected steep but short ups and downs. It does mean scenic views all round, cliffs and villages scattered up and down the coast, and plenty of signs for camping grounds. We start approaching Varna now, and are about 30 kilometres away. We know we can get accommodation in Varna, it looks like a major tourist destination from what we gather, but we are hoping to find a campground as the map shows many tent-icons. We cycle past the entrance to a resort-style campground, pointing down a drive, and we know we'll be camping tonight. Shortly after that campground we come to a place called Balchik, and it is an obvious tourist destination. We conveniently cycle straight past an Irish pub with outdoor seating, on what appears to be a road where we will be easily spotted by the women-team in the support vehicle and perfect for sitting down and having an early lunch. We shall not pass up this opportunity. Bulgaria just gained brownie points with this Irish pub; 'I'll have a Guinness thanks!'... 'Sorry Sir, no Guinness, we've run out for the season and we are closing in 3 days time, very sorry.' Not to worry, there are plenty of alternative ale choices to go with the soup and fresh bread that we greedily order.

Cindy and Heather in the support vehicle are not answering our text messages. When we finally get in touch with them they tell us that none of the campgrounds checked out and they are still looking, but if we could check out Balchik too that would be good. Lucas volunteers and heads into the tourist office across the square from our Irish pub. It is a makeshift little office. I get up to go exchange some money, next to a casino (!). The exchange was easy, we get Bulgarian money; Levs. Lucas is told by the tourist office ladies that all the campgrounds are shut as it is now the end of the tourist season. This end of season business is strange. The entire Black Sea coast apparently shuts down for most of the year, only opening up May till August. What happens the other 8 months of the year? We are told nothing happens the rest of the year.

We ride up the road a bit and find a modestly priced hotel right on the water, with to date the most reasonable price for a hotel on this trip yet. With Heather's birthday coming up shortly, and this place looking ideal for a rest day, I enthusiastically tell the hotel staff that we have a birthday girl coming. They get us a nicer room for Heather and Cindy, the last sea-view room available apparently. Us men are placed in mountain-view rooms at the back. I advise the hotel reception that the girls will come very soon. David sends a message to the girls to come back to Balchik. Apparently Heather had just found a camp ground, but by now we had fallen in love with Balchik.

Balchik...

David texts them the name of the hotel in his best English characters: XOTE? PECTOPAHT. This is written on a big sign above the entrance.

Balchik, as is the rest of the Black Sea coast, is an interesting place, totally equipped for tourism but still looking very run down and dare I say it, looking 'Bulgarian'. Everywhere you look there are signs advertising real estate, ranging from units to resorts, pieces of land and other investments. The prices are often mentioned both in Euros as well as in Levs, and appear very reasonable. Many buildings are either run down or under construction. The weather is great; not too hot, not too cold, and perfect for a few days of relaxation and to 'reward us' for being ahead of schedule.

It is going to be a holiday for us, and we have already fallen in love with the place. Affordability of Balchik, especially the room rates, has a lot to do with that, and the fact that it is sunny and warm today also helps. We are not deterred by the closing

bars and restaurants, there are still plenty to choose from and the lack of crowds is wonderful.

The hotel, хотел ресторант, is situated off the main square, so I go for a walk trying to intercept the girls. Remember I mentioned Conrad the older German man who is also cycling to Istanbul? Well, there he comes, cycling into town towards me with a friend he had picked up along the way. They are looking for accommodation. Enthusiastically I take them to our hotel and try to explain to the man at the desk that these are friends that I just accidentally ran into, and if they can give them a room here as well.

As I walk out of the hotel again I see David on the balcony, hanging out his washing - our trademark. I yell at him, telling him that Conrad and his friend will share the girls' room. I am just kidding of course, and off I go looking for the girls. I find a phone shop where I immediately buy a Bulgarian dual SIM pack, providing me with two different SIMS, which we can use it in two different phones, and make communications between us cheaper, instead of using the internationally roaming phones that Cindy, David and Troy carry.

On returning to the hotel David sourly greets me from his balcony and tells me I am in big trouble. I soon learn that Cindy and Heather had found the hotel, and that the specially booked room-with-a-view had gone to the Germans, thinking they are the people I had booked it for. So, as I had told David jokingly, the girls were now sharing their room unless they wanted a rear facing room like us boys. They had already chosen the latter, and had showered and settled in. I think David was also a little sour because he had made his first little boo-boo of the trip; the hotel name was not хотел ресторант. The reason why the girls took so long to find us was that David's interpretation of the hotel's name was a very common text written on almost all hotels, it simply means Hotel-Restaurant. The fact it was called Hotel Lotos had escaped him. I must admit they were the biggest words on the building. I had tried hard all trip to catch David out on something, but David has it pretty much together. I did not rub it in of course, as I am the one who decided to plan a trip on Velo 6, the bike route across Europe that is still only a gleam in some keen cyclists' eyes, and assured the team it was all downhill and with favourable trade-winds all the way.

The room situation at hand now requires Wally magic, and I go straight to the reception to see the manager. Minutes later they are also given a room with a view. They must be keeping them up their sleeve, giving them out sparingly. Good strategy, as they now booked out two of their rear facing rooms by saying we could have the last ocean front room almost as a favour!

They also promise to do an after dinner birthday cake for Heather's birthday and get the singer, who is performing that night, to sing her happy birthday. Although this birthday cake is now going to be done one night too early I do not want to push my luck. I am also not entirely sure if we decide to have dinner there the next day, and so the early birthday dinner is now officially planned for tonight.

Day 61, 3842 km Balchik, Bulgaria

Nothing like a little sun and sea for rejuvenation! We are waterfront in a cute little resort-like town called Balchik, just north of Varna, Bulgaria. We passed through the border on September 24, again with no troubles – even when Cindy and I were singing Hit the Road, Jack while they checked our passports (we'd found a great radio station!). After the successful crossing, Cindy and I headed on in the van with big ambitions to find a campsite for the night.

For the past month or so, it has been quite difficult to camp, what with lack of open spaces, security and, well, official campgrounds, but our road map looked promising, showing us many tent logos along the sea. In a 100km stretch, the map showed at least four potentials – we were pretty confident that we'd find somewhere to laze for the evening.

Nope. We drove the whole distance seeing no camping and ended up in the big city of Varna, where we had a tricky time finding an info centre, (by the way, KFC came through for us again when it offered a much needed toilet, refreshing juice and a local info package!). Once we did find the tourist info centre, the poor woman helping us didn't know much about camping…

We got back into the van and started back tracking to where the map showed tent sites. In all but one place, there was nothing but dirt and abandoned gas stations. The one place we did find was perfect. It had a security gate to get inside, actual tent sites, looked like showers and everything and - ! ... The men had already gone ahead and booked into a hotel. After the initial shock wore off that we had spent five hours looking for dirt and the guys had given up and found a hotel 30kms up the road, we were excited to learn that the guys had generously left the last sea-facing room to us girls – nice! Except reception thought the two cyclists who'd come in just before Cindy and I, were us and gave them the room...

Luckily, the horseshoe up Wally's butt was working yet again, and he managed to get Cindy and I a room facing the sea – yes, we are spoiled – must be that Walter Charm!

Last night, we had a gorgeous sunset float out on the sea in a boat for an hour. We've decided we like this place so much, we are staying another night!

FYI: our hotel here is only 50 levs (about $50) per night for two: so for a resort town, that is a killer deal, being right on the water. We have paid double that for really crappy hotels, where we had to deal with 'the only hotel in town' prices. They sometimes see us coming a mile away.

With our sponsored van and flash team jackets, we must look like we can afford more because on more than a few occasions, we have been quoted a price and when we've gone to pay the next day, the price has suddenly gone up and no one conveniently speaks English anymore. So it is nice to find little gems like Balchik, Bulgaria!"- Heather's Blog September 26.

Cold Mastika served with Airan is the traditional drink in Bulgaria.

Indeed, at the early birthday dinner Heather is serenaded by the entertainer of the night and the restaurant staff present her with a luscious looking cake complete with a rocket candle - which is un-extinguishable while it's burning, singeing anything near it. Appropriate amounts of alcohol are consumed again and we are introduced to the Bulgarian national drink; Mastika. It is served frozen so it looks like a sparkling silver thickish liquid. As an accompaniment people here drink it with Airan, a salty yoghurt drink unceremoniously served in its commercial plastic container at the table.

Heather's birthday soon becomes an entire weekend celebration in Balchik. Heather arranges a sunset boat cruise in a dinky vessel that needs last minute repairs which require the steering wheel to come off and the dash removed. Troy is worried that he might have to get his hands dirty on this trip.

The boat is really makeshift and David refuses on principle to not come as it is a 'smoker', and not only a possible disaster waiting to happen, but a disgrace to be photographed or filmed on. Heather brings the last bottle of French wine from the support vehicle. It must have been chilled and warmed a hundred times, knocked about but probably still alcoholic. We take lots of photos and enjoy the sunset ride on the bay. Lots of little fishing boats are about, going in or out of the bay, plenty of seabirds, the white cliffs of Balchik in the distance. And above all I enjoy the feeling of being propelled forward without having to pedal.

With the birthday celebrations, the location, the scenery, everything just came together here and we have no intention to leave, ever!

The restaurant at the hotel had accepted the birthday kit which I had purchased for Heather's birthday in the members only store in Constanta. The kit includes a birthday themed tablecloth, hats, cups and so forth, and with a little hand-grease the hotel staff managed to set up a table for the birthday breakfast. The birthday breakfast at a leisurely 9am has us seated at the specially decorated table with balloons and hats, the works! Normally by this time we are on the road, and most of us are starving except for Cindy who is still blow-drying her hair in the girls' room with sea views. Maybe she had to answer a few SMS messages from her daughter Melanie in England as well, but she almost misses the balloon breakfast.

There are no presents as we have not passed any bike shops lately. Had we passed one Troy, David and I had all planned on getting a bike-stand each for her. Not sure how three stands would work. It is what Heather very regularly wished for during the trip but never bought. Presents for our birthdays were just not feasible; the support vehicle is too full as it is already!

Heather is treated to a massage at the Three Star Holiday Beach Hotel nearby to celebrate her birthday. The massages on offer include wine and chocolate wrap, which much to our disappointment are not consumable products. I have to get the chocolate-wrap just to make sure. Cindy tries licking my arm afterwards and discovers I still taste salty. People with CF always taste salty. Lick your baby and if he or she tastes salty it just about the definitive diagnosis of CF (The sweat-test is still used today to be one of the main affirmative tests to diagnose cystic fibrosis). Heather also tries to lick my arm to see if it tastes of chocolate after I come from my wrap experience and is also disappointed. The wine and chocolate used by the masseurs only smell of it, not taste like it.

Being fairly unaccustomed to massages and beauty treatments, I cannot give an educated opinion on what they did, but I must say that the disposable underwear that they made me wear for the chocolate and wine treatments are totally ridiculous, and a waste of time as far as modesty is concerned. It is all very relaxing I must admit.

The following day is another splendid day in paradise, and we are doing our best to repeat yesterday again today! And so I go and sit on a scenic deck in Balchik for another day, with pleasant music playing in the background, free wireless Internet and very affordable prices all round. I have another massage in the hotel across the road. Cindy has early morning skinny-dips in the Black Sea and Heather does not walk up any of the nearby hills despite threatening to do so for her birthday..

With all this treatment, all this relaxation, good food and good company, we all feel a million dollars again and ready for the final assault!

We had started to see an increasing number of road signs along the way ever since reaching the Black Sea, pointing to Istanbul, and we are excited to finally hit the road after our extended break. Now where did we park the bikes…

# ISTANBUL IN SIGHT

Whilst in Balchik I have been trying to organise a welcoming committee for Istanbul. Lucas is keen to have something significant that we can film. Just riding into Istanbul and stopping somewhere, calling it a day, and saying well this is it, now let's go home, is not a good way to end the documentary. My friend Kathy from London had told me she was going to Istanbul to welcome us with her friend Vicente. I call Kathy and tell her about the lady (Laura) from the Dutch Consulate-General whom I had met on the train in Holland. Kathy tells me she will contact them and ask where would be a good place for us to finish in Istanbul given that the Pera Palas Hotel where we had planned to finish might be closed for renovations. The (not so) funny thing was that I had misplaced Laura's business card, nor could I remember her name. When Kathy calls the Consulate General in Istanbul and mentions The Great COFE they immediately know what it is about and connect her to Laura Bins, the head of press and cultural affairs at the mission, my saviour!

Laura tells Kathy that the Pera Palas Hotel where we had intended to finish is certainly not a suitable place to finish the ride. They toy with a few ideas, email me with suggestions, but in the end we all decide on Laura's initial suggestion that the 'palace', which is the Dutch Consulate General, is in an ideal location for us to finish our ride. Laura offers to arrange a private taxi to guide us into the city if necessary, and Kathy tells me that she will arrange for a ribbon and a bottle of Champagne. I imagine the Consulate to be an office in Istanbul somewhere, not a Palace, as Laura calls it.

Heather: "We are by the sea again in Nesebar. Have had lots of huge, long up and down hills with hot temperatures - we love it! Today's 40kms ended with a huge, long downhill where the girls beat the boys and one recorded speed was 62 km/hr!

We are a little surprised, by signs of prostitution everywhere. Young women stand in the bushes on the side of the highway, some clad in barely more than g-strings, waiting for pick-ups. Billboards for malls have a naked woman with a shopping bag barely covering the goods…" – Heather's blog September 29.

We ride to Byala, our next destination before reaching the ancient world heritage city of Nesebar. We again cycle past an awful lot of signs indicating numerous camping grounds, and Heather is jubilant at the prospect. We are certain to be camping tonight! When the usual message complete with GPS location comes from the support vehicle we assume it is a campground. It is not a campground. All the camping grounds turn out to be either closed or just not there, but Troy and Cindy have found us cheap private lodging run by an old lady and her daughter up in the main street of Byala. It is clean and humble, and the price is modest. We get three rooms, each with a little bathroom attached. Heather believes we can comfortably share two rooms, and valiantly offers to sleep on the floor of one of the rooms.

The lady owner of the hotel is concerned about our numbers, and charges us more for the rooms if we sleep more people than beds in them. In the end we get three bedrooms, paying the extra $20 for the luxury. Troy is upset with Heather for having to renegotiate rooms with the lady; he feels she is never happy. Heather is keen to save us all a buck, but none of the others think a few dollars here or there is a big deal if it means the difference between comfort and discomfort.

The trip has cost us close to $100K in airfares, filming equipment, gear, preparation and other costs, so why watch the last pennies. Of course we are always looking to stay in budget accommodation, and not live lavishly, but we need to stay fit and well. Keeping a small group of 6 diverse individuals happy is not always possible, and concessions need to be made, but if the basics are looked after, the finetuning of our relations towards each other is much easier! It is a good thing we can swap roommates and that we can swap driver and navigator positions so that we are not always stuck with the same face every day.

As it is we have a lot of fun together and know each other pretty well by now. Troy puts in a big effort to please us all when choosing a place to stay and feels let down when people complain. He is not in the best of moods today. Heather is happy, she at least tried to not spend too much money. She knows she is at the end of her budget and hates to 'bludge' from us, which is not the case at all as we are a team and we love her for whom she is and what she does. We all put in our everything for this adventure. She has a nice long shower and manages to even keep the toilet paper dry this time!

The food situation in town is miserable, and again we only find beer. Hoping to find food we go for a stroll down the hill towards the sea. It is a long hill, pretty desolate too, it is relatively warm, and the sun is going down steadily. We find a lone restaurant, part of a little hotel, just before reaching the sea shore.

We sit down and order food. It takes forever to come, but we are comfy sitting outside watching the sun go down. Strolling a kilometre up the hill after dinner is slow and painful for me; I huff and puff and cough as Heather, Cindy and Lucas dart and dance along. David and Troy attract less attention, not wanting to come across as loud tourists to the odd group of young local people that pass us going in the other direction. David is on full alert when it is dark and deserted and we all

act like the noisy tourists we are with cameras and phones. And me coughing and spluttering along.

The next morning we try to eat breakfast from the car's supplies, which involves a big food search resulting in a collection of all sorts of rotten and smelly remnants. Cindy takes the chance to throw out all the offensive items and collects the edible ones together and cleans up the mess. It is always difficult to keep the car clean and under control. It is only a little space for six people with our gear squashed in tightly. Everything is packed in tightly during the day, and anything that needs to be accessed generally ends up on the bottom of everything despite careful planning. The cargo area is not ventilated or cooled, which concentrates and adds to the smell! This is one area that David has virtually no control over, much to his annoyance, and I share that feeling a bit – even though I know it would be no better (especially) if I had anything to do with it!

After breakfast, which was supplemented with a bowl of very old almost inedible apples the kind lady caretaker gave us, we get on our bikes and ride again. We are now approaching Nesebar, a town which has a 3,000-year-old historic part located on a rocky peninsula Originally it was a Thracian settlement called Menebria, which at the beginning of the 6th century BC became a Greek colony. The fortress and other relics that survived the ravages of time date back to the Middle Ages when this was an important Byzantine town. In the first few centuries AD it was an important trading city for the Greek empire, but after a few bloody sieges it was occupied by the Romans. Many of the old fortifications, Byzantium structures from the Roman period, can still be seen on this walled part; the Ancient City of

Nesebar. Lately it has become a very popular, and World Heritage listed, tourist destination in Bulgaria.

Day 61, Wednesday September 26 we arrive in Nesebar. It is around 2pm and we all want to do a million things. The hotel is fantastic. So far each Bulgarian hotel has been affordable and comfortable. All that we want to do (all at once) is to eat in the restaurant; drink a beer, swim in the pool, shower, and go into this World Heritage listed Ancient City of Nesebar. We also want to walk on the beach, and somehow we all want to do it together... But you try organising 6 people all with slightly different priorities, and none lucid enough to discuss 'the plan' or wanting to commit to anything 'quite yet'. Makes Lucas' life hard, trying to film us. He can only be in one place at any one time.

On arrival in any given place we are rarely organised or prepared for anything. Occasionally when we all buzz around randomly like that the one hotel room key would end up in one pocket with another room-mate spending hours looking for it. Sometimes five of us end up somewhere and a sixth would feel left out. But at the same time we are all secretly happy to have some 'alone-time'!

Troy and I intend to go with Lucas to the ancient city of Nesebar, but are distracted by the hotel pool and one more beer. Cindy is going silly in the pool and is splashing innocent bystanders with her dive bombs. Lucas leaves us, embarrassed by our loutish behaviour and he will under no circumstances miss out on the sights. He catches a bus into town, 5 kilometres away. Troy and I finish our beer and catch a cab into town 10 minutes later, expecting to catch up with Lucas in the Ancient City.

Boy is this place touristy. Nothing but shops, market stalls and big crowds. There are festivities, dancers, music and some impressive looking ruins and walls amongst it all. We spot restored churches and other, some better some worse, preserved relics. The entire ancient city is surrounded by impressive looking walls. Troy and I sit down in the first touristy square we see, and (miraculously) expect to see Lucas walk past any time. He does not show. We get up and walk through the town, around the sea shore and follow the wall back to the front entrance. I try to convince some good looking girls to pose for a photo with Troy outside the ancient gates, but they refuse. They are modern girls I guess, and not interested in Roman Gods like us.

Nesebar beach has plenty of still usable paper tissues for me...

 Nesebar is the biggest tourist destination that we visit in Bulgaria and on the beach we run into a comparable garbage pile left over from a busy tourist season. I pretend to look for unused tissues. We walk the remaining 3 or so kilometres back to our hotel, a pleasant walk and therapeutic cough. As we finally cross the dunes to the hotel we walk through what appear to be unofficial toilet areas (bushes). I tell Troy how convenient it is to have these toilet areas where tourists leave lots of toilet paper drying in the bushes, which can be re-used! Troy is grossed out!#*#*. I pee in the bushes just to feel like a real tourist.

During our 'time-out' periods we all lazily lounge around, doing whatever we want to do. I for instance have taken a liking to massages here in Bulgaria - due to the price factor. The hotel reception staff in our Nesebar hotel arranges a masseur to give me a massage after dinner, my fourth massage in 3 days I think! I am not normally a massage kind of person, and I think this will be my last one as I have had enough now. I am still in pain from an extra firm therapeutic massage administered by an older woman over a 90 minute torture period in Balchik; it really sorted out knots in my back that I was not aware of.

On leaving Nesebar we stop at a carwash to clean the bikes and the vehicle, in preparation for our arrival in Istanbul. We are not allowed to do it ourselves, so we watch them spray the bikes clean under close supervision of Troy.

The spray they use is so powerful that it spins the pedals so hard that the reflectors fly off them. It is important not to spray directly into the bearing areas, as it will get water in the grease which can have a devastating effect on the bearings. With clean bikes we get on our way, watching the road-signs slowly countdown to Istanbul, battling head winds as we make slow progress along the main road down the Black Sea coast.

As we approach Burgas, a large tourist town, we notice two cyclists coming up behind us. We try and increase the pace a little. Slowly the pair catch up and start passing us. They cycle along with us for a few minutes, riding along on their road bikes and bright cycling clothing. Partially to check our maps, and partially to let them pass we pull over. They stop too and we officially meet. They are amateur cyclists out for a Saturday ride and one speaks a bit of English. We take the opportunity to ask them about the road ahead and explain we like to cycle to Turkey along the Black Sea coast.

Do we have to go inland to Kirklareli? The map shows no other option but to go inland to cross into Turkey. The men advise that we do not need to follow the Black Sea all the way to Carevo as we had planned, and can take the turnoff past Burgas onto the E87 through Krushevets and cut across to Malko Turnovo - the Bulgarian border town where we hope to spend a night before going into Turkey. David looks at the long distances of nothing on the map along the suggested route, takes note of the brown patches and the blue line (creek/river) crossings, and we decide we are not as fit as they think we are and continue along our way following the Black Sea. The men ride ahead of us into Burgas and disappear.

David leads us into Burgas on the main road, using his trusty GPS. We make a few guesses here or there, where the GPS maps do not correspond with reality, and manage to smoothly find our way through town without a hitch. I breathe a sigh of relief as we leave the pollution and the traffic behind.

At the end of the day Troy rewards us with a fantastic little hotel in Sozopol. If we find a hotel that is about €15 per person we thank our lucky stars. We thank our lucky stars again. This time the hotel is on the Southern end of the beach in Sozopol, a scenic Bulgarian Black Sea town. It is a fair hike up the hill from the beach and we are not at all inclined to go to the beach. The view from the hotel is good enough! It was a hard ride in, I was exhausted. This hotel has a Sauna which David and I immediately put our names down for. But first things first, I have struggled hard to cycle the 80 odd kilometres today and enthusiastically jump in the shower of the new looking room and wallow with my dirty laundry.

For some reason I never imagined Bulgaria to be this comfortable and nice. No doubt this Black Sea coast will also take off and get spoiled by the tourists, just like Kosa Mui in Thailand, Benidorm in Spain and the Gold Coast in Australia. As these thoughts fill my brain, the end of the ride, Istanbul, going home and seeing Katherine again, I suddenly remember the sauna.

Time to go and meet David at the Sauna. One problem, no towels in the bathroom. I yell out for Lucas to pass me a towel. These are things that make Lucas squeamish. He panics as he sees no towels in the room. I threaten him to find me a towel or I'll come out naked and go ask the hotel staff myself. Lucas takes me seriously as he already thinks we are all too promiscuous as it is and fears I would probably pull it off and embarrass him.

Worse still he would feel obliged to film it all. Fear radiates from Lucas as he runs screaming down the hallway of the hotel looking for towels. I start a loud count-down starting at ten. Ten, ... Nine,.... and so I count down to 1. I yell out a few random fractions and then Lucas returns with a towel which he shoves through the door with his arm. I put him through his paces sometimes. I think Lucas knows I am just toying with him!

One day he'll get me back, let's wait for that documentary he is going to make of it all! No photoshopping my wrinkles or hiding my belly. CF is my excuse for a pot belly, and wisdom is my excuse for wrinkles. People with CF often have an extended stomach from all the coughing perhaps. I hope Lucas will be kind in portraying me as the good looking young chap that I (mistakenly) still think I am.

Clean, and dry, I make my way downstairs to the spa and meet David there. We sweat it out for about twenty minutes. By the time I am (well) done. Cindy walks in and takes my place. David still has some baking to do. Not long after I find myself sitting at a table on a sunny terrace under a blue sky complete with Black Sea views ordering food and drinks with Troy, Heather and Lucas. As time ticks away Heather is getting suspicious of what is going on in the sauna with David and Cindy, it has been quite some time and we are making up horrible fantasies.

Heather is almost convinced of the fantasy that Troy and I make up with our fertile gutter minds and is disgusted and disappointed and almost upset with the prospect of an illicit relationship within the team. David is after all a respectable married man! I had actually seen David coming out of the spa shortly after me, and knew he was in fact watching TV in his room as we make up horrid fantasies about him and Cindy..

Eventually a water-wrinkled soaked and relaxed Cindy appears on the terrace looking for her prescription glasses. We decide to pick on her by teasing her endlessly about her eye-sight, or lack there-of. Cindy spots the pool and decides to go in. Just as she jumps into the pool we yell at here her, 'Watch out for the pool Cindy!!, Oh Gosh guys, she fell in!'.

In the mean time Troy has made friends with a pregnant cat. After a few beers the cat looks particularly appealing and he tries to pet its pregnant belly. This immediately results in a small scratch on Troy's arm. Given the fear of rabies, something he is acutely aware of he quickly orders another beer to help him through the panic. He survives without contracting rabies on the spot, but he won't know for sure till however long it takes for rabies to incubate in his body. Troy is going to be nervous till he gets home. From now on he is more cautious with the domestic animals.

Later on, in the room, with my laptop I locate a random encrypted Wireless Network that is named 'call this phone number 80123456'. I dial it immediately and speak to a fellow geek. Within minutes we have wireless Internet arranged. Handy to have entrepreneurial geeks in the vicinity. Maybe refrain from electronic banking perhaps, just to be on the safe side, but heck, I do like living on the edge (It is regarded as unsafe to use unofficial access points as all internet traffic can be recorded. Using encrypted websites does make life very difficult for a hacker, but not impossible.

Typically they can read your emails without a worry. I am not worried, I am grateful). When the geek comes to the hotel to pick up the money he charges for the internet access I ask him if he has many people passing like me. He says I am the first! No one understands, not many find out, even when they discover his network they are unable to connect. He obviously is ahead of his time, even for the Western World I am sure. I am so glad to meet a fellow geek that I gladly parted with my money to support him.

We leisurely leave around 9.30am, one of our more leisurely starts, and still get into Carevo, our next stop, at a reasonable time. It is only a 35 kilometre ride but I am stuffed in any case, totally beat. The miles are getting me I think; I am very low on energy and am grateful for a short day. The Black Sea has been much hillier than I had expected.

The road South down the Black Sea Coast is now forested and fast. The hills are getting longer, and we come across a road construction crew. There is a temporary traffic-light, and we stop with the cars. I am always grateful for any forced break, and have no qualms about waiting. We wait for about ten minutes till the very last car travelling in the opposite direction has passed us, and then the man with the flag and the radio allows our direction of traffic to go through the one sealed lane that is left to drive on.

As soon as we get the go ahead we are moved off to the side, on the wide unpaved but firm and rideable unfinished new road surface. Why we did not get told to ride there immediately is a mystery. Perhaps it was a power thing. In any case, I got my breath back, done some farkeling, had a muesli bar, a drink, some nuts, and thanked my lucky stars for the unscheduled but certainly welcome break.

The scenery along the road becomes more scenic, a little too scenic. We start to see the occasional female hitchhiker alongside the road. Skimpily dressed and reasonably attractive I wonder what they are doing there. Turns out these are prostitutes advertising their wares along the road! Certainly looks scary, they could get raped and murdered instead of getting paid by a customer. Lucas is revolted at the thought they are prostitutes and Heather is fascinated. David tries not to look, and I try not to stop. I love talking to interesting people, but this might not be the appropriate kind of interesting person to talk to.

It bothers me that I am so shy in stopping to take photos of people. I know that some of the best photos I have seen in the past include locals, but I get shy when I see people that I really like to photograph. These prostitutes would make great photographs, standing there looking forlorn and desperate. I briefly forget about the pain and strain and try to look tough, not cough and bravely ride through feigning dis-interest.

We observe the odd trucker stop for the bait. Imagine being a truck driver and stopping for a quickie. Would you feel safe in the forest? I would be scared of the ladies' accomplices to rob me or steal my truck! Depending on what the 'quickie' included I would also gravely fear for my health. I now try to forget these women in their bikinis along the side of the forested road that we ride through; I am starting to get nauseous!

Occasionally we now also ride through entire 'clouds' of gnats, the little flies going into my nostrils and I have to watch out not to swallow them by the dozen. If I were to cough in one of these clouds that is what would happen. Great way to eat flies, just cough enough while riding and you are bound to swallow a mouth full of these innocent insects. I take care not to cough too much, and keep my mouth closed. I hypothesise to Lucas that these spots with flies indicate where the prostitutes do their deed. Lucas goes green.

Close to Carevo Troy and Cindy text us the location of a hotel they found for us. I watch my trip computer's odometer clock over to 4000 kilometres. A long distance for a bicycle holiday, and as the digits flick to the three zeroes and the three becomes a four I feel I am accomplishing something really big now, Heather and Lucas are very excited too when they hear we passed the 4000 kilometres.

Four thousand kilometres ago Lucas could not ride his bike! We have come a long way. We ride into town past a deserted tourist office, locked shut and vacated for the season, find Troy and settle in the hotel – on the top floor of course with plenty of stairs to climb.

We have pretty much the whole day here now, which is good as we intend to celebrate Cindy's birthday tonight. We have no idea what we are going to find tomorrow night when it is her actual birthday. Tomorrow we are heading inland towards the Turkish border and we have no idea what we are to find once leaving the touristy Black Sea coast. Images of crashed planes and naughty children chasing us still haunt us.

Shortly after arriving and refreshing we all go our ways. It is clear which direction Cindy goes in as we soon hear the church bells of the little church next door. It is not a Sunday and it is not on the hour. It is Cindy, our birthday girl ringing in another 16th birthday...

Carevo is a more tightly built village, houses closer together, cobblestone streets, wooden houses, and a less touristy feel. The little shops in the streets seem to be geared towards the locals. Lucas heads down a path to the beach for some filming, Troy goes down the stairs for a beer, David and I follow Cindy down the road. We do not want to get her arrested on her birthday. In the end we all end up on the little beach, throwing sand at each other. This would be OK except the sand has a lot of litter in it and it is too cold to get in the water.

For Cindy's birthday dinner we first walk around town hoping to run into a perfect birthday venue. Eventually we veer back towards the port side of town and settle down at the Windmill restaurant where we can sit outside. We enjoy a meal with some birthday ales. David wants to make sure we all eat at the same time this time. He is sick of the mixed up orders that we are always getting, always served at random intervals which ensures that one of us eats early, another late, an appetiser arrives after a dessert and so forth. We always have that happen to us, but David has come up with a theory. He thinks that perhaps it is customary, east of Vienna, for people eating at restaurants to all order the same food. Who knows we have been doing it wrong all along, and maybe this explains why we always have such slow and terrible service, and receiving botched up food orders. David discusses our requests and sensibly orders the same courses for all of us. It is a bit of a birthday dinner and he orders lots. We wait with abated breath. We are hungry. We are served more beers... We wait... Eventually one bowl of soup arrives, and no more. Cindy gets it. She has to start it before it gets cold. Two plates of schnitzel and another bowl of soup arrives. Some pieces of bread five minutes later,... and so our food dribbles in as per usual until we have all been fed over a two hour period. That blows that theory.

The desserts at our own hotel seemed more appetising then what we see on the menu here, so it is back to our hotel. Walking up the ramp from the port into the empty cobble stoned streets I huff and puff away and Cindy is excessively jubilant about having survived another year of living dangerously. She tries to push her luck. David has to physically restrain her from climbing a flagpole at the local council office. She wants to retrieve a Bulgarian flag. Fortunately we all arrive at our hotel together and without getting arrested. Like Troy says she makes a pretty good 16 year old for someone who will in not too many years be heading into her 5th decade. Long live Cindy!

We consume a few desserts each to celebrate Cindy's birthday and to ensure we sleep well before the big ride ahead we sample some fancy local drinks, the umbrella kind. Even Lucas gets into the alcohol tonight, although he does not show it. He proclaims to be drunk, but he could have fooled us seasoned drinkers who think he is quite sober. It is all relative. We are leaving the Black Sea, we are excited.

No rest for the wicked as they say, and we push on early the next morning to leave the by now familiar Black Sea shore and head inlands into the unknown. It has been a good for us for the past 10 days with reasonably good roads, reasonably good weather, great places to stay, good food,... We will miss Bulgaria; we were all impressed by this country – even though we only cycled through the touristy Black Sea part of it. We all hope to revisit the Black Sea coast in the future again.

We have reason to believe that the terrain going inland to the Turkish border is going to be tough and we like to make the ride as small as possible that day. David has seen on the map that we are going to cross some big creeks and rivers, meaning we need to ride up and down and in and out of valleys. The map has ominous looking brown patches on it.

It is Monday 1 October today, day 66 on the road. Today I will also start back on oral antibiotics in preparation for the next few weeks. In Istanbul I can expect lack of exercise and an abundance of pollution, and after that driving 3000km back to Amsterdam is not exactly what my lungs need, and not to mention flying home in a plane for 36 hours or more... The end of the ride really is nigh!

David had studied the meagre maps more and more and was getting increasingly worried about the road into Turkey. There really is no way we can avoid going inland to Kirklareli in Turkey. It looks so inviting to just ride on along the coast, cross into Turkey, and follow the coast till you come to the Bosphorus River which you follow down to Istanbul. Alas, there are no roads. I had checked this carefully in my trip preparations and had also come to the conclusion that Kirklareli is the only way to go. David has come to the conclusion it will also be hilly. The rivers running across our path (not alongside our path) indicate hills, and this theory is supported by the green and sometimes brown shaded areas on our road map.

On this map we can see one last Bulgarian town before the Turkish border; Malko Turnovo. We plan to spend the night there if it has a hotel. Heather secretly buys a cake for Cindy before we leave. Only Troy knows, and mum's the word.

If only we could follow the Black Sea into Turkey... For some reason the only Turkish border is inland at Kirklareli.

East of the border, our last and least camp.

Sure enough we barely left Carevo and the road starts winding and heads up and down... It is tough riding, hill after hill after hill. The forests are wonderfully fertile and thick. The road is quiet and has a nice surface. I cough up each hill slowly and race down the other side. It is pretty tough and we are not making great progress, the single digit speed on my bike computer agrees. We ride through some more clouds of gnats, but see no more prostitutes anywhere near.

We do see some kids in the bushes along the road, and David fears we'll get chased again. In any case we are not going to stop anywhere near them or near any other small settlement. We ride past a few very poor looking villages that look more like inhabited dumps or ruins of old houses where handfuls of people are congregating. We see the odd tent and caravan there too. Kids and dogs running around complete the picture. We think they are Gypsies – not that there is anything wrong with that! (In reference to Seinfeld's fifty-seventh episode 'The Outing') The kids seem friendly and wave, the dogs are enthusiastic too and trot along with us, seemingly friendly. The dogs are probably hoping to meet Heather, but she is in the vehicle with Troy today.

The hills go up and down and also get bigger and bigger. The downhill rides are awesome but each uphill stretch is harder than the preceding one. I am getting hungry. Losing my mojo. A message comes in from Troy; he is having trouble finding anything in Malko Turnovo.

We call the car at 130pm, hoping to get rescued with food. Heather, who is navigating today, tells me we should be able to get some lunch at the markets they had seen in Malko Turnovo, but there is no hotel. Troy suggests we not waste our time and head straight for the border, 10 kilometres past the town further up the hills. I ask if they can make it back to us so we can raid the vehicle for lunch. Troy explains he is out of Bulgaria and just waiting for the Turkish customs as we speak, and he thinks it is too late to turn around now. They will look for accommodation on the Turkish side. We are spread over two different countries now, and this does not sound good to me. The Turkish township of Kirklareli is another 25 kilometres from the Turkish border, presumably downhill as Troy tells us it is all uphill to the Turkish border which is situated on top of a ridge some 750 metres high.

We are hungry and tired and have another 15 kilometres to go before we possibly get to a market that may or may not have food.

In the mean time Cindy's phone is making text sounds and ringing often. Her phone, as is Troy's, is often buzzing and jingling with text messages from loved ones, but today Cindy is getting actual calls as well! They are birthday calls and messages from friends and family. Some calls are from her daughter Mel(anie). Mel is living and working in London but on the spur of the moment decides to try and meet us in Istanbul. The logistics are difficult to arrange as we are arriving in not too many days (is it really that close to the end?). Daughter Mel is making frantic last minute arrangements and updating Cindy regularly. We cycle up each next hill, around each next corner, over each next bridge, and make our way closer to Turkey. Troy texts us; he is having a hard time finding accommodation in the first town across the border, Derekoy.

At 2:30pm we arrive in Malko Tornovo. As we ride into town we notice a large tourist map on the side of the road, and it shows two hotels. We ride a little bit further and see a tiny shop. With a rumbling stomach I stop and frantically start searching the one little shop for lunch ingredients. The chance of finding something edible here is pretty slim - unless we settle for tinned food. I try to explain to the lady we need some lunch, and miraculously she understands and tells me to continue another hundred metres down the road to the restaurant! And so we end up in a quaint little restaurant, where we actually find nice food! We are greeted by an English speaking fellow diner with his kid. The man who introduces himself as Milka speaks fluent English! He is surprised to see foreigners in his town and asks us if we are staying in the newly renovated hotel in town. Oh how I wished Troy had run into this guy! He is a marathon runner on the international circuit, working here as a teacher. With all the mountains around I can imagine how he stays fit.

Troy calls us when he receives an offer to camp on somebody's land just past Derekoy, and he is asking if we would be happy doing that. We cannot give him advice as we are still in Bulgaria about to cycle up to the border, and have no idea what the Turkish people on the other side are like. We envisage a small poor village like the ones we are reluctant to stop at even for lunch. Now what is going to happen to us tonight, it will be getting dark in 2 or 3 hours.

Well fed we reluctantly climb back on the bicycles around 3pm. We are on our way up the hill to the border crossing ten kilometres away. David is worried we will reach the border too close to closing time which might cause complications. There is no support vehicle to come to the rescue now.

In my lowest possible tree climbing gear I make the ascent to the border. Lucas is on my heels, stopping regularly to film the scenery and catching up to me each time. Troy sometimes reminds Lucas that he should ride ahead of me so I can get some draught off him as he is obviously much fitter then me. But Lucas has to stop regularly to film the changing landscape, and then race up to me to film me coughing up my meal... I am sure he is pushing himself hard to get all that footage. In any case, riding behind Lucas is a little tricky as he is not as steady on his bike yet and rides less smoothly. This means that if you follow him closely you risk bumping into him. I have the same problem with Heather. She likes to have an occasional good stretch on her bike as she rides along. A Heather-stretch involves stopping with pedalling, a few occasional erratic turns followed by a foot off the pedals and swing-of-the-hips stretch. If I am too close to her I run into her rear end. So drafting is perhaps a good idea in the Tour de France, but not too practical for us amateurs having fun! David is a very steady rider and I don't mind drafting off him – that is if I can keep my speed up and stay within spitting distance of him. In any case, we rarely manage to effectively draught off each other. It is nice of Troy to think of these issues, he is a thoughtful man; I am pleased he is with us.

This part of the ride, approaching the Turkish border, just like the first part of our day, is extremely scenic. There are great hills and trees, drifting clouds, fresh air, minimal traffic, and so we slowly approach the border.

Four o'clock we make it to the border and find a surprising number of buildings there. All looking very official, and terribly confusing. There is a tourist bus with Bulgarian tourists waiting to cross. Custom agents point us towards another building, they only do busses. The officers at the next building points us back to a third building we had cycled around, the actual customs office. It is a huge building, cavernous inside. At this time it is empty and sounds echo around it. I see a money exchange point, duty free shops that are closed now, and a closed restaurant across the road. I change some money. This is the first country where we have to pay for visas to enter. Australia does it to foreigners too.

I had not expected that the ride inland from the Black Sea to Turkey was going to be this hard! I believe we climbed three mountain ranges ending up at a border crossing around the 700+ metres. It was worth the climb, we are crossing into the country of our destination!

Speeding down the road, barely staying within the dividing line on the road, hitting the high forties we see some raised eyebrows from green official looking custom vehicles that we narrowly avoid on the way up. We are flying down the mountain towards where Troy and Heather have set up camp alongside the road!

The village of Derekoy that we soon get to is totally different from all the Bulgarian towns we were accustomed to. It is not a tourist area that is obvious. The little main street that we ride through is full of friendly waving people, young and old. We dare not stop. It is late and it looks like we might be mopped by friendly inquisitive people. We are too worried about where we will find Troy! We have coordinates punched into David's GPS.

No trouble spotting Troy, only a couple of kilometres further downhill from the village we see the tents set up on someone's land alongside the road. It is 6pm and we are exhausted. We had cycled 78 hard kilometres and my knees are a little wobbly by now. Heather and Troy are waiting for us at the tents. It is always most appreciated when the support vehicle sets up the tents for us as it is the last thing you feel like doing when you flop off your bike feeling like jelly!

We immediately start our frantic farkeling. Farkeling as you may have gathered is the term we have all adopted by now. It is meant to describe the packing and unpacking of bits and pieces in a random order, trying to get things arranged for departure or in preparation of leaving the bikes. I am the king of Farkelers, much to David's annoyance. David is lousy at farkeling; he knows where everything is and is well organised. Organisation has been crucial to his past careers where life and death depended on quick action and organisation.

As we farkel with our gear Troy and Heather drive up the hill to the township to get dinner and beverages. They were not keen to leave the tents set up unattended, and were not keen to split up. Lucky we had exchanged some money at the border because this place is most certainly not going to accept credit cards. We are in a very rural area, still way up in the mountains, and we are attracting a lot of attention just cycling through town.

As expected Troy and Heather get ambushed by friendly Turkish people and are immediately shown where to buy beer. With the help of half the village they eventually return with beers and kebabs.

Day 70, 4,213 km, Pinarhisar, Turkey

Can it be true? Only three more days until what will surely be a teary ride into Istanbul. How is this possible? It was just a couple days ago that we were halfway, wasn't it?

I don't think it has really hit any of us yet as we have just entered our last country – Turkey - and it always feels exciting to enter new territory and spot the differences. This time, it is bordering on extreme. Having spent the last week feeling like we'd stumbled into all-inclusive vacation resorts along the Black Sea, we are once again confronted with adventure as we search small, crowded towns for obscure hotels and find the only restaurant in town with hopes the food is decent.

The border crossing into Turkey was more complicated than any of our crossings to-date, though the people offer easy smiles and are very welcoming. Today, a nice man waved us into a café for coffee and then paid for it.

Turkey is the first country we were required to purchase Visas for entry. While the Australian's got away with paying 15 Euros each, I had to pay 45 Euros for my Canadian status.

The riders this day were Walter, Lucas, David and Cindy and they had a longer day than the 54km first expected. Troy and I had little luck finding a hotel in the original destination on the Bulgarian side, and so made an executive decision to see what the next town had to offer. This meant going through the border and subsequently stalled the riders by at least an hour.

When Troy and I pulled into the next town, it was much smaller than the last Bulgarian one. I went into a shop to ask the man if there was a hotel nearby and he said no, but the Turks are not ones to watch idly while a visitor suffers. The next thing I knew, there were five or six people around me and three around the car, all offering us any help they could. Of course, it was all in Turkish, but one man did speak English and soon we were escorted to another man's fish farm one kilometre down the road where we were urged to camp for the night.

Camping is fun and all, but this night, not so much. It would save us the cost of a hotel, but it was hard to watch the faces of our tired rider's when they showed up and surveyed the scene: three tents perched on uneven ground, not a drop of water for showers or toilet needs in sight and the worst part, it was Cindy's birthday and we hadn't secured a beer stash yet!

Troy and I left the team to 'get comfortable' and drove back into the nearby town where we immediately got escorted to a restaurant and a nice woman made us kebabs-to-go. A young man did a beer run. Luckily, the Bulgarian town we had stayed at the previous night had a good store and we were able to get Cindy a yummy cake that survived the day in the car.

We drove back to the team who didn't look much happier than when we'd left and tried to brighten their mood with food and beverages. Birthday or not, the night ended early and we were all asleep before 10pm, that is until a stray dog woke some of us up with its midnight prowl through the garbage bag we left out...ooops." - Heather's blog, 3 October 2007.

The campsite is frequented by the odd random person arriving on mopeds that occasionally ride through our grassy area and return with fish. Turns out the land we are on is part of a fish farm of sorts. We do not venture into the nearby fish farm as we are too buggered to meet people and try and make ourselves understood with pleasantries. A man arrives on a small motorbike and picks up a vehicle parked in the grass nearby. The car looks like a taxi, he must be starting his night shift.

Cyclists like us are rare as hen's teeth in this area, but just after we arrived we see these two cyclists heading the other way, up the hill towards Bulgaria. We would love to stop them and quiz them about the road they have just come from. It is past

6pm, and I am sure they are frantically trying to get somewhere for the night. We give them a friendly wave.

There are no toilets, and there is no running water, and tonight is Cindy's actual birthday! We sure chose a good spot to celebrate it. All pretending to have forgotten the birthday we sit on our colourful rubber backed picnic mat and eat our kebabs like a hungry pack of wolves, washing it down with Turkish beer. Troy sadly reports that this is the first time that beer here is actually the more expensive choice of beverage, and that water and soft drinks are now cheaper. We sadly take note of this alarming fact, and mentally prepare ourselves for de-tox in Turkey

After our Turkish non-schnitzel meal David and Heather start farkeling at the back of the car, Troy joins them, and one by one we get all of us except Cindy at the back of the car. We have a cake waiting, complete with candles. Heather had managed to not only find a cake in Bulgaria, but also keep it out of harm's way and undamaged throughout the day in the fully stuffed support vehicle.

I call out to Cindy; 'Cindy, is this your bag? Can you move it?' She probably thinks there is something bad, as we all stand around looking into the car. This is all she needs on her birthday, complaints from a team ganging up on her. Wasn't the fuss with Mel enough? Mel is not coming now; it is just too hard to arrange this short notice.

So when Cindy reluctantly comes over and sees the cake she is pleasantly surprised. We lit the candles before she came and now sing her a happy birthday. We eat the cake for dessert, and bring out the alcoholic beverages that we still have hiding in the car: leftover slivovitz, vodka and other nasty stuff. And before we knew what was happening Cindy was singing, 'It's my party, and I'll cry if I want to...', with a bottle of Jim Beam in her hand when a tired looking couple on bicycles rides into our makeshift camp. It is the same people from a couple of hours ago. They obviously had no luck finding a place to stay and rode back down to where we are camped.  Losing altitude, especially with full gear on the bikes, is not a desirable thing to do straight after lugging it up a hill. It is pretty much dark now. Immediately we invite them to camp with us. It is a young Polish couple who are cycling from Istanbul back to Poland. They set up their tent on the other side of the non-functional overgrown old water-well that we are camping next to, and we give them beer and cake. Safety in numbers is also what we are thinking as well as 'do unto thy neighbour'.

# WELCOME TO TURKEY!

The playing cards come out, and the fellow Polish riders join in. David and I crawl into our tent for an early night. The real reason that I think we retire early is because there is no cold beer, and besides, we are exhausted. David's own secret reason for sleep is that he has no trust in the non-secured campground arrangement we have.

Any sleep he can get before shit hits the fan would be gold. Disaster is inevitable, or at least a high chance. Why would people ask us to camp in their run-down paddock like this unless they wanted to come back with the dudes and machetes! It is our first night in Turkey, anything can happen.

Listening to the others playing cards we almost doze off when we hear a moped arrive. David, fully on alert even when asleep is ready for the unexpected, and he immediately expresses an expletive. He assumes that if this is not the gang of thugs, at best this means stranger(s) are coming into camp, and with the alcohol going around deduced that it will likely end in trouble for us. David is more aware than others of potential problems because of his policing background. He rarely gets called out to happy campers playing cards, but usually to a crime scene, which could well be a remote piece of land next to an abandoned well where hitchhikers (or cyclists) were camping till they got murdered... This also explains why David's hair is more salt than pepper.

Whoever showed up on the moped fortunately is not troubling the party. The person does whatever he has to do, visiting the fish farm or picking up another overgrown taxi from the paddock. Danger passes, we fall asleep again.

I sleep instantly at any given time, even during the day I can lie down and nap. I call these naps man-naps; it is hard work just being a man – or at least that is how I explain it. Maybe my higher blood sugar levels have something to do with that. I will address that back in Australia. Not long now!

We wake up with the sun and all have to use a toilet. There is no toilet. A stark reminder to the fact we are in our first primitive camp of the ride. Every other occasion we were able to ride the distance to an official campground or a hotel, but last night, smack bank on Cindy's birthday, we had to rough it. Naturally all of us had expected to do this on many occasions, and the fact we have been able to avoid it all this time does not make it much easier to deal with. We are not used to it, and the support vehicle is unprepared. We have no breakfast either. This is what a cycling adventure is all about, we try reminding ourselves, as we straighten our sore backs and dream of coffee, a bathroom and breakfast.

I walk away from the tents and cross the road to the other side to find a quiet spot to do my morning business. At some point on this mini-outing I glance backwards to the tents to appreciate the scene, take it in and amuse myself with possibly the only road-side camp of our trip for future memories. I crane my neck and feel something strain. I find a stick to dig a little shallow grave and successfully make a humble contribution to the environment and modestly cover it with foliage for some innocent person to step on. My neck has now become stiff and sore. My stomach rumbles.

We exchange information with the Polish cyclists, tell them what to expect on their way into Bulgaria, and in return they tell us what we can expect on our way into Turkey. They had come from Istanbul and just followed the major highways. Apparently they thought that was OK. They tell us there is ample space to cycle on but the heavy traffic flying by is friendly to cyclists. This is not our cup of tea! Unfortunately they also report lots of ups and downs to Kirklareli, where we plan to have breakfast. It is the next major town and we hoped it was going to be downhill.

We start our day with empty stomachs. My emergency caffeine (and guarana spiked) power drinks are all finished. Now would be an ideal time to gulp down one of these energy drinks that I usually have in the support vehicle exactly for such 'emergencies'. The energy drinks have come to my salvation on several occasions when there was no coffee or should I say no adequate coffee. The caffeine content of these drinks acts as a fine substitute and lifts my mood immensely in the mornings when I have trouble waking up. This is my regular status quo, even at home. I wake up slowly. Maybe this is the process of re-oxygenation of my body, or maybe I am just not a morning person. But this morning I find I had run out of the caffeine loaded coffee substitutes. My last one was consumed yesterday on the way up the mountains.

Troy cruises off with Cindy to scout for breakfast opportunities. We cycle up a few hills and down a few hills, and after about an hour, on a good little downhill stretch, we see the support vehicle on the side of the road in front of a corner. Desperate for breakfast I still manage to pull a funny and fly past the car and around the corner out of view. I see Troy looking at me, starting to raise his hand and watching me disappear with disbelief wondering if he had to chase after me or wait for me to realise my mistake and cycle back up the hill. Of course I stop around the corner and re-appear at the vehicle in seconds.

Troy and Cindy had breakfast of sorts for us, consisting of strange sausage, strange bread, some juice and some water. Greedily we consume. The vehicle is searched for any other leftovers, but none is found. No coffee, still no caffeine drink. I am craving a cuppa!

After breakfast we cycle up a few more hills, but eventually come to an amazingly long and fast downhill section with little traffic on it. We cruise at a fat 40km/hr pace towards the town of Kirklareli, from where we had planned to head back to the Black Sea and follow it to the Bosphorus river. Now that we know how bad these brown patches on the map can be we expect this to be a hilly detour and we decide against it. With road signs telling us Istanbul is only about 200 kilometres away we just want to get there without getting troubled by mountain ranges of possibly 700 metres high. Fortunately there are lots of little roads and we will not have to drive on busy highways, although we may need to ride more than the posted 200kms to get to Istanbul if we follow the minor roads.

We bypass the fairly major town of Kirklareli as our route does not take us through it, but just skirts past. We had our breakfast and we feel we should be on our way and not make more detours. Though I am seriously hanging out for a cup of coffee, a cup of Turkish coffee, one of those your spoon can stand up straight in, but we are not passing any cafes. David is desperate for a detailed roadmap of Western Turkey. We do have a big fold-out map of Turkey with us, but on a map that covers Turkey, a country that is more than 1000 miles wide, the small roads we want to cycle on are barely mentioned, if at all.

We have seen not one cafe or shop along the road, even though we are now riding on fairly busy roads passing Kirklareli. Coffee coffee coffee, my brain screams coffee. Without coffee my mornings are just not right.

I alert the others about my urgent need to stop at the first place we see. David concurs, he needs his coffee too. Heather and Lucas do not understand the gravity of the situation. I keep a sharp eye out for anything that looks like café, and eventually about 10 kilometres out of Kirklareli as we enter a little township called Kizilcikdere we spot one.

It appears to be full of old men that are eyeing us curiously, and there appears to be no spare table. All eyes are upon us, and we quickly decide to hop back on the bikes and continue. It does look like there might be more coming up shortly - we see small crowds of people in the streets of Kizilcikdere. Eventually we see a quiet little café, with only a few people in it. There we finally stop for our coffee, and this is the first time we socialise with Turkish people.

Very very friendly people, wanting to buy our coffees, and trying hard to talk to us. Communication is very difficult as English and Turkish are very different. We see mostly men in the streets here, women appear to be the minority. The men are very friendly, and they team up with the one Turkish man who speaks a little English. We cannot possibly start explaining about Cystic Fibrosis, so we try to tell them that we are cycling from Paris to Istanbul and come from Australia and Canada.

The writing on our jerseys is not exactly clear to the men either as their alphabet is quite different from ours, although it looks close. Turkish script is interesting. They have changed their script many a times through history, ranging from the original Orkhon script to Arab and Cyrillic alphabets. The current Latin based variety now in use was not implemented till Ataturk's cultural reforms in the early 20th Century. It does not have the letters Q, W and X in it.

The coffee we are served is believe it or not, Nescafe. Nescafe is not meant to be served in a tiny little glass with lots of sugar, and this certainly does not satisfy my urgent needs. We are not allowed to pay. We get on the bikes, and on our way. My coffee thirst is not quenched.

We cycle on, past army bases, past garbage dumps with burning incinerators, through clouds of pollution and through fields of sunflowers. Sunflowers are still a common sight on our trip, and, presumably because of the southern location of Turkey, these flowers are still blooming as opposed to the wilting ones we saw a month ago after leaving Vienna.

We stop in every place where I think we can find coffee, and every place where David thinks he might find a map. Turkish people do not appear to use road maps, or if they do it certainly appears to be a covert operation, nobody knows where to get one. The names of the towns are now virtually unpronounceable for us, even though the script is very much phonetically equivalent to their language.

The town we cycled into after our 'coffee break' is called Űsküpdere, and then there is one called Kizilcikdere. There are large Turkish flags hanging in these towns, and we now see mosques instead of churches. We feel far from Paris, and very far from home. We really have cycled across a continent, a satisfying feeling to make it this far.

The roadside is dusty and the hills are mostly barren here. There are bigger dogs, but they do not seem to chase us too much, except for Heather who already had a dog chase of sorts this morning straight after breakfast. We almost don't count her dog chases anymore, they are too frequent. Heather on the other hand has a frighteningly clear recollection of each of these chases. The rain has held back for us, and we slowly wind our way through the countryside with Istanbul in our sights. One thing we notice is the increase of rubbish along the roads, especially when approaching the towns. It has been getting progressively worse ever since leaving Hungary, but now it is getting ridiculous! Tractors ploughing the fields have plastic bags blowing past them, and all fences along the road are decorated with colourful litter.

We ride through Kaynarca when I spot a promising looking café. Enthusiastically I jump of the bike and inquire within. From what they tell me I gather they only have Nescafe instant coffee. In the mean time David is enquiring for maps at a large petrol station across the road. No luck for him either, but he did find English speaking Turks. They are friendly, and try to show us the way. We are not lost, but just want to have some detailed local maps to ensure we are on the best possible route for the bicycle, away from the traffic yet heading in a desirable direction. I wonder if I could ask them how to ask for normal Turkish coffee in Turkish. Turkish words are difficult for us westerners.

The word for thank you is teşekkür ederim. We always make a point to learn some local words of the prevailing languages, but after having tried to master one or two pleasantries in Serbian, Croatian, Romanian, Bulgarian, not to mention the French and German ones, it is getting harder and harder not to mix them all up in our heads. Anyway, the friendly Turks try to teach me how to say it, but it is a lost cause.

They point to the café I had just come out of, and lead us back across the road and order Turkish coffee. We get Turkish coffee, or at least some kind of Turkish coffee. Maybe it was made weaker for us foreigners.

# ANOTHER CREDIT CARD DRAMA!

Troy awaits us at a hotel in the main part of the next town, Pinarhisar. The town feels distinctly non-Western, we are close to leaving Europe, and are heading for Eurasia!

Hotel Onder that Troy had found is good, and we should consider staying here despite it being only 1pm and we have only done 65 odd kilometres. There is no accommodation in Vize, 25 kilometres further down the road and the one after that is another 25 kilometres past Vize. We do not want to arrive in Istanbul too early either.

Lucas tells us how he filmed the manager asleep behind the desk on arrival in the hotel, and waking him up. The sleepy hotel manager and his son, who appears out of nowhere, are very friendly and let us use their one and only computer to access the Internet for our blog. After we farkel long enough to get comfortable in our rooms we go looking for a late lunch. We find lunch in a little lokanta. I ask for Ayran, my favourite salty yoghurt drink which I know they have in Turkey. When I was in Turkey as a young back packer almost 20 years ago, I saw a street vendor selling Ayran in the street. Thinking it was milk I bought a glass and was surprised to discover it was a salty thin yogurt drink. It is an acquired taste, and I really do like it, especially with a meal.

We sit down and the waiter walks up to us within a minute, and asks if we want chicken. We say yes. The chicken served with rice comes quick and tastes good. We certainly welcome the change of schnitzel based food.

Happy as a pig in mud not having to struggle with menus and getting decent plain food quickly we ask for the bill. The bill is a shock. We suspect we are taken for a ride. It is about $20 per person, and this little plain looking restaurant with plastic table cloths, nothing fancy, sure does not look like an expensive place to eat. We just pay and leave.

When we return to our hotel Lucas and I find the young teenage son in our room, hanging out the window swinging a string. For some reason he has to get some key to another room where somebody is locked in, or at least that is what I understand from the hand and word gestures. In the end I decide to hang out the window and throw this key on a string to another person hanging out another window.

With my successful throw I am now roped into throwing a long computer cable along the same way; no idea what they are doing. It is fun helping them throw things around outside the window, although it is worrying to find a young kid in our hotel room full of electronic toys that we cannot easily hide or keep discreet!

After all this excitement I get my still stiff neck rubbed by Cindy. Cindy is busy massaging all of us, as we'd all had a bit of a hard ride these last few days. Cindy was suffering too, but none of us are offering to rub her back or neck. David occasionally offers to massage her a bit. I wished I could help her out, but I equate giving massages to sex, even my dear wife Katherine does not ask for massages anymore as she claims that when she really is in need of a massage I can't keep my mind on the job for more than one minute. I should leave massaging to the professionals. After my neck rub I go out looking for a SIM card so I can have a local mobile phone to use for Turkey. This is our first Turkish town where I have the opportunity to get a local phone, and it is important that I find a SIM chip quick smart. We have serious planning to do prior to arrival in Istanbul, which will certainly involve the telephone.

Getting a SIM chip proves to be much more difficult than in the other countries. First of all there is the language barrier, which is much more severe than any other place we had come to, resulting in great confusion at the local phone shops. In the first phone shop I ask for a prepaid mobile phone chip and being pretty sure I am buying the correct product I start filling in the multitude of forms the shop assistant gives me. A surprising amount of paperwork for a mere prepaid mobile phone, and the questions ask for my bank account details and mother maiden names. It occurs to me that I could possibly be filling in the paper work for a 10 year contract, and not a prepaid SIM. I quickly abort the mission. Maybe I should just relax in the hotel room, just like the others.

Before going for dinner I ask the hotel manager for 'restaurant' advice, asking him how much we can expect to pay for a basic meal. Although we have trouble communicating he does seem to agree that $10-$20 per person is pretty normal. He asks the key-throwing son to walk us to a recommended restaurant in town for us to have dinner. The kid takes us to the same restaurant. We walk to a neighbouring restaurant. We are all given food in a matter of minutes, and again not really given a choice. It is nice and plain, and again it is a good meal for us. We even indulge in the dessert we are offered. It is almost as if the waiters are giving the food away, it comes so easily without seeing menus, without too many questions. We like it. Although the food is fresh and plentiful, it is not exactly Turkish like we had hoped, but maybe this is just what we need. David had a bad belly for over a week, and this food is only going to be good, being non fatty, reasonably fresh and healthy. I think we were very spoiled in Bulgaria with modest pricing and excellent hotels. We pay our $20 per person with a smile.

David and I decide to go find a cool beverage after dinner and wander off to look for an establishment that might serve it. You can buy beer anywhere in these Turkish streets, from little one room shops attended by kids to the larger stores, but to find a pub is more difficult. We find one and as we walk in are greeted by a thick blue cloud of oppressive cigarette smoke. Trying to peer through the unhealthy atmosphere we see no one in the pub except the bar-man; smoking. Turkish tobacco seems to be on par with French tobacco. Being a sucker for punishment we continue with our quest for beer. Like the food in this town, the beer choice is pretty much confined to one brand; Efes Pilsen. We get one, drink it down and get out before we choke.

David retires to the hotel and I venture out to find a phone SIM again. This time I am lucky to find an English speaking customer in one of the shops, and when I am again confronted with the same forms as in the afternoon I can ask the kind customer to clarify the situation. He assures me that this is normal procedure for obtaining a prepaid SIM chip.

It is amazing how the whole world has accepted serious privacy invasion on all fronts in the name of national security and the war against terror.

Patiently filling out all the personal details that the form demands, the friendly English speaking customer translates for the shopkeeper that my new SIM will not be activated for a few hours, and perhaps not until the next morning.

A few hours later when playing cards in the hotel room my phone starts working, and I appear to be on a prepaid plan. As soon as I realise the phone is up and running I load the phone up with credits and immediately send a text message to Kathy in London to see if she has any news on our arrival plan. She tells me her tickets are in order and that her Spanish mate Vicente is also coming! Cool, I like Vicente.

We are all excited to be so close to our final destination, and we cannot wait to get on the bikes in the morning. We swallow the hotel breakfast in quick gulps; white bread and jam, tea and fake Turkish coffee (instant coffee in small cups) on request. A quick checkout with cash and we are on our bikes heading for Istanbul. There are plenty of long hills and lots of wind. The wind is not blowing in entirely the correct direction, and progress is slow. This is going to be a long day. The basic maps we have show lots of brown patches, indicating hills, and we are in for some serious riding in the next few days.

Troy and Cindy meet us along the road as we ride into Saray for lunch. We rode 45 kilometres so far. Troy tells us there is not much in the form of accommodation before we hit Istanbul from what he gathers. I have had enough for one day, a common feeling as the mornings are always the hardest. Troy finds us a comfortable hotel, hotel Viyana and we check in before we even find lunch. Once again we have two rooms. I get to sleep with the women folks this time. Scary! Scary for them perhaps. They are scared of my toilet smells I think. In fact I have less trouble with my guts then most of the others. By the time we left Romania it got so bad for all of us that Cindy often asked us, at breakfast, what number we were on a scale of 1-10, where 10 represents a perfect bowel movement and 1 represents liquid and 'uncontrollable'.

The numbers were regularly below five and some of us were close to zero. How you cycle with that kind of bowel issue is beyond me. Thank goodness I can take pancreatic enzymes that digest my food better! I still out-smell them! I don't think I smell that bad, but I am assured by people I travel with that I do smell! At least I am regular as clockwork and have no worries with my digestion as long as I take my 10-20 pills a day!  It is especially typical for young people with Cystic Fibrosis to have digestion and belly issues, but as you get older and know exactly how your digestion works, what it likes and doesn't like, digestion is less and less an issue. I also seem to notice that when my lungs are bad my stomach (read stools) is particularly good, and the opposite also applies to some extent.

The pancreatic enzymes that I bought along the way are different to what I usually use; the various brands all have different mixes of the various types of enzymes. One has more lipase, the other more protease, and so on. Hard to say which one is stronger or weaker, leaving me to guess the right amounts. The juggling of enzymes is not too difficult as it is more problematic to take too few than too many. They are just dehydrated pig organs – therapeutic meat!

And so I move on to the subject of food and credit cards again. Across the road from our comfy Turkish hotel is a supermarket. Considering the hotel has no food or drinks available it seems appropriate for me to investigate this supermarket. Wow, what an amazing discovery. Not since Vienna have I seen such a well stocked supermarket. This is it, they even accept my American Express card and I go berserk. Buying all sorts of snacks ranging from Turkish delights to fresh figs and everything in between. They even sell some cold beverages to our liking; Efes. I am out of control, especially since we are just about to walk into town to find a Turkish café, and we are not planning on sitting in a hotel room pigging out on groceries.

As I walk across the street with my bags of groceries I find most of the team gathered in the hotel lobby ready to investigate the town of Saray. On our ride in we had noticed some festive looking vegetable and fruit markets; apparently Wednesday is market day here. If our hotel was a little closer we would have checked it out. But as is the norm, our bicycles are securely locked away in a garage behind the hotel and not to be seen again till the morning. My groceries now attract interest and we go up to the room to check out the delicacies. David is disappointed that we need to eat strange foods in a hotel room instead of checking out this cool town. He is pretty right, but this booty of interesting food peeked our interests, and checking out town can wait till we go on our dinner mission in a few hours. We indulge in fresh figs and chickpeas.

The next few hours are spent drinking beer and snacking. We spoil our appetite for dinner, but David had gone out and scouted out a couple of suitable places for us to eat where we can see the food and hopefully point at what we want. David has a plan of attack, and come 6pm - with half filled bellies - we dutifully head out to check the scene. We are stuffed with snacks. Restaurants are still not as cheap as they were in Romania and Bulgaria, but we are getting used to the prices now. The food is good, complete with eggplant dishes! This time we go straight for the kitchen, where you can actually point at large containers with food. I am sure it wasn't quite the way they expected us to order, but we get what we want this time; Turkish food!

Walking back to the hotel we are dragged into a Turkish bakery where there is a flurry of activity as many excited men make Turkish pida breads. The place is covered in flour, and as is expected, it is hot in here. The men want to show us their flamboyant bread making skills. They are not trying to sell anything, they are genuinely friendly. We sure seem to be off the tourist route here, we see no other white faces, and we seem to be the ones attracting attention out here. Lucas films the bakers at work, Heather and I look on, David is standing outside, looking embarrassed, and Cindy is darting in between. The Turkish street scene is pretty interesting, there is always something happening. When we part with the friendly bakers I get approached by a salesman with a suitcase full of perfumes. Everybody wisely says thanks and brush him off, but I see opportunity. Opportunity to have a chat that is. I almost get sold some huge containers of fake perfume for $5. I would've bought some if not for the scepticism of the team. Glad I didn't because there is no way I, or any of us, are going home with everything we have in our possession as is!

Hotel Sezen served us up a nice breakfast, the usual white bread and jam trick. We ate as much as we could, another big day ahead. Who knows where we will be tonight, but it is going to be a stone's throw from Istanbul! I decide to pay with a credit card as the hotel shows every credit card mankind has invented on the front door. 'Sorry Sir, this is not a valid card.' 'No Sir, this one is not a valid card either', and this one? 'No, not a valid card either.' For more excruciating fun I pull out every card in my possession; My ANZ card, my MasterCard (which always runs out of credit), the American Express from Australia and the Blue Sky Amex card from the USA... Then Cindy pulled out her cards as well,... 'No, I am sorry none of these are valid.' I felt like scraping the credit card stickers of this hotel's front door. This is not the first time as you understand, and it is infuriating when you literally bank on it. In the mean time the rest of the gang is roaring to go, heading for Istanbul, our second last day riding our great bikes, and the last day with a good distance to cover – over 100kms. David and Troy are ready and have sorted out the route out of town. Lucas and Heather are also ready to do it, but Cindy and I are checking out... I tell the checkout man at the hotel to call the support phone number which is clearly printed on the card reader. He dials it and passes it on to me. I steadfastly refuse to handle this matter! Imagine me trying to tell a Turkish technician that the machine doesn't work. Come to think of it, the technician may well be based in the Philippines or India – in which case the chances of them speaking English is actually quite good. 'The lines are down Sir.'... I throw up my hands. The man has a new idea, his mate across the road.

As David and the troops are waiting at the support vehicle ready to get on the road, I am fuming at the hotel reception. The hotel manager takes me across the road to a car accessories store. There the transaction is done in under a minute.

Our final country; Turkey!

# ISTANBUL

A minute later we are heading further East towards Istanbul! I am not in a good mood, must've been a combination of the white bread breakfast with tea in combination with a 30 minute check out. I never expected these minor issues to be amongst my biggest challenges! Waking up for me is generally problematic. My brain never really kicks in till 11am, and without coffee that process tends to be painful for me and those around me as well! Grumpiness is also typically a sign of me getting infection but let's hope it is just coffee withdrawal symptoms.

Where we are riding now the roads are very quiet and almost void of traffic. The road surface is good too, apart from the steep edges and the by now howling wind. The road is long and winding and goes up and down. We are heading in a mostly South Easterly direction, pretty much directly into the wind. I am lagging behind quite a bit. My lungs are in relatively good shape, but that does not mean that I don't cough and spit for hours every morning. I am not exactly feeling ready for more kilometres after lunch. Wearing the helmet cam I try to do some filming but almost fall of the edge of the road on a downhill stretch. I am low on energy and not concentrating. It would be a disaster to have a high speed stack so close to the finish. The going is tough now; we are riding up and down many hills. I cough up all the hills. Lucas either cycles with me or waits for me on top of many hills with his camera pointing at me. I am struggling up the crest of these hills. The wind is a killer here. The hills are bare and far reaching, I am tired. We do not see Istanbul yet, but we must be getting close. Today we should see signs of Istanbul in the distance. I was hoping we'd get really close today, but the going is slow.

I am imagining smog in the far distance. Could it be Istanbul already? We are 100 kilometres away as the bird flies. Going up and down is proving tough, and following the road towards the Northern end of Istanbul is going to be difficult. We had planned to approach Istanbul from the North as no major arterial routes come in that way, and we are hoping for the traffic to be less dangerous there. But now we definitely need to ditch the idea as the going is tough. We agree on just following the road signs to Istanbul and dealing with the traffic as we get closer. Looking at the map we estimate it to be a small distance on the highway into Istanbul, approaching from the West. The Polish cyclist proclaimed not to have experienced any problems following the major roads, so why should we.

We are now starting to see smog appearing in the distance, and this time I am actually very pleased to see it as this means the end of our long journey; Istanbul on the horizon. Every hill we cycled up I expected to be the last, as surely we have to go downhill to sea level. Some of these hills are pretty high, with nice distant views of forested regions ahead. There are many more hills, one after the other.

We have lunch on the road, with Cindy and Troy who had arranged a nice selection of Turkish goodies for us riders. Shortly after we get on the road after lunch Kathy calls from London to tell me that Laura at the Consulate-General can arrange a 'secure car' to guide us in from where we are staying on Friday night. I am not sure if this is good news or not, will we need a 'secure' car? Our plan right now is to ride our bikes to as close to our end destination as is feasible, preferably 20 kilometres from the city. The road signs are steadily counting down to Istanbul.

Will we need guiding in? I suppose we still have no proper map of Turkey or Istanbul, and the chances of obtaining one are slim it seems. I struggle up a few more hills, and ride hard against the wind down some other big hills when we suddenly see a large mosque on the edge of a ploughed field, this looks like the beginning of a big town, maybe this is the first outlying suburb of Istanbul.

We enter a very busy traffic area of a town called Habibla with steep roads going up and down. At one point I catch a tractor going up a hill, and holding on to it I pass Lucas and Heather and finally David who is most surprised to see me up the hill this quick. These gold opportunities rarely arise, which is a good thing as it is obviously dangerous to hold on to slow moving vehicles going up hills. In fact the last time I was able to do this was perhaps ten years ago in Canberra when the truck I was holding onto slowly accelerated to 50 kilometres an hour and I had to let go, but not after having gained a nice distance up a hill. Opportunities like this rarely present themselves, moments of adrenaline, accelerating up hills with one hand on the handlebar and one hand clinging to motorised metal.

After a few kilometres into the urban sprawl we have to consult our navigation aids. David is quite paranoid when all of us pull out fancy looking toys and start farkeling with them, making us an easy target for robbers. I try really hard not to use my fancy phone or my camera. The maps on my phone are very up to date it seems and occasionally it is worth waiting for. Traffic here is absolutely ludicrous, dangerous and not much fun. We see an old man with a long grey beard on an industrial looking trike, battling through the traffic and we instantly feel better on our nice bikes with no loads. Slowly we are heading out of this town, which indicates that we are not in the urban sprawl of Istanbul yet. The road is very busy and crowded with fast traffic in all lanes all winding in and out seeming randomly. The fumes are bad here, the dust is no better. We are riding in the dirt on the side or on the road as we see fit. We are fed onto a major highway which still appears to be under construction. The wind is in the right direction now, and the road is downhill; we are flying with the traffic at dizzying speeds towards the next cluster of concrete buildings. We see minarets poking out amongst the roofs in the distance. It looks like what could be Istanbul.

No idea how we are going to find Troy in this metropolitan mess that we are heading into, or whether he is driving along the same route as us! Eventually we get an SMS with a location. By now the traffic is getting clogged up, side streets steadily feed more cars in our path. I am weaving in and out of traffic like a madman. Renewed energy has come with my adrenalin rush which overcomes all physiological and psychological obstacles such as sore muscles, tiredness, and above all fear. Heavy traffic like this I had encountered in Tokyo on the bicycle a few years ago when I visited ex-pat van Praag family, this is fun. I switch to video game mode; one life left and I must win! David is OK running through the traffic like this, but for Heather and Lucas this is a frustrating and horrible experience, but we all stick together. We manage to find our way into what looks like Istanbul proper.

David's GPS leads us to the location where we find Troy in an alcohol free hotel. We are in Hotel Viyana on Eski Edirne Asfalti. I assume asfalti means road. It is late afternoon, we are buggered, and we rode over 100 kilometres today. The bar downstairs looks good enough to have an early celebration drink in, but it is closed as we are in the period of Ramadan.

It is Thursday, tomorrow is going to be a rest day as we are practically in Istanbul now, and Saturday we ride into Istanbul proper. I catch Troy's eyes. I can't say 'we are in Istanbul mate', or I'll cry! I mumble something like 'we're not far now!' and I see he understands. Troy and I feel the same way. It has been a long ride and we are ready to arrive at our final destination. It was hell on two wheels today, and on four wheels for Troy. We are seriously in Istanbul, this is practically it. Troy and I are close to tears when we catch each other's eyes, we know this has been our last day of proper riding; we are as good as at the end of our adventure.

We are shown our rooms. This hotel is as pricey as it is musty. Perhaps Lucas and I have the smelliest room of all because our floor is currently under renovation.

The hotel sure does not seem full, but we are several floors apart again. We walk out and find a fast food joint of sorts that sells hamburgers. It also sells Turkish goodies, so we eat well. Even my credit card is accepted! There is a bottle shop of sorts across the road where we can buy beer too. The night is spent playing cards and chatting over a big map that we have. We need to decide on a plan of attack. Tomorrow is Friday, and we have less than 20 kilometres to ride. We decide that we'll spend the last day getting ready, as in finding a clean shirt to wear to begin with! Lucas also needs to interview Heather about the ride, something he will need for the documentary. She will be back in Canada where she is from before we know it, and now is probably the only opportunity for Lucas. Too bad we don't have good wireless microphones for the camera here, but we have no choice.

David and Troy will use the rest-day to conduct a reconnaissance mission to the Consul-General so that we are assured to make the grand entrance on time on Saturday. Imagine if we get lost and the Dutch Consul General and all the people waiting for us have to have lunch without us on Saturday. We also figured that we should perhaps drive Lucas and Troy into the Marmara hotel on Saturday morning. They can leave the car there, take a cab back to us, and then we can keep the taxi (or the 'secure car') to drive ahead of us with Lucas filming inside. This way Lucas can get ahead regularly and Troy can cycle in as part of our team. After breakfast in our newly adopted restaurant, the burger joint, Troy and David cycle off on their mission into the big smoke to find out exactly where the Dutch Consul-General is. They find the consulate after battling the traffic and fumes on the bikes, and briefly meet with Laura Bins, our contact. They find the very deluxe lots of stars Marmara hotel that we are booked into. They think it will only take us an hour to ride in from where we are now; about 15 kilometres from our destination. We need not worry about a special 'secure' taxi now that they know where it is, and have noted waypoints into the GPS.

Seeing it all makes it also look more doable. They devise the following plan. Troy will drop the car at the hotel in the morning and catch a cab back. Lucas can get in that cab and ride ahead of us and film as the rest of us ride.

Troy in particular has a good ride in the horrid traffic knowing the car was safely parked in front of the hotel and he did not have to drive through the crazy traffic! Traffic is chaotic and random and driving on the wrong side of the road around traffic medium strips appears to be acceptable. From our hotel window we see this happen on the street below where buses impatiently push the oncoming traffic out of the way in an effort to bypass a minor crash scene. The excited vehicle occupants involved in the bingle insisting on not moving their cars till the police arrive to determine exactly who is to blame.

I try to make a local phone call from the hotel to Kathy, but am unable to do it. I have to use my mobile phone as there is a 'communication' problem! Even from the front desk I cannot make a call! In the end I get a text message to her. She replies reassuring me that she is on her way to Istanbul with Vicente. Things are going to plan!

None of us get a chance to relax or do any touristy stuff on this rest-day. It is Friday, the last day before the big finish, we are freaking out with excitement! It wasn't till 7pm that we realised we still had nothing special to wear for the Consulate lunch. Nothing we have is clean or ironed, and so we decide to all go for a shopping mission. Most shops sport an American Express sticker I am glad to report. When I find the shoes I want the credit card machine does not work. Sure enough this salesman also has ties with a nearby store; he takes me to his mates nearby, but their machine also failed to work for us. Out of principle I am not paying cash, they should have a manual swipe machine. My patience with these stores advertising credit card acceptance is wearing very thin. The sales-man is seriously apologetic, and I am nice to him and promise to return in an hour. He explained it was a communication problem, so that might be resolved in one hour. At least this man was offering us tea and grapes in his shop and genuinely seemed apologetic. I guess even the phones in the hotel are out. But a few hours ago I paid for lunch with a card.

Cindy goes for a special hair-do minutes before we decide to have dinner. She wants to get her hair shampooed. As we order food her hair is washed and styled by 12 people upstairs in a salon where foreigners rarely venture. It is a highlight for Cindy who has owned a salon herself in Tasmania. We are treated to a humungous Turkish platter. Lots of pide bread, aubergines, olives, kebabs with marinated meat and much more. I polish it off with a glass of Ayran. Cindy comes in looking no different to us, but she feels a million dollars. She helps polish off the food and we order her some more. This is our last dinner 'on the road'. We are all buzzing with excitement and none of us are thinking clearly. Certainly not me or Cindy, we are both naturally absent-minded.

After dinner I venture back into the shoe shop and try to use my card again to no avail. I give the guy cash and tell him to keep the change for all the trouble he had with me, as it really does not appear to be their fault. The shop across the road where we buy some more clothing does not have the credit card stickers, and I pay for my purchases in hard cash. It just annoys me if they draw me in the shop by displaying credit cards and then do not accept them. If they say they accept cards, they should accept cards!

Back at the hotel Cindy takes Troy's hair clippers, she has not seen her own hair dressing kit since we left the Danube in Romania, and sculpted our heads to read Cofe4CF. Troy, David and I are happy to sport our cause, but Cindy herself is not game to let any of us attempt to shave her head. Heather is not game and neither is Lucas who is in fact very vein.

We discuss tomorrow's arrival plan again and now that we know the way and roughly how long it will take we are changing our mind again. We now figure it would be easier if we leave two hours for the ride, leave here at a leisurely 10am, stop at the Marmara hotel, which should be a casual 60 minute ride, do our check-in, and then cycle all together into the Consulate's palace around the corner from the hotel. This means Troy can drive the vehicle through the horrible traffic on Saturday morning, which we expect not to be too bad, and Lucas will not have to speak Turkish in a taxi in order to make him stop and go to film us.

We play a couple of nervous card games before retiring. We sleep well, knowing that Troy and David know the way in tomorrow and that it is only a one hour ride if that. Troy did report his throat hurt from the pollution and his head buzzed from the traffic, we are so close that nothing really matters other then the fact the end is a mere one hour ride from where we are.

# SEEING THE PINK MIST

After a good breakfast at our newly favourite restaurant that served food during the day, which due to Ramadan is hard to find, we leave on our final ride. We had left boxes with food and other stuff in the street, stuff that none of us could carry home. As we jump on the bikes for the very last time I see the boxes on the side of the road. We are leaving behind pieces of our adventure. Maybe we should have left a note on it in Turkish to say; 'please take'. There are our plates and cooking gear, our food, clothing, and so forth left out on the streets. We are on our way to the final destination!

Heather: "The riders were Walter, Cindy, David and Heather. Troy and Lucas were in the support vehicle laden with cameras and no small amount of adrenaline to cope with Turkish drivers.

At about 9:30am, we rode out into the streets, squeezing our way through narrow gaps between sidewalks and buses, metal and flesh. We soon saw that biking through the streets of Istanbul, although completely damaging to even healthy lungs was THE way to travel. The support vehicle drove approximately 6km before it was wedged deep into the worst kind of metal-hell jam. This was when Lucas got nervous. Our lunch meeting at the Consulate was slated for noon and it was clear nothing bigger than a human body was going anywhere fast." - Heather's blog.7 October.

Despite being a Saturday morning the traffic is unbelievably heavy. The bicycles easily negotiate the traffic (well, within inches of our lives that is), but the car is held back. We stop and wait for the car to catch up. After 30 minutes we call Troy to ask if we had missed them going by. No, they have not passed the road works at the roundabout yet, which is where we are waiting for them. Time is ticking away. A journalist calls me on the mobile to ask how we are riding in so he can intercept us. I have trouble understanding him with all the traffic noise. I understand he wants to know where we are now. I pass the phone to a random stranger who looks strangely at me giving him my phone. He puts it to his ear and gets to speak to the journalist. He seems to know what to say and after a few words he hands me back my phone with a smile. The journalist tells me he will catch up with us. Yes, in this traffic? I don't think so!

While waiting for the car to catch up I climb up some steps, away from the road, and get a nice view of Istanbul. One huge mess of small buildings with a huge highway in the distance and one right in front of me. Minarets and mosques dotted regularly amongst it all. Traffic noise and fumes abound. I gag. The fumes are disgusting. I just stand as far away from the traffic as possible. Every centimetre seems to make a difference. Fully loaded buses with people who look as if they have been on the bus for a while, full cars, motorbikes, and people walking through the lanes of stalled traffic. It all appears very outlandish to us. Troy and Lucas finally catch up in the car, and we continue on our way. Time is ticking away. This traffic congestion is most unexpected, and the car gets stuck in traffic again. We are going to have to ride to the hotel and hopefully Troy can catch up on less congested bits of road. Two hours to drive under fifteen kilometres on a road we are not going to get lost on seemed easy enough last night. No way could we need longer. But it now looks as though we may not have allowed enough time.

David, Cindy, Heather and I battle through the traffic, past the big roundabout through a Roman Aquaduct, and we cross the Ottoman bridge into the heart of Istanbul. This is where the press catches us. We are filmed from a car by Turk CNN. It is the journalist who had spoken to me earlier. They find a dubious spot to pull over and quickly speak to us as we confirm the quickest way to the Marmara hotel. We follow the CNN car up the last hill to Taksim square, where our hotel is. It was fifteen minutes to go to our scheduled noon arrival! No sign of Troy, we had left him behind. We struggle through the fumes up this last hill. We are doing the final yards and there is no Lucas filming us, he must be freaking stuck in the traffic with Troy!

Lucas is panicking. He is going to film us going into the consulate; he is going to be there, it is impossible for him not to be there. We cannot re-stage this event of all events, our finale, the coup-de-grace; our arrival! Lucas is stuck in traffic with Troy. In a wave of panic he asks Troy for directions – none of us have decent maps except for the most inaccurate ones on the GPS unit. Lucas has a compass, but that is not going to help him now. Troy tells him the bearing and distance from his GPS, and Lucas looks blank at the compass in his hand. It goes into his pocket and he grips his camera tight. He jumps out of the car and starts running, 'pick me up when you pass me, if you pass me!' are his last words.

Troy is not exactly relaxed himself. No way is he going to miss the ride in! He has to ride with us; he has to be there too! It is a nightmare in development for Troy. After doing the reconnaissance mission yesterday how can things still not work out!! Cold sweat breaks. We are all sensing that the finish may not go as planned, and we might have to arrive at the consulate late, or go in as half a team, we are going to have to make big decisions. There is press and people waiting for us. People with Champagne and lunch. We are determined to get there at noon. Where are Troy and Lucas? Are they lost?

Lucas is running … He runs along the busy road, sweat pouring out of him again, and camera in hand and probably filming at the same time. He has to cross the road and he sprints through a pedestrian underpass, aware that this might just be the point where Troy could pass him! He sprints through, and surfaces on the other side just in time to see the support vehicle disappear in the distance. Eyes glazed in panic, 'seeing the pink mist'. Seeing the pink mist is a made up phrase I have come across that figuratively describes what you do when you are very anxious, and Lucas was seeing it. All that Lucas can do now is wave frantically and film Troy disappearing in the distance at a rate of knots. Quick thinking Lucas immediately flags down a taxi which he must have conjured up out of thin air. Lucas barks at the taxi-driver; 'Follow that car!'

Troy got a break in the traffic and pushed the little VW hard along the sections where he could, not noticing a panicked figure in the rear vision mirror waving at him. He is on the final mile through the Aquaduct, across the bridge over the Golden Horn (part of the Bosphorus River), up the hill… There he finds us in front of the Intercontinental Hotel finishing off our interviews with the press. It is now three minutes to noon. Dying for a leak he darts out of the car. Returns two minutes to noon and asks where Lucas is. Lucas? Why is he not in the car with

Troy? Troy tells us on how Lucas had bailed from the car and had started running. We all mount the bikes, we are ready to go in, we are dying to go the final hundred metres into İstiklal Caddesi; a street closed off to traffic. There we will find the Dutch Consulate-General situated in a palace behind a large ornamental iron gate. Can we go in without Lucas filming? Where is he? What about all the times we bet on him and he always came out with the best possible outcome, never lost a bike, never got home after dark, never failed in his missions. Where is he?

We had seen Lucas run on his sandals before, he is surprisingly fit, but he has no idea where he is going this time. In fact I don't think he knows much more than the name of the hotel and the consulate, but has no phone or written addresses on him. The time ticks away steadily.

We are on our bikes now, and about to set off on the bicycles to cycle the final yards to our welcoming committee! The CNN Turk film crew is with us, and they promise to exchange footage of the last 200 metres in exchange for some footage of our ride. We feel bad for Lucas, but we have to go in, we are itching to go! And just as we are on the bikes we hear Lucas' voice, "Guys! I made it!", and spot him emerge from a taxi.

The feeling of elation, the feeling of success and completion, joy and exhilaration is radiating from us. We are all together, as a team, riding our bikes to the finish line. We have no idea what to expect as we ride very slowly down the alleyway with cameras rolling and people walking and jogging with us. At the end of the alleyway we enter a very busy walking mall, full of activity; we are in İstiklal Caddesi. We carefully make our way through the crowd for no more than 200m, carefully crossing the tram line tracks as we cross over to the big wrought iron gate where we see Kathy and Vicente waving at us surrounded by other people in party spirit".

I lead the team through the gate into the Dutch Consul General's front garden which appears as a little piece of heaven behind the gate with the busy shopping street.

Together we ride through the gates to the sound of hands clapping and corks popping. Here we all get wet eyes. I try to pop a wheelie, but almost fall of the bike. I steer towards the ribbon, that is held up and we cycle through it as people cheer and pop open bottles of French champagne. This is it, we have arrived. We drop our bikes inelegantly around the place and accept the glasses of champagne. Photographers and press, friendly consulate related people who speak Dutch, a huge bunch of flowers, we have it all.

Cindy getting interviewd by Turk CNN!

And next thing I know a complete brass band walks in! All wearing T-shirts with the word Chaupiques on it. They enter through the royal gate and rip into a cheerful March. We are received like royalty, complete with a brass band. The

Chaupiques stay for lunch, they are a Dutch band! I ask Laura, who was responsible for the entire reception, how they managed to get the band. 'The band? No idea who arranged them, it wasn't me!' she tells me. Of course I do not believe that. Someone surely must have arranged for them, they do not just appear out of thin air – although anything is possible. They are certainly warmly received, they play lots for us, and they join us for lunch. If there was enough food for all then surely they must have been expected!

"There we sat in the garden with our smelly, sweaty biking clothes around dignitaries of the Consulate, but no one seemed to mind. During dessert, we were again surprised by a letter from the Australian Ambassador expressing his admiration for Walter and his mission to inspire people with CF." – Saturday October 7, Heather's blog

We feel a million dollars as The Chaupiques play a festive tune at the Dutch Consul General's palace.

During the lunch I speak to Mr Hennis the Consul General of the mission, and he tells me they had planned lunch around the table, he points towards a table. I take another sip of champagne. Mr Hennis walks inside the palace, the actual consulate, and comes out with the cook. A little welcome speech is given to welcome us officially. And a fax is read out from the Australian Ambassador to Turkey, Mr Doyle, to congratulate us as well. It makes us feel much more important than what we believe we are. After all we are just scrubbed up friends who just had a great time coughing the distance. The cook is also thanked for catering for the unexpected visitors. It is time for me to have a good chat to these Chaupiques!

They are indeed Dutch speaking; I verify that by speaking to them in Dutch! The story unfolds. They are indeed unexpected. They are a group of friends who regularly played together 20 years ago. They have all gone their own ways in life now, have their own families and lives, but once a year the band meets for a weekend of jamming and to decide on where to go for a week; a cheap airfare is chosen to go to a different place each year for a week of busking.

This year the band's busking week was destined for Istanbul. They were just walking to Istanbul's China town to busk for the afternoon when they walked past the gate. They noticed the commotion with the cyclists riding in, asked if they could play for us, and someone said yes! As they wondered into the gardens they were still unaware they were actually entering on a piece of their homeland! It slowly dawned on them that by chance they were at the Dutch Consulate, which they thought was pretty funny. Funny? Funny? It was hilarious, what timing! No one had arranged it, this was totally accidental. Some stars were in the right position, our Christmas had come early, and we are just utterly blessed. Yes, we have arrived in style!

A good few glasses of champagne and a belly full of nice fish later we stumble out, but not without a quick look inside the palace. It has a long Dutch history, built in the 18th Century by the Dutch representatives. The palace's chapel was opened to the public in the mid 19th Century when practising religion other than Islamic ones were frowned upon. As the Dutch had opened up their arms to welcome other nationalities in those days, they still continue with that tradition today as we found out first hand!

Heather: "Day 73, Istanbul, Turkey, 4,395km: YAHOOOOOOOO!!!!

My God, where do we even start...?! How to possibly capture what it feels like to have finished The Great COFE for Cystic Fibrosis? Well, for starters, you can bet there were wet eyes, wide grins and a few "I can't believe it's. And what would the final day be like without a giant helping of Wally Luck?

Whether you believe in coincidence or fate, our final day on the COFE challenge was most certainly accompanied by something other than the ordinary. It started with the insane traffic of Istanbul. We had spent the previous night on the outskirts of the giant city hoping for a relatively straightforward ride to the finish line, which was to be the front gates of the Dutch Consulate General smack in the middle of the Istanbul.

Two friends of Walter's, Kathy, a journalist from London, and Laura, in charge of Press and Cultural Affairs for the Consulate (whom Walter just happened to meet on a train in Amsterdam at the beginning of the trip), had exchanged countless emails and phone calls in order to plan a reception for the COFE team at the Consulate. We had no idea what to expect and boy, were we surprised!"- Heather's blog.7 October.

# MORE MIRACLES

"A more perfect day could not have been thought up and we would like to extend our dearest thanks to everyone involved in the reception and to those of you who journeyed along with us for the last 73 days. We are all very proud of Walter and the kind of person he is. Surely each one of us has ingested some of this man's happiness for life and may we all be able to draw from it throughout our lives.

Way to go, Wally!!!!!!!!!!" – Heather's last blog entry.

The hotel the consulate had booked for us is a tad expensive, but we are prepared for it, they also accept my American Express card! Not only is it one of the best hotels in Turkey where you are totally isolated from the culture around you except for the magnificent views of Istanbul, it is also the location of the best restaurant in Istanbul. Kathy and Vicente would go and book a table for dinner for us.

You like to make a booking at the Safran Restaurant for tonight? Saturday night on the last weekend of Ramadan? I don't think that is possible Sir.

The lady at the hotel reception makes a call up to the top floor to speak to the restaurant. 'Alright, I'll send them up', she ends her conversation, and Kathy and Vicente catch the elevator to the top floor. There she is told that a booking for one or two could possibly be arranged in an emergency, 'but EIGHT, no way! Not for any Saturday night soon. Maybe we can fit you in for Monday night'. The phone rings. 'Excuse me for one moment' she picks up the phone; 'You like to cancel your reservation tonight Mr. Johnson? No problem Sir, thank you for calling'.

She grabs a pen and a ruler and neatly draws a line across a booking on the full booking sheet. She turns to Kathy again,' I believe we can fit you in!'

Heather and Lucas lapping up luxury pre-dinner drinks overlooking Istanbul.

The cancellation just called in was the only booking for eight on the list; it is truly our lucky day.

Pre-dinner drinks on the roof top bar taste better than anything we have tasted ever. We are all dossed out in our cleanest outfits, shaven and brushed up, looking indistinguishable from the rest of the crowd. Only difference is that our smiles are bigger than anyone else. We had been glowing all day, and are ready to glow for the next few hours to come! The view of the Bosphorus, the lights of Istanbul, the lusciousness of the bar, the elation of being finished. What a rush.

At dinner I present the biggest honour of all; The Phlegm Cup. I had purchased a new stainless steel camping mug exactly like the one I use to spit in when I do my nebulising, but this one was to be engraved and used as a trophy. The decision who to award it to was a tough one, everyone had participated fully in our ride, no one had slacked off or given up, all had pulled their weight. But in the end the winner was David as he had navigated the entire trip, looked after our safety and more than anyone else, had financially contributed a significant dollar amount into the ride and on top of that had used up his long service leave to come along. If I had medals to give out we all deserved one as the ride could not have been as big a success without every one of us. We are a hell of a team; they helped me cough the distance!

Troy is particularly proud of our achievements and drinks accordingly. After one of his toilet visits during the dinner he comes out with a new friend; a Canadian man whom he had proudly told about our achievement while relieving himself of recycled beer. The man and his wife soon joined us with a nice bottle of Dom Pérignon. When minutes later Troy topples over a few of the elegant glasses full of champagne he excuses himself and retires, and shortly after we all just about pass out from exhaustion.

Lucas' blog entry: "It is finally starting to sink in that we have reached the end of this incredible journey. From the vibrancy of Paris to the splendour of Vienna and to the calming beaches of the Black Sea - and now we find ourselves here, on the outskirts of Istanbul, within a day's ride of our finish line. This has been my first trip to Europe and what a trip it has been, there is far too much for me to tell in this short entry - but suffice to say that it has certainly been a milestone in my budding career.

Looking back on what we have overcome and accomplished (and I mean that literally because I've filmed and reviewed the clips repeatedly already) it is utterly amazing that we have made it this far, and this well. Whether it be the physically demanding stretches of endless rolling hills or the nerve-racking chaos of city traffic, somehow we managed to get through it all in one piece.

It is a true testament to David's spot-on navigation, Troy's technical ingenuity and Walter's sheer utter determination (as well as the almost indefinable 'Wally factor') that we are here now. And of course the trip would not nearly have been as enjoyable without the accompaniment of Heather who has done a fantastic job of keeping the blog updated, as well as Cindy, whose incredible energy and enthusiasm brought fresh air to our team.

To be honest I had hoped for this crazy group of people to get into far more trouble than we did, good for the doco you know - but at this point I am simply relieved and very proud of what we have accomplished. And I must say we certainly had a good dose of mishaps and hardships - mountains, rain, mud, head wind, blazing sun, heavy traffic, as well as Hungarian con artists, Romanian Weddings that never end, feral dogs or even that wonderfully nasty Slivovitz- just to name a few things, in all the 60+ hours of footage that we have amassed I am absolutely confident that we will have something to show that is worthy of Walter's vision.

My real work is now about to begin, I can look forward to many months of intensive editing sessions in front of the computer to shape this documentary into something that will entertain and inspire. Though it will take time, it is not a hard task - for Walter's story is that of a person who refuses to consider himself a victim, and there is definitely something in that for all of us."

Troy's blog entry: "Well it is all over, I can't believe we all got here in one piece. I have had the time of my life on this journey and to do it with a group of people I never knew before the trip (except for Walter and Cindy) has made it more exciting in some ways. I must say a special thanks to Walter and his lovely wife Katherine for asking me to join Walter on this trip. To see what it is like on this side of the world is amazing. I have had good and bad days in and out of the car the only real trouble was coming into Istanbul. I have never seen traffic like that (after all I do live in a small town with only about three roads). Anyway I also would like to say to the other guys and girls that have help on the trip a very special thank you."

Cindy's blog entry: "I know Walter through the Devonport Hash House Harriers – a local running group we both attend. On our first meeting, I could see that Walter had something I didn't have: a bright smile, acceptance of everyone and always a joke. I wanted to find out why he loved life so much.

After our first run together, I noticed Walter coughing a lot. I suggested, 'I would be home in bed with a cough like that.' Walter said, 'I'm living with Cystic Fibrosis' and told me a little to satisfy my curiosity.

He asked me to come on the COFE trip as I was travelling Europe at the same time.

One day, I followed Walter out of Budapest after a rest day. The effects the polluted city had on his lungs was very obvious to me as I watched Walter struggling in front of me. Physically, he juggled balancing his bike in traffic between consistent coughing, blowing his nose, vomiting and just getting enough air in his lungs. This was a bad day for him.

I estimate the coughing/vomiting bouts were about every twenty turns of the pedal - even more if the terrain was uphill. Gradually, the coughing lessened, but what I hadn't seen before was his breakfast coming up - masses of it over several coughing bouts.

As always, he soldiers on and continues riding. I ask if he's alright and he says, 'This is normal.' It's definitely not for me. If I had to cope with all this, I would be crying and home in bed.

Being on this trip has awakened my senses to Walter's plight and made me aware of his daily routine: using the nebuliser at night and in the morning to cleanse his lungs and make them user friendly for the day. It reminds me of my worst experience with influenza, when you keep coughing until you vomit, and your whole body aches, just from coughing. I feel totally worn out from listening to Walter and have to leave the room because of the extreme nature of the lung clearing that he has to do to survive.

I now know how lucky I am to be supporting him in his efforts towards creating a positive awareness about CF. The next time you hear someone clearing their lungs, just think it may be a person with Cystic Fibrosis trying to live with CF."

# AND FINALLY, THE OPENING OF THE BOTTLE

Sunday October 7, Day 1 post COFE is sightseeing in Istanbul for us, but David and Troy are happier just hanging around the hotel, lapping up the peace and tranquillity in preference to subjecting themselves to the hustle and the bustle of Istanbul. The rest of us scatter in all directions, absorbing ourselves into the Eastern culture. The Blue Mosque, the Topkapi Palace, the food…

After visiting the Grand Bazaar we did not want to take a taxi back as all the taxis were charging incredible amounts for the ride home. We had caught a taxi from the hotel to get there and were advised by the concierge that the ride back was likely to be ten times more expensive, so we were prepared. It is pleasant enough walking around. The walk back is mostly along the Bosphorus River, heading for the Ataturk Bridge. Just on dusk when I was chatting with Vicente, who had come over from London with Kathy, we come across a good con: It was a hustle and bustle near the food markets along the river that had sprung up as soon as the sun went down to cater for the fasting Muslim population whose religion allows them to eat again. Some Samaritans are handing out special Ramadan food packs for the hungry Muslims. Vicente, who is in fact Spanish, is also handed a food pack just when a shoe-polisher drops a shoe polishing brush as he rushes past. Vicente sees him drop it and picks up the brush. We call out to the poor shoe-polisher. When the man hears us he hurries back and is very grateful for Vicente's action and insists on giving him a shoe polish.

'I am so poor, I cannot afford to lose a single brush, let me polish your shoes, I have a family, do you have a family, I have kids, do you have kids, one is sick and needs medical treatment, and oh I am so poor…' Vicente tries hard to avoid a shoe shine, as he does not need it. He wears perfectly clean brown suede shoes. The grateful soul with his reunited brush literally grabs him by the ankles and enthusiastically starts polishing his shoes black. They are ruined now, that is obvious. Vicente looks at me, but he allows the man to pay back the favour, after he unsuccessfully tried to stop him from painting his brown shoes black.

'Right, there you go, that is 20 Liras please Sir', the shoe polisher exclaims enthusiastically. Vicente is not impressed and tells the man in no uncertain terms that he is being unreasonable and this is unwarranted especially since he did specifically ask not get a polish. In the end Vicente shoves 5 Liras (about $5) in his hand to shake him and we run off. When minutes later I walk past fisherman fishing off the bridge I see a pretty woman 'lose' a handkerchief in front of me. I have no trouble stepping on it as I walk straight on, staring at infinity, knowing the woman is probably picking it up to try whatever the trick is on the next tourist. Am I getting paranoid?

After two nights it is time to clear out. Istanbul has been a fun and exciting place for us. We have bought lots of souvenirs including little carpets. We have all spent a lot of time packing up and our last dinner together had come. We choose a modest Mexican restaurant in the neighbourhood and settle in. We have one more ceremony to perform, the opening of the bottle: The time has come; it is our last night together.

Cindy is very excited to read the messages in the bottle!

We ask the valet of our fancy hotel to fetch the car and we search for the bottle. We find it. But we also find that condensation inside the bottle may have ruined the messages, changing the bits of paper with crayon writing into mere coloured bits of paper. The micro climate of the support vehicle had apparently caused some dew inside the bottle.

Not to be dispirited by such minor detail we are sitting at the restaurant and look for implements. The bottle has assumed a mystical status by now, and we are reluctant to unceremoniously smash it. My suggestion to smash the bottle is not accepted in case we need to take this bottle to Bondi Beach! So not wanting to break the bottle we painfully extract the bits of rolled up paper using the implements from the restaurant; chopsticks! After much fiddling, and drawing attention of nearby tables, all we find inside are indeed the nicely blotched coloured bits of paper with no legible script left to read. Nothing identifiable as letters at all. Beware all you potential shipwrecks out there!! Use waterproof ink!

We are still exhausted, exhausted from 72 days of riding, and retreat to our luxury hotel for our last night. We all stay up late, farkeling with our gear.

After a big breakfast the next day we summon the car from the valet, a final group hug and goodbyes in front of the hotel, and David and I get in the VW Caddy to drive back to Amsterdam – a ride that will take us three or more days – to return the car to Martin.

Cindy flies to London to go have a break with her daughter in Ireland, Troy flies to Brisbane to have a naughty catch-up weekend with his girl. Lucas will soon be flying home to Canberra from Istanbul and Heather is going back to Canada via Scotland to visit her very pregnant girlfriend before leaving Europe.

David and I get into the support vehicle and head for Holland, a long trip! We leave at 11am that Monday morning with panic in our eyes. Two GPS units on the job, and complete with our Europe Road Map book we nervously negotiate the Turkish traffic and drive out of Istanbul.

# THE LAST PILL

Calculating the number of required pancreatic enzymes that I need for any trip is always tricky. How fatty will the food be in all these countries, will I get muesli and sandwiches or fried bacon and pancakes, ox-tongue, tribe or sheep brains for breakfast? I calculated 800 pills would see me through 80 days. It became clear that this was not enough very soon, and I could've known that 10 a day is not enough in any case. I expected very lean healthy meals. So in Germany I managed to buy two more bottles of enzymes, another 500 pills. As we neared the end of the trip I realised I was still going to be short.

When we arrived in Holland at midnight I was down to one pill, not even enough for breakfast. The Dutch pharmacy came to the rescue.

# SPECIAL THANKS

Special thanks again must go to the Mad Bomber Company for sponsoring us, Martin Quelle for providing the VW Caddy support vehicle, Batavus for providing the excellent bikes and Patagonia for doing their best to dress us well! To ride a bicycle like we did on some of the worst roads imaginable for 4395 kilometres requires tough equipment. The Batavus AM400 did the job admirably! No breakdowns of significance. Considering we had 5 bikes doing the trip and we only had one seat break off, and one bike which lost a couple of gears off the cluster on the second last day we cannot complain!

Thank you to all of you out there that read our blog, donated money and product and thought of us. Without all of you this trip would never be made into a documentary, I probably would never have written it all down, and we never would have reached so many people affected by Cystic Fibrosis.

One thing we failed to do was get a Turkish Bath in Turkey. But Heather was brave enough to attempt one on her own. She emailed us the following report:

# HEATHER'S SCRUB

This has got to go down as one of the most hilarious travel experiences I have ever had…first, I'll explain the idea of a Turkish bath: you get scrubbed by someone armed with a lofah sponge until you are gleaming. Sounds easy enough, if not a wee bit intimate and right horrific, yes, but I had to try it

First, I walked to the Hamam (Bath) from my hostel and in my hurry to get off the busy street full of locals staring at me; I enter the MEN's baths. There was a crescendo of murmuring and a flurry of towels and I was immediately rushed out and across the street to the Women Only Bath. Oooops! Teehee…

I was not too excited when I entered the bath as it seemed kind of seedy in there, but I had asked at my hostel for a good bath that was not touristy, so I had committed. Plus, I was more curious than I was scared.

I changed into the cracked, well-used flip flops and a rather tatty-looking towel and was shown into the bath area.

Creepy! Shafts of dim light came through open holes in the tower above my head and the room was steamy and claustrophobic-feeling with its wetness.

I was told to WASH! By an angry looking old lady and she motioned for me to sit on the marble. I was a little creeped out sitting el nude-o on the wet marble where everyone else's parts had been, but again with the curiosity....

The old lady left and I splashed water over myself from an urn beside me that looked like a toilet mounted on the wall. There was a 'fresh' water supply coming in from a tap that lent a sort of calm-watery sound to the air with its constant drip.

Somewhat doused in water, now, I sort of just sat there, all modestly trying to cover myself with my hands while I watched what the woman across from me was doing. She seemed to be overly enjoying herself and hardly noticed me until I got up to leave and she said, finished? With a look of shock. I had NO idea what I was supposed to be doing! Was I supposed to have brought my soap? She had some... did I ask to borrow hers? Was anyone going to come a scrub me, or what?

Being impatient, I walked back out into the foyer and there again was much murmuring and the angry old lady came over and pushed me back into the bath saying WASH! I suddenly wondered if I'd stumbled into a Turkish women's prison...

So I just sat there, splashing bowl after bowl of water over myself until finally the fat, angry old lady was back. But she was naked. Except for a black pair of bikini underwear - Yuk! I had visions of a more nurturing, motherly sort! Maybe she was just coming to bath herself - nope!

She slapped her hand on the giant slab of marble in the middle of the room and barked something. I went over and she pushed me down onto the marble. The next thing I know, I'm being vigorously rubbed down with a loofah sponge by the naked, fat, nasty old lady! She kept slapping me on the ass to signify that I had to turn over! And there were breast and stuff, in my face, dangling over my eyelids!

She reefed me up into a sitting position and scrubbed my arms and my hands kept brushing her saggy parts! I did look down at my arm through all this and was astonished to see these gloppy balls of dead skin all over me - Yuk! But somehow, fascinating...

WASH! She says.

Then she's back and slaps the marble again. I come over and lay down and she goes at me with soap and another sponge. There is so much lather that I keep slipping around like a soapy fish and she keeps trying to grasp my leg or my arm, but I'm all over the big marble table and barely clinging to it. I am laughing uncontrollably under my breath and this is aggravating her, which makes it funnier.

WASH!

After, there is a shampoo session complete with my face between her breasts as she massages my scalp; I emerge from her flesh with soap in my eyes and frantically trying to breathe.

There is another wash and then I'm ushered to the sauna where she doesn't let me out until I have all but melted and am starting to feel faint.

Then, blessedly, it's over with a cold WASH!

And that, ladies and gents, was my Turkish Bath Experience NEVER to be had again unless I can afford the fancy hotel ones where the woman may be better looking and a bit more 'firm'...

I'm sorry for any family members that read this far. Family gatherings may be awkward now...

Well, time to go shopping for cashmeres and carpets!"

www.ingramcontent.com/pod-product-compliance
Lightning Source LLC
Chambersburg PA
CBHW051828090426
42736CB00011B/1705